Persuasive
Business Proposals

WRITING TO WIN MORE CUSTOMERS,
CLIENTS, AND CONTRACTS

Tom Sant

AMACOM

AMERICAN MANAGEMENT ASSOCIATION

New York • Atlanta • Brussels • Chicago • Mexico City
San Francisco • Shanghai • Tokyo • Toronto • Washington, D.C.

Library of Congress Cataloging-in-Publication Data

Sant, Tom.
    Persuasive business proposals : writing to win more customers, clients, and contracts / Tom Sant.
        p.   cm.
    Includes index.
    ISBN-10: 0-8144-7153-6
    ISBN-13: 978-0-8144-7153-1
    1. Proposal writing in business.   2. Persuasion (Rhetoric)   I. Title.

HF5718.5.S26   2004
658.15'224—dc22

                                                      2003018709

Printing number

10   9   8   7   6

Contents

Section IV
Writing to Win

Preface

The goal of *Persuasive Business Proposals* is to teach you how to write winning proposals. More than ever, effective proposal writing is a skill that you need if you hope to be successful in sales.

When the first edition of *Persuasive Business Proposals* appeared, proposals were a staple item in government contracting and were appearing with increasing frequency in the commercial sector. Now, it has become extremely difficult to win large deals without a proposal. From high technology to waste hauling, customers in all sectors of industry now require a written proposal before they will award their business. You need to know how to do the best possible job as quickly as you can.

Why are decision makers requiring proposals more frequently? Five business developments in particular have had a profound impact:

1. **Federal buying behavior.** First, there's the influence of the federal government's procurement policies. Billions of dollars are up for grabs each year in federal contracts for everything from defense systems to janitorial services. Virtually all of that money is awarded on the basis of written proposals. Many government contractors, especially those in the defense industry, imitate federal procurement policies and procedures when seeking subcontractors of their own. They require written proposals, and the trend trickles down.

2. **Increasing complexity.** A second factor that's boosted the demand for written proposals is the increasingly complex, technical nature of many of the products and services being delivered. In technology-oriented industries and those involving complex or specialized solutions, including telecommunications, transportation, insurance, information technology, and dozens more, the customer faces a bewildering assortment of information and options. As a result, decision makers ask for proposals so they can slow down the sales process and clarify what is complex and confusing.

3. **More competition.** The business environment has become increasingly competitive. Clients and prospects who once were willing to make buying decisions based on face-to-face contact are now delaying the decision process, encouraging competition, and—here's the irritating part—requesting formal proposals from all potential vendors. Clients want to compare sources. They want to study their options. They want to compare prices to make sure they're getting the best possible deal. Often they want to be convinced, reassured, impressed. It doesn't matter

whether they're buying accounting services or aerospace products, technical writing or touch probe systems. Everything is a competitive opportunity. Some sectors of the economy have been deregulated, opening them up to competition. When the first edition of this book appeared, no one was writing proposals for energy services, because the entire energy industry was regulated. Now it has become extremely competitive and confusing.

4. **Team decision making.** Over the past few years, many companies have embraced the notion of pushing decision making downward and outward to include as many perspectives as possible. Decisions are often made by a "self-empowered work group" that embodies a variety of expectations and assumptions, a wide range of responsibilities, and very distinct information needs. Selling to a group means you must deliver a message that shows users of your systems, services, or products how the features you will provide can make their lives easier. Technical evaluators will need to receive data on the application fit, operational impact, specifications, and similar details. And other subsets within the team might look at the general business impact, the return on investment, the total cost of ownership, the effect on productivity, and other measures of outcome. You will need to provide content appropriate to each group, and may face the additional challenge of trying to communicate without having personal contact with some members of the team. As a result, you need to create a proposal that walks the corridors of the customer's organization on your behalf, speaking to each type of decision maker as clearly as possible so that those decision makers can join their colleagues in approving your recommendations.

5. **The need to calculate costs accurately.** The smart buyer doesn't select a vendor based on price alone. Smart buyers look closely at the business impact of the various solutions they receive. They may try to determine the total cost of ownership by looking at "hidden costs" associated with acquisition, planning, shipping, implementation, training, or maintenance. And they will try to determine whether a particular recommendation will require process changes that could be costly or difficult to accomplish.

   Besides cost factors, they may also want to see which solution delivers the greatest overall value. They may be looking for impact on operations, revenue generation, operational efficiency, customer retention, employee productivity, product quality, or regulatory compliance. Whatever the criteria may be, they want to choose the product or service that gives them the most of what they need. As a result, they will request a proposal and try to find information and evidence that enables them to calculate true costs and project a realistic return.

These are just some of the reasons you need to know how to write a winning proposal. Your job, your company, your prosperity may depend on it. Unfortunately, if you're like most proposal writers, you probably do not have a clue how to do it.

But don't worry. I've taught thousands of people how to write a winning proposal. In fact, during our workshops students have written proposals that directly resulted in six- and seven-figure sales. I've received phone calls, e-mails, and hearty handshakes from people who have been thrilled to tell me that they used what they learned and it worked. They won the contract, they sold the service, they closed the deal.

They did it by following some simple guidelines. You can do it, too. This book will show you how.

The methods I advocate have been successful in all kinds of environments, for all kinds of businesses. How can that be? How can a method that produces a winning multivolume, multibillion-dollar aerospace proposal also produce a successful two-page letter proposal to fund a recycling center?

The answer is simple, but it's important. You need to understand it so that you know what to expect. *Writing a winning proposal isn't a matter of content. It's a matter of structure and process.* Say the right things in the right order and you'll win.

What we will focus on in this book is the process, the steps you need to follow to develop and write a clear, compelling, persuasive proposal. I'll show you the same methodology I use when I work directly with a client.

Persuasive Business Proposals is divided into four broad topical areas: the proposal writing problem, general principles of persuasion, project management as it applies to producing a proposal, and writing tips to help you communicate clearly and persuasively. Here's a summary of each area:

- ▨ **Section I: Why You Need This Book.** You may already believe that you need help with your proposals, but this section briefly defines what a proposal is (and what it isn't), the elements that are common to winners, the most damaging mistakes (the ones you *must* avoid), and a few other foundational concepts.

- ▨ **Section II: A Primer on Persuasion.** At its most basic, a proposal is a form of communication. But in its controlling purpose it differs from a technical memo or a job appraisal. A proposal is written to persuade. As a result, it's vital to understand what persuasion is, how it happens, and what you need to think about when writing a proposal.

- ▨ **Section III: How to Manage the Process and Keep Your Sanity.** I once heard the manager of proposal operations at a major telecommunications firm describe his job as "directing traffic in the middle of a stampede." Developing and publishing a proposal, whether it's a two-page letter or a twenty-volume formal bid, can be maddening. But if you understand the basic steps and have a structured approach to managing a proposal project, you can make the work much more bearable and increase your efficiency. We will look at the process from pre-RFP activities all the way through to the steps you should take after the contract has been awarded.

■ **Section IV: Writing to Win.** You can have the best idea, the best product, the best plan. But if you can't communicate what you have to offer in a way that the decision maker understands and accepts, none of that will matter. Your choice of words and the way you structure your sentences can either attract or repel the decision maker, helping you win or guaranteeing your loss.

Throughout the book I have included examples of both good and bad proposals to illustrate techniques, processes, and formats. The good examples aren't intended for you to copy and use, although if you want to do that, go ahead. You'll be better off if you take the time to grasp the principles that underlie the examples. Learn the techniques. Understand the process. Then you will have the skills to write tailored, persuasive proposals of your own, proposals that speak directly to your clients' needs and values. Proposals that *win*.

I know you're busy and I know writing is probably not your favorite job, so I promise that throughout the book I'll maintain a dual focus: First, to make sure your proposals are as *effective* as possible, to maximize your chance of winning. Second, to improve your *efficiency*, so you can get those proposals done as quickly as possible.

No one can guarantee that your proposals will always win. There is no magic that can transform a weak performance into a masterpiece. But there are techniques and methods that can help you produce a strong proposal in the first place. That's the goal of this book.

1

Why You Need This Book

1   *The Challenges You Face*

Suppose you're a sales professional representing a vendor of specialized computer systems. You make a powerful presentation to representatives of a potential client, and you can tell it's gone beautifully. They're clearly impressed. They're flashing all kinds of buying signals, asking questions, focusing on their particular concerns. Then the chief decision maker says, "Well, this looks very promising. Why don't you put together a proposal for us that covers what we've talked about, the pricing issues, and some kind of basic delivery and installation schedule, and then we'll go from there. Okay?"

No problem, right?

Or suppose you represent a company that specializes in reducing energy consumption in large buildings. You're going through your e-mail one morning and come across a message announcing a competitive bid to retrofit an entire school district! You open the attached RFP document and glance through it. You can see that it's perfect for you. In fact, this is a job you really want. You can handle it well. You can make money on it and deliver a big ROI for the school district. All you have to do is respond to the attached 125-page Request for Proposal and create a convincing argument as to why you're the right choice.

No problem, right?

One more: You're a partner in a mid-size accounting firm. You've managed to grow and develop a solid client base in your region by personally selling to small and medium-size businesses. But now you want to win some larger projects, take on bigger clients, perform complex audits, move into general business consulting, and generally move the level of the firm's activity up a notch or two. What that means, of course, is that now you'll be competing for jobs against other firms like your own and sometimes against the big, international firms. And instead of face-to-face selling and relationship building, you'll be competing through your proposals.

No problem, right?

Chances are, it is a problem. If you're like most people, you find writing proposals a big challenge.

Some of the very best account executives, program managers, engineers, designers, consultants, and business owners freeze up when they get back to their desks and have to put what they know and what they're recommending on paper. These are people who are capable of making outstanding presentations face to face and who can manage a complex program with exceptional skill. But when it comes to writing a proposal, they don't know how to begin. They don't know how to organize their information and ideas. They aren't sure of the format to use, the pattern to follow, or the details to include.

What's worse, if you're like most professionals, you probably hate writing in general and proposals in particular. That's too bad, because it's hard to do something well if you hate it.

Recently I was speaking at an international conference sponsored by Microsoft. The attendees were integrators, developers, and resellers from all over North and South America and Europe. More than eight hundred people attended my session, so I thought it was a great opportunity to do some informal polling. I asked them a question I've asked many other groups over the years.

"How many of you honestly enjoy writing proposals?" I asked.

From that group of over eight hundred attendees, fewer than twenty hands went up! And that response is fairly typical. Most people—95 percent or more—do not like proposal writing.

Maybe that's why they've figured out clever ways to escape the job.

The most popular technique involves cloning. Proposal cloning. Have you ever seen a salesperson stride into the office and ask, "Who has a proposal I can use?" He or she grabs an electronic copy of somebody else's proposal, does a global find/replace to change the former client's name to that of the new prospect, and then fires it off. The fact that the original proposal was to the Southern Regional Medical Center and the new proposal is to Oscar's Cigar Shop doesn't seem to matter. Of course, the client is a little confused when it sees itself referred to as the region's leading cancer specialist, but that's a minor detail.

You and I have both seen the consequences of proposal cloning, of cutting and pasting old boilerplate together. The proposal doesn't flow. It doesn't really address what the customer cares about. It may even contain embarrassing errors. I've even seen proposals that had the wrong client's name in the cover letter!

Recently, I was called by the president of one of the largest direct mail marketing firms in the country. He wanted some advice on how to turn a bad situation around.

"We just responded to an RFP from Microsoft," he said. "We worked like crazy people, cutting and pasting from previous proposals to make sure we gave them a complete response, and then sent it overnight to Redmond. A couple of days later I called the manager there who was the primary decision maker and asked her how our proposal looked. She said it was a little early to say, but she could offer two observations. First of all, she said, our proposal was so long that no one had time to actually read the whole thing yet. And then she said, 'The second thing is, we don't call ourselves Oracle.'"

I talked with the president for over an hour, and we came up with a few ideas for salvaging the situation, but I truthfully doubt the opportunity could be saved. Putting the wrong client's name in the proposal is bad enough, even though everybody has probably done it. But putting in the name of Microsoft's archenemy is probably the kiss of death.

Another escape technique that people sometimes use is the "data dump" approach to proposal writing. The author gathers up all the internal marketing documentation, product slicks, case studies, white papers, technical specifications, and anything else not clearly labeled "proprietary," forms it into a neat stack, drills three holes along the left-hand margin, and puts it all into a binder. The basic attitude behind this approach is "Here's a bunch of stuff. I'm sure something in here will convince you to buy from us. Just keep looking until you find it."

For obvious reasons, this approach yields very little in terms of positive impact. Customers don't want bulk. They don't want irrelevant detail. And they don't want to do more work than is strictly necessary to understand your proposal.

Finally, and perhaps most damaging of all, is the "graveyard" technique some salespeople use to bury opportunities that will require too much work. They hide the deals that will require a complex proposal or bid response. If they can make their quota with easier sales and smaller deals, they think, where's the harm?

While doing a consulting engagement with one of the most successful sales training organizations in the United States, I had the opportunity to interview several of the firm's star producers about how they handled proposals and RFP responses. Noses wrinkled. Lips lifted in sneers.

"I avoid them," one woman said. "Trying to get anybody to help on a big RFP is impossible. Announcing you have to respond to an RFP is like turning on the lights in a dark room and watching the cockroaches scatter."

They all preferred to sell a lot of small deals rather than a single million-dollar deal that involved a complex RFP response. One of them admitted that he hadn't bothered to go after a seven-figure contract with a major high-tech firm because the RFP was too complicated. What's more, he had buried the same deal two years in a row!

I suspect that sales managers would be stunned to learn how many deals their own salespeople manage to bury in the same way for the same reason.

If you can close business without writing a proposal, you should do so. The fact is, writing a proposal can be a lot of work. Sometimes the task involves tons of annoying details that you may find tiresome. But proposal writing can be extremely rewarding, too, both professionally and financially. To create a winning proposal, you have to give your best effort. You need to combine your business savvy, your psychological insights, your communication skill, and your creativity, all in one package. When does a mere memo or e-mail message allow you to do so much? And how often are the stakes so high?

Your proposal may be the only means you have of communicating to the highest levels of your customer's organization. When you write a proposal, you never know where it may end up. Will it be read by the manager to whom it was addressed? By a committee of evaluators? By the CEO of the corporation? Your proposal is your surrogate, representing your ideas, your products and services, and your company to these people. By creating a powerful proposal, you create a better impression. You cast a larger shadow.

So learning how to write a great proposal can be one of the most important business skills you ever acquire. It will enable you to communicate your solutions effectively and persuasively to your customers, your colleagues, and your own management. In doing so, you'll be meeting their needs for information and insight while achieving your own goals.

Besides, writing a proposal is often the most truly professional thing you do.

Professionals and Writers

Over the years, I've worked with thousands of professionals in companies large and small, in government agencies, in universities, in health care organizations, and in engineering, manufacturing, and consulting firms. One opinion I've heard voiced time and again: "I like my job, but I hate all of the writing I have to do!"

The underlying attitude seems to be that the writing isn't really part of the job. Instead, it's some kind of onerous burden slapped on top of your real responsibilities by a devious or unsympathetic management.

But wait a minute. What are "professionals," anyway? Are they merely people who do for money what amateurs do for fun? That may be true in sports and romance, but not in the business world. No, being a professional means something more, something rooted in the origins of the word.

The first true *professions*—the law and the clergy—arose in the Middle Ages. (In spite of what you may have heard to the contrary, these really are the oldest professions.) Since then, the number of professions has multiplied, but the fundamental meaning has remained the same: A professional is someone who has mastered a complex body of knowledge and who can therefore guide, advise, and tutor others in that area. A professional is somebody who can and does *profess*.

What that means, of course, is that communication is the very essence of the job. It's what separates the professional from the laborer. You expect your doctor, lawyer, I.T. manager, account executive, or other professional to communicate—to explain in simple language what's going on, how it affects you, and what your options are.

Believe me, if you're smart enough to master your chunk of the business world, you're more than smart enough to write well. You *can* produce a good proposal, a winning proposal. You can do it! You can even have fun doing it! All you need are a few techniques and a little self-confidence.

Let's Get Personal

I love books. Always have. They're a source of entertainment, information, wisdom, solace, and more. If I'm feeling down, getting my hands on a new book lifts my spirits immediately.

Now I'm lucky enough to live just a few blocks from a wonderful bookstore. In fact, if I stroll up to the end of my street, cut through a lovely neighborhood park, and walk a couple more blocks through the nice, old neighborhood where I live, I arrive at the front door of a store that *Publisher's Weekly* named "the best bookstore in America."

It's a beautiful place. As you enter, there's a fireplace with comfortable chairs and leather couches to the right. There's a gourmet restaurant to the left where the chef makes dishes from a featured cookbook each week. The staff is friendly, the selection is comprehensive, there's even a solid collection of classical and jazz CDs. For a bibliophile like me, it's a little slice of heaven.

So where do you think I bought most of my books last year?

That's right: Amazon.com.

Why? How could I betray my neighborhood store this way?

Well, for one thing, I can go to Amazon pretty much any time, day or night. And I can shop in my underwear (or less), if I choose to. (I'm pretty sure if I tried that at my neighborhood bookstore, they wouldn't be happy about it.)

But the biggest reason I buy more at Amazon is the *personalization* of the experience. When I enter my local store, the employees may look up and smile (or not). But they never greet me by name, and they have no idea what I bought the last time I was there. On the other hand, when I go to Amazon, I'm always greeted by name and they have several suggestions for me, many of which are pretty darn interesting.

Now I know Amazon's apparent personalization of my shopping experience is just a form of collaborative filtering using database technology in a Web-based e-commerce application. But it still *seems* more personal than the store does, and it has created a level of expectations in my mind that a traditional retailer will find hard to match.

What does this have to do with your proposals? Simply this: If your proposal isn't at least as personal as the Amazon Web site, you may actually alienate the customer. It will look like boilerplate.

Consider these two examples:

A company that advertised itself as the world's leader in customer relationship technology asked us to review their proposals. They were losing a lot more than they were winning, and they thought we might be able to tweak the message a little. When we looked at the executive summary to see how they were approaching the customer, we saw a revealing pattern. The first word of the first paragraph was their name—not merely printed, but an actual reproduction of their bold logo. The first word of the second paragraph was the same logo. And the third paragraph, the fourth, and so on. For four solid pages. Nothing in that executive summary focused on the customer. In fact, it looked like an exercise in egotism. How personal was that experience for their prospective customers? What kind of attitude did it communicate?

In another case, a company that provides integration services for enterprise resource planning software asked me to review their proposals and train their sales force. They sent half a dozen sample proposals so I could prepare. One of the samples was a fifty-page proposal for outsourcing help desk functions. But the proposal began with the vendor's history, then presented their vision statement and their mission statement, then went into their quality philosophy, then discussed their affiliations with major software providers, and on and on. It was all about them, not the customer. *In fact, the customer's name didn't even appear until page seventeen!* Unbelievable.

If you submit a proposal that is filled with boilerplate text that focuses on yourself, you are giving the customer an *impersonal* experience. You are delivering a document that fails to acknowledge the customer's unique needs, values, or interests. Your self-centered proposal communicates to the customer that the information they shared with you during the sales process has made no difference to your proposal at all. Ultimately, you are undercutting the notion that you are offering a solution. Instead, you are providing the customer with a generic experience that suggests what you have to offer is a commodity—it's the exact same thing for everyone.

This is particularly damaging if you or your colleagues have done a good job of establishing rapport with the client and if you have taken the time to uncover and articulate the client's needs during the sales cycle. To do all that work and then submit a proposal that is not based on those insights inevitably creates doubts in the client's mind. "What's going on here? Who am I dealing with?" they wonder. "If I choose these people as my vendor, will my future experience be more like what I saw during the sales process, which focused on me and what I need, or more like this proposal, which is just a bunch of boilerplate and bragging?"

Today, in the wake of Enron, WorldCom, Andersen, and other debacles, customer expectations for honesty, clarity, and credibility are higher than ever. A salesperson who communicates with customers as individuals wields far more power and influence in today's marketplace than the well-oiled front-office marketing machine. People buy from people, and they always prefer to buy from people they trust. We just happen to live in a time when customers have more options than ever and when they have been conditioned by experiences online to expect personalized treatment.

So what does this mean for you and me when we write proposals?

■ Delivering big slabs of boilerplate may be worse than delivering no message at all because the boilerplate will sound "canned" and will undercut the rapport we've created with customers. I saw a demonstration of a proposal tool that claimed to help salespeople write better proposals. One of its first options was to "retrieve" the executive summary. I started laughing out loud, because there is no way a single executive summary will work for all customers.

■ Effective proposals are built from a combination of content and insight. You must have something worthwhile to say, and you must say it in a way that shows customers that it's relevant to them. This is not as hard as it sounds, and if you make the effort you will differentiate yourself from your competitors in a way that creates a dramatic and positive impression on the customer.

■ Effective salespeople do not deliver one message over and over. They do not treat customers as demographic units. They engage in conversations, they listen, and they view customers as individuals. They create proposals that communicate clearly and specifically to those individuals.

In short, delivering boilerplate proposals and sales letters can put the cold, clammy kiss of death on your sales process. Starting your proposal with your company history or descriptions of your products alienates the reader. Failing to focus on the customer's needs and objectives right in the beginning of your proposal undercuts all the carefully managed, consultative sales methodology that you followed. When you're selling a really big opportunity, you need a really good proposal. A price quote, a bill of materials, a technical spec, or a marketing brochure just won't do the job.

So let's learn how to create a proposal that will do the job. Let's learn how to write a winner.

2   *A Good Proposal Is Hard to Find*

A while back I was invited to speak at the annual sales kick-off meeting for a major software corporation. The morning of my talk, I waited in the ballroom, where breakfast had just been served to 450 salespeople, while they went off to hear the president present the "state of the business" address. After that, it was my turn.

As I sat quietly, sipping one more cup of coffee and gathering my thoughts, a fellow came bustling into the ballroom. He glanced around at the dozens of empty tables, spotted me, walked over, sat down, and said, "You're late for the meeting."

"No, sir," I replied. "I'm the next speaker, so in a way I'm early. But why aren't you in there?"

"Oh, I'd like to be, but I'm waiting for a limo. I have to dash off and close a deal."

My eyebrows went up. "Congratulations. Must be an important deal."

"It is," he said. "It's worth about four million dollars. But before you get the wrong idea, I'm not selling anything. I'm buying. I'm the vice president of purchasing, and I have to go sign papers to bring this to closure."

I was scrambling around, looking for a business card, in case he had any money left over, when he asked me, "What is the subject of your talk?"

"Sales proposals. How to write them."

Suddenly this rather charming and interesting person went through a metamorphosis right before my eyes. He grabbed a fork, pointed it at me, and practically snarled as he said, "Listen, you tell our salespeople that if they produce the kinds of proposals I get, I'll make sure they get fired. You tell them that! I get proposals for deals like the one today, deals that range anywhere from half a million to ten million dollars. And what are they? Nothing but a bunch of product sheets, line item pricing, and boilerplate. There's no ROI, no calculation of the total cost of ownership, no analysis of the payback, nothing I can use to make an informed decision. What a waste!"

I didn't have the heart (or the guts, since he was holding that fork) to tell him that his company's salespeople were producing virtually the same thing for their customers.

Not that they were all that different from the vast majority of firms. In the course of a year, we see thousands of proposals from hundreds of companies. Very few of them produce a persuasive proposal.

Most of them start out focusing on themselves, on their company history, their product, their technology, their mission, or some such thing. In fact, proposals are often fatally damaged by one or more of the "seven deadly sins" of proposal writing.

The Seven Deadly Sins of Proposal Writing

1. Failure to focus on the client's business problems and payoffs—the content sounds generic.

2. No persuasive structure—the proposal is an "information dump."

3. No clear differentiation of this vendor compared to others.

4. Failure to offer a compelling value proposition.

5. Key points are buried—no impact, no highlighting.

6. Difficult to read because they're full of jargon, too long, or too technical.

7. Credibility killers—misspellings, grammar and punctuation errors, use of the wrong client's name, inconsistent formats, and similar mistakes.

So . . . What Is a Good Proposal?

Seems like an easy question. I think most of us agree that "one that's done" isn't an adequate answer. But after years of working in the proposal field, I'd have to say that most businesspeople probably don't have an answer.

For one thing, they tend to confuse proposals with other kinds of documents. Or they fail to understand the proposal's purpose. Or they lose sight of their audience and start writing to themselves.

Some salespeople, even sales managers, treat the proposal as a checkbox item on the overall sales process diagram. Did demo? Check! Submitted proposal? Check!

If that's the attitude you take, the document you deliver may actually end up doing more harm than good. Although good proposals by themselves seldom win deals, bad proposals can definitely lose them. Treating the proposal as a nuisance or a pro forma submission that doesn't really matter can raise doubts in the customer's mind about your commitment and competence. It can throw obstacles in your path and prolong the sales cycle.

So before we define what a proposal is, let's make sure we know what it's *not:*

It's not a price quote. If all you tell the decision maker is the amount he or she has to pay, you've reduced what you're selling down to the level of a commodity. You've said, in effect, "All products or services of this type are basically the same. We have nothing unique to offer. Choose based on cost." Unless you are always the lowest-priced vendor, that's not a strong position to take.

It's not a bill of materials, project plan, or scope of work. In technical and engineering environments, people sometimes take the attitude that if they just explain all the details of the proposed solution very clearly and accurately, the customer will buy. Actually, giving customers a detailed bill of materials or project plan may have exactly the opposite effect. You've just given them a shopping list so detailed they may decide to do the job without your help. Ouch!

It's not the company history, either. Oddly enough, a sizable number of the proposals we see start out that way. Why? From reading dozens and dozens of these things, I can assure you most company histories are not very interesting.

Here's the bottom line: What is a proposal? *It's a sales document.*

What is its job? To move the sales process toward closure.

That's it. Pretty simple. It's safe to say that if the proposal doesn't do that job, it's a lousy proposal. And if it does do that job, no matter how, it's a good one. I truly don't care if you write proposals in crayon on the back of a grocery sack; if you've got a high win ratio with them, good for you.

However, over the years we've found that there are certain specific kinds of content that need to be in your proposals to maximize their chance of winning. And we've found that certain structural formats produce better results.

A good proposal helps you make money by convincing people to choose you to provide the products and services they need. The proposal positions what you have as a solution to a business problem, and helps you justify a slightly higher price than your competitor by showing that you will provide superior value.

To do the proposal writing job well, you need to make sure that your proposal is persuasive, accurate, and complete. Unfortunately, lots of proposal writers invert the order of those qualities, producing proposals that are bloated with detail and scarcely persuasive at all.

In my experience, no one buys based on the "thud factor." The biggest proposal does not automatically win. But thousands of people succumb to the delusion that if they throw everything they have into the proposal, the sheer length of the document is bound to impress the customer.

Just the opposite is true. A study we conducted presented a group of evaluators with three proposals. One was twenty-five pages long, one was about fifty pages, and one was nearly one hundred pages. We told the evaluators that we wanted them to look for certain factors in the documents, but in reality all we wanted to see was which one they picked up first. Overwhelmingly, they reached for the short document before the other two. Wouldn't you?

Why does that matter? Because evaluators are inevitably influenced by what they have already seen as they look at other proposals. Let's suppose they picked your proposal up first, because it was concise. And let's suppose you did an excellent job of showing that you understand their needs, are focused on delivering a big return on investment, offer a realistic solution, have plenty of credentials to prove you can do the job on time and on budget, and have differentiated yourself and your offering from your competition. How well will those other proposals stack up, especially if they're bloated and unfocused?

The Value of Your Proposals to Your Clients

Why do customers ask us for a proposal when the recommendations we have made in person so obviously make sense? Because the proposal has value for them. For example, a good proposal can help the decision maker to:

- Compare vendors, offers, or prices so he or she can make an informed decision

- Clarify complex information

- Make the buying process more "objective"

- Slow down the sales process

- Solicit creative ideas, become educated, or get free consulting

Comparing vendors, offers, or prices. Are you the only vendor this prospect is talking to? It's possible you are being asked for a proposal so that your recommendations, pricing, and evidence can be compared to a competitor's.

Buying products or services can be tough, especially when the decision maker must deal with an array of options, lots of conflicting claims, and little practical knowledge of the area under consideration. "Getting it in writing" is the traditional way to deal with this problem.

Clarifying complex information. Do you sell something so complex that it would take you more than ten minutes to explain it to your mother? If so, it's possible some of your prospects don't understand it, either. A proposal gives the nontechnical customer a chance to read, analyze, ponder, get help, and eventually understand.

Adding objectivity to the buying process. It seems odd, but some people don't want to buy from people they like. They're afraid that if they really like the salesperson, they will somehow make a bad decision based on rapport or friendship. If that strikes you as a goofy way to make a buying decision, join the club. (After all, wouldn't you rather do business after the sale with people you like?) Regardless, it makes enough sense to some customers and prospects that they will try to create an arm's length relationship by asking you for a written proposal.

Slowing down the sales process. Sales is a little bit like courtship. The very word "proposal" applies to the final stages of both activities. In the early stages of both, the process can take on a momentum of its own. We get excited, we become enchanted with new possibilities, and we rush forward. Asking for a written proposal slows the sales process down. The buyer figures that it will take several days, maybe even a couple of weeks, for the salesperson to put together a proposal, which gives the buyer time to think about this decision calmly, to weigh the options, to determine whether this opportunity will look as good the morning after as it does right now.

Soliciting creative ideas, becoming educated, or getting free consulting. Decision makers face a tremendous number of demands on their time and abilities. They need to know what's out there, who has it, and how much it costs. They need to know if there are new ways of handling old problems. What are the trends in the industry? Who are the new players in the game? It's all a bit overwhelming.

One way to establish a base of information is to ask for proposals. As long as you are honest with the salesperson about your time frame, there is nothing wrong with this practice.

What about clients who issue RFPs or request proposals with no intention of buying anything? They're looking for free consulting, and to the extent you answer all of their questions, you may be giving away the solution. Or the client may solicit bids in an effort to "beat up" the existing vendor. Does this happen? Yes. Is it ethical? No. If you're selling a product, you have wasted time and energy, because you've prepared a proposal for somebody who never intended to buy anything. But if you're selling a creative solution, an idea, a system design, or other intellectual property, you may have lost much more. The potential client may glean enough substance from your proposal that he or she tries to do it without you, using your concepts but developing them internally. Or, even more galling, the client may use your proposal as the basis for soliciting bids from your competitors. This doesn't happen frequently, but it happens often enough that you should be careful.

The important lesson is that you should always do some prudent qualifying before committing yourself to the time and effort of writing a quality proposal. There is no point in submitting to someone who has no budget, no authority, or no real interest in working with you. And there is even less point in submitting to someone who may take your material and share it with your competitors.

The Value of Your Proposals to You

Look at your proposals broadly as part of your overall sales and marketing activities, rather than narrowly as the formal means of responding to a specific request. Seen that way, a proposal can help you build your business in several ways, including some that extend beyond the immediate opportunity to which you are responding.

The obvious: helping you sell. The proposal's most important job is to help you sell something. (In the nonprofit realm, it should help you obtain funding in support of your mission and objectives.) To go a little further, though, a high-quality, carefully constructed proposal can help you:

- **Sell on value instead of price**: Use your proposal to move the decision maker's focus away from price and toward such measures of value as lower total cost of ownership, higher reliability, direct customer support, documented technical superiority, or some other message that separates you from your competitors.

- **Compete successfully without having personal contact with every member of the decision team**: You may never have the opportunity to meet every member of the team in person. A good proposal can speak to each member of the team, helping make your case.

- **Demonstrate your competence and professionalism**: It's probably not fair and it's definitely not logical, but almost everybody does it: We judge a vendor's ability to deliver goods or services from the quality of the proposal they submit. Our conscious, rational mind tells us that spelling and grammar have nothing to do with the ability to provide help desk support for our PC users, yet we find those misspellings and grammar mistakes raising doubt and uncertainty in our mind.

- **Offer a bundled solution**: The customer may ask you for a proposal for basic bookkeeping services. In your proposal, though, you can add a brief description of your ability to provide tax preparation, too, as part of a total solution. That will increase the size of the deal, it may differentiate you from other bookkeepers who submit a proposal, or it may just make the customer aware that you also do taxes. All of these are good things.

- **Sell the "smarter" buyer**: Smart buyers want to gain as much as possible while spending as little as possible. If you don't show them what they gain by choosing your recommendations, they will inevitably focus on the other half of the equation: spending very little.

- **Sell a complex, technical product to nontechnical buyers**: Speaking the buyer's language is an important part of winning his or her trust. A flexible proposal process can help you communicate effectively even if the customer lacks in-depth knowledge of what you're offering.

The proposal as a marketing tool. Think about your company's image. What do your clients think of you? What do prospects who have never worked with you assume about you?

Try this exercise. Take a clean sheet of paper and list all the characteristics, traits, or attributes that are typically associated with your company. List them all, positive and negative. Be honest, but be fair. (I find that people are often extremely hard on themselves and their companies, demanding a level of perfection that their own customers don't expect. Try to get out of your head and see things the way a customer or prospect probably does.)

A typical list might look something like this:

- Expensive

- High-quality vendor

- Reliable

- Difficult to deal with/bureaucratic

- Good product knowledge

- Innovative, willing to come up with new solutions (for a price)

- Financially stable/solid

- Lots of experience

- Significant local presence

- Not interested in small jobs or small clients

Obviously, this is a mixed list, as virtually any company's would be. The question is how to use your proposals to capitalize on the positives and to minimize or overcome the negatives. One of the negatives on the list is the fact that clients perceive your company to be expensive. Doesn't it make sense to issue an unsolicited letter proposal every time you have a price reduction? In particular, you might want to target current customers whose costs can be reduced if they adopt the recommendations you're proposing.

One of the positives on the list is that your company has a significant local presence in your market. Why not play that up in each proposal you submit? Remind the decision maker that he or she will be dealing with a vendor who can respond to problems or concerns immediately, in person, rather than in a day or two or over the phone.

Each proposal should also emphasize and promote your perceived strengths and offer evidence, if possible, to overturn preconceptions about your weaknesses or shortcomings. Even if you don't win a given bid, you may have a positive impact on the decision maker's assumptions about you and your company. Over the long term that can be extremely valuable.

Influencing clients. Good account management requires you to think about the future of your business relationships, not merely the immediate opportunity. Reacting to a customer's problems or needs when the customer brings them up is all right, but it's not nearly as effective as working with the customer collaboratively to develop a business direction.

Each time you write a proposal, think in terms of your long-term plan for a given client. Where do you want the relationship to be in six months? In a year? In five years? What intermediate steps are necessary to get the relationship there? Perhaps you're currently providing system software to the client, but you'd also like to take on developmental projects. Or perhaps you are currently providing call center operations on an outsourced basis, but you'd eventually like to expand that to include outbound telemarketing and help desk functions, too. By keeping those long-range objectives in mind as you write each proposal, you may be able to spot leverage points. If you have a choice between two or more equally legitimate solutions, recommend the one that will move the business relationship in the direction you want it to go.

In other words, start looking at your proposals as tools and opportunities. Rather than seeing them as a kind of test that's been set up by clients to exclude you, look at each business proposal as a means of accomplishing your objectives. That's the real challenge you face—not merely getting the proposal done on time so you can check it off your list of sales "activities," but making sure that when it is done, it accomplishes exactly what you want.

Of course, it's one thing to recognize the challenge. It's quite another to know what to do about it. That's the topic of Section 2.

2

A Primer on Persuasion

3 *Why the Inuit Hunt Whales and Other Secrets of Customer Behavior*

A specific practice group within one of the world's largest consulting firms hired me some years ago to look at their proposals. They were mystified why they weren't winning more. They were always one of a final two or three vendors. But for some reason, they almost never won the deal. They wanted some tips that would push them over the finish line.

When I looked at the dozen or so sample proposals they sent, I wasn't really surprised they were losing. I was actually surprised they were making it to the final. The proposals were all very technical. They were written in an informative style, as though they were white papers or journal articles. In addition, the tone tended to be condescending or patronizing toward the client. They contained no specific evidence of recent, relevant experience, provided no cost justification or value proposition, and sometimes did not follow the customer's instructions in the original RFP. So it didn't seem too surprising that they were losing. What appeared to be happening was that they were making it to the final cut based on name recognition alone, but when the decision maker moved to a more advanced kind of evaluation, they were losing out.

The defining moment in any sales process is the customer's decision. From the moment we first find a lead and qualify it as a real opportunity, through all the meetings, presentations, conversations, and communications between salesperson and prospect, our focus is on getting the customer to make a decision in our favor.

Obviously, understanding how people make decisions will help us sell more effectively. With insight into the customer's decision process, we can deliver the right message in the right way at the right time.

The Myths of Decision Making

For centuries, the assumption has been that people make decisions in a rational, careful, and thorough manner. Certainly since the triumph of rationalism after Descartes, the model for human thinking has been highly analytical and structured.

For example, Benjamin Franklin claimed in a letter he wrote to the British chemist Joseph Priestley that when confronted with a significant decision, he would divide a sheet of paper into two columns, label them Pro and Con, and then list all the evidence he could think of on each side.

Next, he would compare the evidence from each column, striking out those that balanced each other out, until he was left with a preponderance of evidence on one side or another.

Sounds reasonable, doesn't it?

The problem is that virtually nobody makes decisions that way. Franklin was describing an idealized process that simply doesn't work in the real world and never has.

Imagine for a moment that you are the unfortunate victim of an accident. While cleaning leaves and twigs from your roof, your ladder slips, plunging through a couple of layers of bushes and a porch railing. Luckily for you, someone sees the accident and calls for an emergency medical team. How would you feel if that team used Franklin's process for deciding how to treat you? By the time they divided a sheet of paper in half, wrote down all the positives and negatives associated with each course of action, and began to eliminate them, you'd be beyond help.

Obviously, emergency room nurses and physicians, medical response teams, police officers, firefighters, soldiers, and others who work in fast-paced, life-and-death environments don't function that way. And neither do businesspeople, students, government employees, or anybody else.

When we and our customers must make a decision, we usually find ourselves dealing with huge amounts of complex, confusing, often conflicting information. We are often under tremendous time pressure. We need to make the "right" decision because the consequences of a bad one could be catastrophic for our business or careers. So how do we do it?

How People Really Make Decisions

Recent research has documented for the first time how people actually make decisions. An interdisciplinary team, based at the Max Planck Institute for Human Development (Berlin and Munich) and the University of Chicago, has published results of extensive inquiries into the methods people use in all kinds of situations. This study, *Simple Heuristics That Make Us Smart* (Oxford University Press, 2000), documents the specific techniques people use for making decisions quickly based on a minimal amount of information.

It turns out that people use a limited set of decision-making strategies or techniques. We use them from the time we're children (kids who are taking "multiple-guess" tests in school resort to these techniques for narrowing their choices), in college, in our personal lives, and of course in our business activities.

The researchers speculate that these techniques, or "fast and frugal heuristics" as the authors of *Simple Heuristics* call them, are hard-wired into our brains, part of our evolutionary survival package. Our ancestors didn't have the biggest teeth or the sharpest claws, so they needed to make good decisions. Those decisions helped them survive, and they help us function today.

To determine whether people use these techniques in making a proposal-related business decision, I conducted experiments for over a year in which I distributed a proposal for Internet security services to groups of business professionals. I asked them to evaluate the proposal, noting the time when they reach a decision either in favor of or against the offer being made in the proposal.

They are looking at a real proposal, one that deals with a complex, important problem and offers a solution priced at approximately $250,000. So how long does it take people to make a "keep/discard" decision? On average, a little over six minutes.

Fast and frugal, indeed!

By understanding how people gather and process information, we can gain good insight into the best way to organize our proposals. Also, we can structure our evidence for maximum effectiveness and can prioritize the content to match the kind of information the customer is looking for, based on the decision techniques he or she is using.

In *Simple Heuristics* the authors describe seven heuristics of choice, but of those there are three that are particularly important for making business decisions.

Recognition

The first and simplest technique relies on recognition as a simple cue to make decisions. The basic principle is that given two objects, one recognizable, the other not, we infer that the recognized object has higher value.

Here's an example: Suppose your laptop computer suddenly died. You go to your I.T. manager and tell her that you need a new one. She says, "Well, you're in luck, because I happen to have two brand new laptops with all the software installed. You can have either this IBM ThinkPad or this Kretzenheimer Millennial. Which one do you want?"

Chances are you'll take the IBM. Why? Because you've never heard of the other one.

To test this principle, I have often distributed a "lunch menu" at the outset of seminars. The so-called menu gives attendees two choices: a turkey club sandwich or baked gravlox with cremora sauce. As you might expect, over 90 percent of participants will choose the turkey club sandwich. A few adventurous souls choose the gravlox, and a few will complain that there's no vegetarian option. But people for the most part are not willing to eat something for lunch that they've never heard of.

So what does this mean for our proposal efforts?

First, it suggests how important pre-proposal activities are. If the evaluator has never heard of us and our proposal lands on his or her desk, chances are we won't get much more than a cursory glance. (Conversely, if you work for a Fortune 500 company, you may get passed along to the next stage of evaluation based on recognition alone.)

The recognition heuristic indicates the importance of repeated exposure, in the form of advertising and branding activities at the corporate level, and repeated contacts, in the form of phone calls, e-mails, and other forms of what the marketing guru Jim Cecil calls "nurturing" the account. Our pre-proposal activities lay the foundation for choice by establishing recognition.

What else does the recognition heuristic tell us? Well, it certainly suggests that if we represent a small or new company and our prospects have never heard of us, we may have a difficult time winning deals. Conversely, if we receive an RFP from a potential client we have never heard of and with whom we have absolutely no relationship, we probably ought to "no bid" it. Our chances of winning are minimal.

Finally, it means that if you are a sales professional, you can't depend solely on the corporation to handle recognition building activities. You should make the effort to communicate with your prospects and leads on a regular basis to maintain recognition. Send the prospect a clipping, drop the prospect an e-mail with an interesting Web link, leave a voice mail, and make other efforts to communicate something of interest or value every six weeks or so. That way, when the customer is ready to buy, you won't be relegated to the discard pile because the decision maker doesn't recognize you.

Single-Factor Decision Making

But how do customers decide if they recognize both us and our competitors? Or if they have never heard of any of us?

Typically, at that point they move to a slightly more complex heuristic and choose among the options based on a single criterion or factor. This single factor is assumed by the decision maker to be a useful indicator to sort among the options. (Sometimes there are as many as two or three criteria, but seldom more than that.)

For example, suppose a company issues an RFP and receives twenty proposals in response. Someone at that company has to sort through those submissions to quickly eliminate most of them. At this stage of the evaluation, there is not much in the way of careful analysis, no real weighing of the evidence. An initial set of "no names" will be discarded. That's the recognition heuristic in action. Then the evaluator will begin to apply a decision factor or two. For example, some of the proposals will be eliminated because they did not follow the RFP instructions. Some will be cut because they didn't answer all of the questions or indicated by their answer that they were noncompliant with a key requirement. The decision process will move very quickly until the evaluator has the pile down to something more manageable.

Even if your customer has not issued an RFP, he or she will probably evaluate competitive offers on the basis of a key criterion. It might be price.

It might be timeline. It might be references or relevant experience or the "business fit" of your solution.

What if you and your competitor are roughly equal on the first criterion? Then the customer moves on to a second and compares. If you are roughly equal there, the customer will choose a third. But decision makers seldom go beyond two or three factors before reaching a decision.

There are three varieties of single-factor decision making that your customer may use. At the simplest level, he or she may use what the experts call "minimalist" criteria, but which we might call arbitrary. The programmers who work at my company provided a rather amusing example of this kind of decision making when it comes to choosing a lunch destination. They used to waste a sizable portion of their lunch period arguing and debating about where to go. Finally, they resolved it as only programmers would—they wrote a piece of software that makes the decision for them. At first, it was a random lunch generator, but then they got a bit more sophisticated. Now they enter a single factor, such as proximity or price, and click the mouse. The system generates a lunch destination based on that factor. And off they go, content with the choice.

A slightly more sophisticated version of single-factor decision making involves asking ourselves what criterion we used the last time we made the same or a similar decision and whether that produced a good outcome. This is called "using the last," and some examples might be:

- "The last time I entered the office pool, I chose teams by flipping a coin and I won $20. I'll do the same thing again."

- "When we bought our annuals for planting last spring, we chose specimens with dark green leaves and they did really well in the garden."

- "Whenever we've hired a vendor who has done the same kind of project before, things have turned out pretty well."

Finally, decision makers sometimes go a step further and develop a limited set of criteria by thinking back over several situations in which similar decisions were made. Which criteria produced the best results? Which didn't work? This heuristic, called "taking the best," assumes that some criteria will produce better results than others.

What does this mean for our sales efforts?

First, it suggests that during our sales contacts with a prospect, we should probe to find out what factors they will use to make a decision. We can uncover their decision criteria rather simply. We just have to ask:

- "When you compare different vendors, what is the most important factor for you in choosing one?"

- "The last time you made this kind of decision, what factors did you use to guide your decision? What did you look for? Did that work for you?"

Second, this technique opens up opportunities for us to help the decision maker during the sales process. A naïve or inexperienced customer may take a simplistic approach, looking only at price. By using the sales process to educate the buyer, we can introduce other factors beyond price that may be more helpful to the buyer in making a good decision and that may give us more of a competitive position.

Third, we need to differentiate between opportunities where we are reacting to the customer's request for a proposal and opportunities where we are offering a solution proactively. When we submit a proposal in response to an RFP, we must recognize that our first job is to avoid elimination based on some arbitrary or trivial issue. That means following directions carefully, answering all of the questions and requirements, and making our compliance to the bid as obvious as possible. An effective tool in this area is the compliance matrix, a table in which you list each of the customer's requirements, give your level of compliance with that requirement, and possibly offer a brief comment or explanation. (An evaluator who works for the U.S. Postal Service told me that he looks at all the proposals and sets the ones that do not include a compliance matrix on the floor. That leaves him with a manageable few.) It's also a good idea to highlight your proposal so the customer can quickly find the high-value content that directly addresses the factors he or she thinks are important.

For proactive opportunities, customers tend to search on their own key criteria until they find a differentiator. Then they stop and make a decision. This implies that it's vital that we organize our sales presentations and proposals to focus right away on the criteria that the customer thinks are most important. Often, these factors will address issues such as:

- Are we getting what we need? Does this solve a significant business problem? Will the proposed solution work in our environment?

- Can this vendor really do it? Do they have the experience and resources to perform on time and on budget? Are they competent?

- Does this represent good value for the money? Is the proposed pricing fair? What kind of return on our investment will we receive?

Estimating the Rate of Return

For thousands of years, the Inuit people of Alaska and Canada have hunted whales as their primary source of food. They go out into the ocean in small boats, and pound on drums and the sides of their boats to drive the whales toward shore (whales have very sensitive hearing, you know). Then, when the whales are in shallow water, they attack and kill them. Now they use harpoon guns and more advanced weapons, but they used to do it with little more than spears.

Now why on earth would they do that? There are much simpler and less dangerous game they could hunt—geese, rabbits, seals, walruses even. They could fish. Why go after the largest, most powerful mammal on earth?

For that matter, why did primitive humans hunt mastodons? We've all seen the "artist's recreations" of a tribe of scantily clad Neanderthals surrounding a wooly mammoth the size of a beachfront condo, attacking it with little more than sharpened sticks.

Okay. So why did they do that? Why not pick on something your own size?

The experts who contributed to *Simple Heuristics* have come up with an answer. Their research suggests that one of the built-in decision heuristics people use is an innate capacity to calculate the "rate of return" for their efforts, particularly as they pertain to the group as a whole. In other words, hunting a whale or a wooly mammoth has a bigger ROI for the tribe than hunting a rabbit does.

These researchers even went so far as to calculate the calories required to kill a whale compared to the calories the community will get from that animal, then calculated the calories expended versus the calories obtained for other prey. The result: The whale was by far the best investment of the tribe's energies.

The fact is that when people are making decisions on behalf of a group, they instinctively want to make a decision that gives their organization the best possible ROI. They'll even buy something more expensive and complex if they're convinced it's the best choice for their company.

How can we help them use the estimation heuristic to our advantage?

First, every proposal should include calculations and graphic displays of ROI, total cost of ownership, payback period, productivity improvements, speed of delivery, or other measures of gain.

Second, provide your decision maker with case studies that show how other customers got big rewards from selecting your products or services. Quantify the impact your solutions had for those customers whenever possible.

Third, find out what kind of outcome the key decision maker thinks is most important for his or her company. Is it increased revenue? Regulatory compliance? Greater customer loyalty? Extended useful life for critical equipment? Elimination of downtime? Whatever the customer thinks is important defines the value proposition.

Finally, emphasize your differentiators and explain how they add value for the customer. Customers want to know what makes us different from our competitors. They also want to know why those differences will matter to them and their companies.

If we provide the right information in the right way, one that corresponds to the processes our customers use to make decisions, our chances of winning business will soar. And, after all, winning business is what writing proposals is all about.

4   *The Structure of Persuasion*

M ost people are comfortable providing information. That's a writing or speaking task you probably feel good about. Evaluations are a little tougher for most of us, and if they involve touchy material, as a performance appraisal might, we may actually dread doing them. However, for the majority of people, persuasive writing is by far the most difficult communication task. It involves a step-level increase in complexity and difficulty over what the other types of communication require.

Unfortunately, when we're short of time or feel uncertain about our readiness to proceed, we're likely to revert to the type of writing we find easiest. For most writers, that's presenting information, usually to an audience that's about as knowledgeable on the subject as we are. For proposals, that's a lethal combination. Factual information presented at a high level of technical expertise not only doesn't persuade, but may actually alienate the reader.

We have to move away from the kind of writing that's easy for us (factual, technical) and into the style that's effective (persuasive, clear), as Figure 4-1 shows. So let's distinguish among the primary reasons people write in a business setting and look at how those different purposes require different approaches.

Figure 4-1. Move out of the Comfort Zone to Persuade Effectively.

	Information	Evaluation	Persuasion
Expert	Comfort Zone		
Highly informed			
Somewhat informed			Persuasion Zone
Lay			

Information

When people present facts that other people need to do their jobs, they're writing to inform. The goal of informative writing is to be concise and accurate. The focus should be on transferring the information quickly and easily. The communication fails if the reader doesn't understand the facts or, worse yet, misunderstands them.

The best way to communicate informatively is to use the pattern taught in journalism classes: the funnel. (See Figure 4-2.) Start with the fact or set of facts that is most important to the reader. In journalism, that's often *who, what, when, where, why,* and *how?* Then go to the next most important fact. Then the third level of importance. The fourth, the fifth, and so on, until there is nothing left to say. By structuring your document this way, you allow your readers to stop reading as soon as they have seen enough.

The challenge in writing informatively is to figure out which fact is most important to the reader. The most common mistakes are writing chronologically, which usually leads to wordiness, or starting with facts that matter to the writer but not to the reader, which usually leads to confusion or false emphasis.

Now wait a minute, you might be thinking. In the previous chapter we talked about decision heuristics and putting the kind of stuff up front that matters the most to the decision maker. Isn't that the same as the informative pattern? It's similar, and none of the structural patterns we'll be looking at can afford to start with content that the reader doesn't care about. But remember that the goal of persuasion is to motivate the decision maker to take action. Simply listing facts in a descending order of priority doesn't create any momentum toward action.

Figure 4-2. The Funnel-Shaped Structure of Informative Writing.

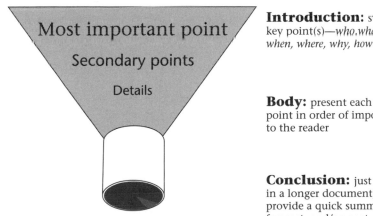

Most important point

Secondary points

Details

Introduction: state key point(s)—*who, what, when, where, why, how*

Body: present each point in order of importance to the reader

Conclusion: just stop or, in a longer document, provide a quick summary, forecast, and/or next steps

Evaluation

Sometimes people aren't trying to communicate facts alone. Instead, they're offering an opinion about the significance of a certain group of facts, what those facts imply.

For example, consider what happens in a court case when one side calls in an expert witness. Such a witness isn't asked to establish facts about the case—"Where was the defendant on the night of July 15?" Instead, the expert witness is asked to offer an opinion about what a certain body of facts indicates. "On the basis of these facts, do you think the defendant is mentally competent?" "Given this sequence of events, did the defendant act in accordance with the profession's current standard of conduct?"

In the business world, each time you write a performance appraisal or do a competitive analysis, you're writing an evaluation. If you merely recite the facts but don't offer your opinion, you aren't doing the whole job.

The pattern for evaluative writing is depicted in Figure 4-3, below, where an evaluation is compared to a hamburger. The point of the illustration is that you need a top bun (the introduction), a bottom bun (the conclusion), and lots of meat in the middle. Informative writing doesn't need a conclusion and it really doesn't require any setting of the stage or introductory content.

Good examples of evaluative writing can be found in *Consumer Reports*. If you were thinking about buying a DVD player or a refrigerator or snow tires, you could find articles there that would evaluate the various models available. First, they define what they are discussing, why you as a reader might care about this kind of product, and what criteria are being used to evaluate the options. Next, they evaluate every model or brand point by

Figure 4-3. The Three-Part Structure of Evaluation.

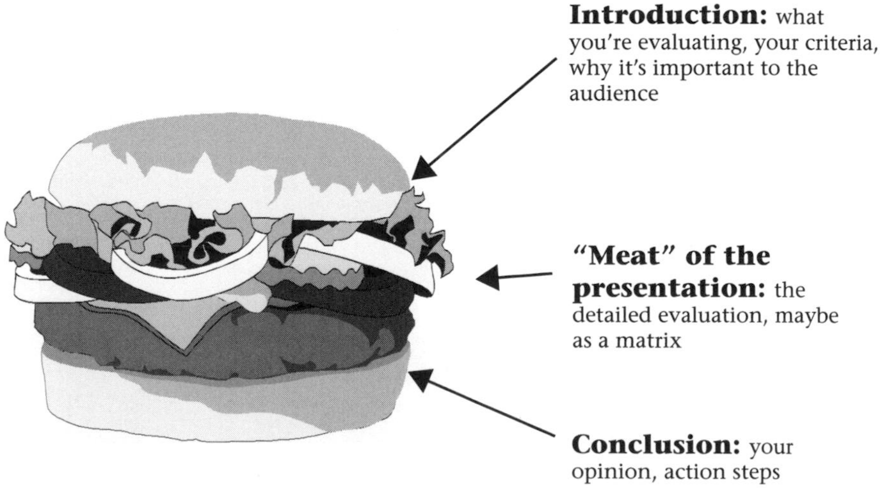

Introduction: what you're evaluating, your criteria, why it's important to the audience

"Meat" of the presentation: the detailed evaluation, maybe as a matrix

Conclusion: your opinion, action steps

point according to the criteria they listed. Usually this part is a combination of text containing anecdotal information about their testing and a table or matrix in which every brand or model is presented. Finally, they conclude the article by indicating which model is the "best buy" in their opinion. Do they care if you buy a DVD player or an ice maker or snow tires? No. It doesn't matter to them if you never buy anything. Their sole purpose is to take a look at what's available and offer an expert opinion about the various choices.

Persuasion

With persuasion, we care very much about whether the reader is motivated to buy. Persuasion combines elements of information and evaluation. It should present facts accurately, and it should offer intelligent, informed opinions. But to be successful as persuasion, what we write or say should influence what the audience thinks, how they feel, or what they do.

Fortunately, the most effective pattern for persuasion, which I call the persuasive paradigm, is simple to understand and use. It consists of four steps.

First: The customer's needs. The initial step in persuading is to demonstrate you understand the customer's needs, issues, or problems. Your first job is to summarize the business situation briefly, focusing on the gap to be closed or the competency to be acquired.

The vice president of sales for a large HVAC firm once asked me, "Why should I tell the customer what their problem is? They already know that. If they didn't think they had a problem, they wouldn't have called us."

The answer, of course, is that we are not telling the customers something they don't already know. We're reducing their anxiety. They're worried that the solution we propose won't work because it's the right solution to the wrong problem. By showing customers that we "get" it, that we listened to them and understood what they told us, we raise their level of confidence. We help them feel confident that what we propose will be appropriate for them.

Second: Outcomes. Next, focus on the outcomes or results the customer wants to achieve. How will he or she measure success? What must the organization see in terms of results to make their investment in your products and services worthwhile?

This part of the persuasive paradigm is probably a bit counterintuitive. After all, wouldn't it be more logical to state the problem and then give the solution? The thing to remember is that our goal is motivation. If we don't create a sense of urgency in the decision maker to go forward with our recommendation, we have not been successful in our persuasion effort. However, motivation does not come from problems and needs. Most businesses are faced with dozens and dozens of problems or needs, most of which will never get solved. Why? Because in the mind of the decision maker, "it's just not worth it." In other words, the return to be gained from fixing the problem doesn't outweigh its cost.

You don't want your solution to fall into the category of "not worth it." You create a sense of motivation in your customer by showing that the problem you are addressing is one that really should be fixed. The potential outcome, the return on investment or improvement in productivity or whatever, is so big that the customer can't afford to wait.

Focus on customers' pain to get their attention; focus on their gain to get their commitment.

Third: Recommend a solution. Most proposals don't recommend anything. They lapse into informative writing and merely describe products or services in a flat, factual way. To be a solution, the products and services you are recommending must be linked to the customer's specific problem. "One of the problems you are facing is declining transaction value in your e-commerce transactions. The aspect of our recommendation that will help increase transaction value is . . ."

Also, when you recommend a solution, sound like you believe in it. Say the words: "*We recommend* the immediate installation of LeadPoint asset management software." "*We urge you* . . ." "*We are confident* . . ." Don't be wishy-washy. Don't depend on telepathy to get your point across.

Fourth: Prove you can do it. The last step in persuasion is to provide the evidence necessary to prove you can do the job on time and on budget. Typical kinds of evidence that you might put in a proposal include references, testimonials, case studies, resumes of team members, project plans, guarantees, third-party validation such as awards, details about your management philosophy, your company history, and so on.

Note that I am not saying your proposal should contain every one of these types of substantiation. Include only what the decision maker needs to see to feel confident about choosing you. That will be determined largely by the criteria that matter to this decision maker and by the specific requirements of the RFP, if there is one. Also, in a situation where you're responding to an RFP, your actual answers will be part of the evidence you provide—basically, evidence of your ability to comply with the customer's requirements and meet their objectives.

The four steps to persuasion are summarized in the staircase diagram depicted in Figure 4-4.

Lots of really bad proposals begin with a history of the vendor or with a technical description of the solution. These proposals don't work because they don't address the most important factor that will motivate the reader to decide to buy: a specific problem or need, the resolution of which offers a big payoff for the customer.

Let's take a look at what happens when we use the right structure to create a persuasive message. Normally I prefer not to teach from bad examples, but sometimes it's instructive to look at how somebody has mishan-

Figure 4-4. The Persuasive Paradigm.

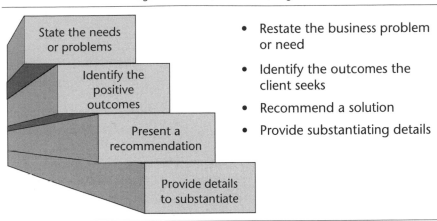

- Restate the business problem or need

- Identify the outcomes the client seeks

- Recommend a solution

- Provide substantiating details

dled a project in order to learn from his or her mistakes. In that spirit, I present here a couple of "proposals." The first is a memo written to an internal audience; the second is a letter proposal.

Sample Proposal 1

To: Bill Henderson
From: Woolie Crofft
Subject: Data Base Software

Today Mike Hinger stopper to explain the software available from his company which could give our executives personal access to the corporate data base in a way that would provide information to facilitate the decision-making process.

There are all kinds of things wrong with this memo, so many that it's difficult to begin to enumerate them. There's the vague subject line, the typo that transforms the verb into something that sounds like a Swedish surname ("Hinger-stopper"), the incredible sentence length, the use of nonspecific language ("personal access," "decision-making process"), and the fact that its chief organizing principle seems to be a loosely chronological stream of consciousness. But the most glaring problem, I think, is that it has no clear purpose. If you were Woolie's manager, Bill Henderson, your reaction to this memo would probably be a hearty "So what?" This memo sounds like one of those worthless scraps headed "FYI," most of which end up being deleted from our e-mail inbox or tossed into the garbage. It certainly doesn't look or sound persuasive. It's not addressing a problem. It doesn't clearly recommend a solution.

Sadly, the author of this memo (yes, it's an example drawn from real life, as all of the samples in this book are; only the names have been changed to protect the guilty) told me how frustrated he was that "nothing had happened." "Management complains about these problems we have with the database," he said, "but then, you when you make a recommendation on how to fix it, they just ignore you." He honestly did not perceive that his memo hadn't recommended anything, that it failed to propose a solution. He was surprised when I suggested that it could be clearer and more persuasive.

Sample Proposal 2

August 3, 2002

Mr. Larry Barns
Director, Telecommunications Services
Information Systems Center
Challenger Automotive
P.O. Box 1476
Moreno Valley, California

Dear Larry:

It was a pleasure having dinner with you last week, and I appreciate the opportunity you gave me to present my telemarketing application.

Challenger Automotive is perceived as a leading component supplier to original equipment manufacturers of on/off highway heavy equipment, heavy duty trucks, and passenger cars and light trucks. The majority of your products are marketed to original equipment manufacturers. For this reason, Challenger product identity is usually lost to the vehicle purchaser. Advertising is aimed at equipment buyers so that when equipment purchases are made, Challenger components are specified.

In the text of its advertisement, Challenger encourages the consumer to write in for further information concerning the product. In some instances, a catalog which is published periodically listing the name, telephone number, and address of dealers and distributors who stock Challenger components is mailed to the consumer.

The risk inherent in this method of advertising involves consumers contacting distributors who no longer carry Challenger components or who are simply out of stock. On the low end of the risk scale, the distributor will refer the buyer to another distributor. This lengthens the buying cycle. On the high end, the distributor will sell the buyer a similar component supplied by a manufacturer other than Challenger.

The solution to this problem is telemarketing, specifically a product we refer to as "Dealer On-Line." Here is a brief description of how it works: The advertisement for the component will carry an 800 number. The consumer will call in on this number and reach a Challenger representative for the After-Market Sales Group. Using an electronic data base, the representative can direct the consumer to the nearest distributor of Challenger components.

Considering your initial response to my presentation of this concept, I know we have a solid application with "Dealer On-Line," and I am looking forward to presenting it to the Sales and Marketing group at the division with your support.

Sincerely,

André LeToille

This letter is truly awful. It starts with a hackneyed, cliché opening that is both inappropriate and weak. It's inappropriate because it implies that the salesperson was allowed to deliver his ideas only because he bought the client dinner. And it's weak because the tone is not one of partnership, but rather of subservience: "Thank you for letting me present . . ."

Then the letter wastes the client's time telling him what kind of business he's in. That's helpful. Is the client supposed to deduce from this information that the salesperson has done his homework and understands the client thoroughly?

It's not until the fourth paragraph that there is anything substantive—a hint of a business problem, namely that the advertising is probably not as effective as it could be. But the solution sounds so canned that the reader begins to suspect that perhaps the salesperson was somebody with a product in search of a need.

Finally, the ending is even weaker than the beginning. The writer completely abdicates responsibility for the selling process and doesn't really ask for anything. Certainly not for a sale.

Both of these sample proposals suffer from the same fundamental weakness. They're not organized in a way that clearly, effectively, *persuasively* communicates to the audience. In other words, they're not broadcasting their message in a way that it will penetrate the noise and clutter surrounding their customer.

So what happens if we restructure them using the persuasive paradigm? If we apply the persuasive paradigm to them, we see some dramatic changes:

Revised Sample 1

To: Bill Henderson
From: Woolie Crofft
Subject: Improving Executive Access to the Database

Our executives need access to the corporate database. The informa-
tion it contains will be invaluable in helping them develop strate-
gies, make decisions, and respond quickly to changing market
conditions. Unfortunately, they are currently blocked from obtaining
that information by a number of system-related problems.

Software available from Hinger Associates will remedy the situa-
tion. It interfaces easily with our existing system, creating a user-
friendly "shell" that allows even nontechnical people to select,
format, and manipulate the data they need without affecting the
database itself. I recommend we lease this software system for a six-
month trial with an option to buy.

Mike Hinger, the developer of the system, indicated that installation
will take about four days. He will provide all the necessary docu-
mentation and support. A six-month lease runs $2,500 a month,
with the full amount credited toward the purchase price of $30,000.
If this software offers even a modest increase in executive productiv-
ity—saving each member of the executive team just two hours a
month, for example—it will pay for itself well before the trial period
is completed.

Shall we proceed?

You can see the difference immediately in this first revision. Notice how
it gets right to the point: executives need access to make good decisions.
Anyone who looks at this memo will see immediately why it's important
and what kind of problem it's trying to solve.

Also, the solution is now clearly stated in the form of a recommendation: "I recommend we lease this software system . . ." No ambiguity there.

The final paragraph adds an extra fillip by providing a value proposition
of sorts. It would be better if we had a bit more development in this area,
perhaps, but at least the recipient's thinking has been turned toward impact.

Here's the other sample, revised using the persuasive paradigm:

Revised Sample 2

August 3, 2002

Mr. Larry Barns
Director, Telecommunications Services

Information Systems Center
Challenger Automotive
P.O. Box 1476
Moreno Valley, California

Dear Larry:

As you mentioned during our meeting on Tuesday, these are extremely competitive times for the automotive after-market parts industry. In such an environment, Challenger Automotive cannot
afford to advertise in ways that benefit your competitors.

Unfortunately, that may be what's happening each time Challenger
runs an ad aimed at the consumer segment of the parts market without also including a toll-free number that can connect consumers
immediately with the nearest Challenger dealer.

Your current advertisement encourages consumers to write in for information about the product and for a catalog that lists the names,
telephone numbers, and addresses of dealers who stock Challenger
components. You also offer an option in the ad in the form of your
Web site URL, although there is no obvious link from the home page
to help a consumer find the nearest dealer.

Consumers want convenience. They don't want to wait. Most of
your target customers are still reluctant to use the Internet to find
information, and are not likely to go more than three clicks deep to
find what they want. Even for those consumers who are willing to
wait to receive a catalog or who have the persistence to use the Web
site, there's no guarantee the information they get will be current.
The nearest dealer might be out of stock or may no longer carry
Challenger components. The net result? You have spent advertising
dollars that ended up benefiting a competitor.

I recommend the installation of a toll-free number: 1-888-CHAL-
LENGER. This number will automatically connect a potential customer to a Challenger representative in your After-Market Sales
Group. Through an interface between the telephone switch and the
representative's computer, he or she will see where the caller is located and will be able to identify the nearest distributor of Challenger components with parts in stock.

Challenger's advertising campaign is a winner. With the addition
of a customer-focused tool like the CHALLENGER toll-free number,
it can yield breakthrough results. Attached are brief descriptions of

the results a similar system delivered for other companies and a pricing summary. We can install the system and have it fully functional within six weeks of your go-ahead. And sales can begin to soar immediately!

Sincerely,

André LeToille

Once again, I think the improvement is so dramatic that it hardly needs to be pointed out. The first paragraph immediately states a problem in clear terms, and from there develops a case for the recommendation. There's not much evidence or substantiation offered here, but it may not be necessary for a recommendation like this. After all, using a toll-free number isn't exactly a risky business proposition.

Going Deeper Into Persuasion

For thousands of years, people have tried to figure out the best way to persuade other people to do things. We know that persuasion has been the subject of serious study since the days of classical Greece. Plato worried about the rhapsodes' ability to appeal to citizens' emotions and persuade them to do things that were not in the best of interest of the city or themselves. And Aristotle wrote one of the great treatises on persuasion. Among the Romans the ability to persuade was considered a hallmark of responsible citizenship.

Since World War II, researchers have worked particularly hard to identify the elements of persuasion. Why? They have some practical motives: improving advertising and marketing campaigns, motivating audiences, influencing the electorate, girding consumers and voters against propaganda, understanding the dynamics of brainwashing, and—yes—writing better proposals.

From all this speculation and research, four elements have consistently been a vital part of nearly every theory of persuasion: the *message*, the *receiver*, the *channel*, and the *source*. Giving them some consideration will give us a deeper understanding of the process of persuasion.

Message

The impact of your *message* depends in part on whether the receiver is receptive to it to begin with. If the evidence or logic in a particular persuasive message is in line with the audience's basic values, beliefs, or biases, the receiver is more likely to accept it and modify his or her attitudes accordingly. If the evidence runs counter to the receiver's basic beliefs, persuasion is far less likely to occur. Thus, the way you frame your message with regard to your audience's preferences is critical.

That may seem circular: You can persuade people to accept only the things they already accept or to do the things they already want to do. But that's not quite what's going on here. There is a difference between a *belief* and an *attitude*. Someone may issue an RFP for new equipment because he or she believes that production efficiency can be improved by using more modern technology. If you can base your proposal on the same belief and then demonstrate how your equipment will introduce labor-saving enhancements, the receiver's attitude toward *you* as the most suitable vendor will change in a positive way. However, if you send out a canned proposal, one that emphasizes the ruggedness and durability of your machines, instead of their impact on production efficiency, you will be not be addressing the client's basic belief. As a result, you may not persuade him or her to choose you.

This is the fundamental problem in submitting boilerplate proposals. Because customers vary widely in their beliefs and values, using the same text for everybody guarantees that a large percentage of them will find your message irrelevant or unconvincing. We will examine how to develop a client-centered message in the next chapter.

Receiver

The *receiver* is a vital component of persuasion, because it's the receiver who must take action, who must make a decision, or whose attitudes must change.

A message that persuades one person may leave another unmoved. Why? For now we can simply note that two of the factors determining how much influence a persuasive message has on an individual are the receiver's personality and his or her personal involvement in the issue. A person who feels threatened by change will be much harder to influence than one who feels confident and secure. Similarly, a decision maker will be particularly cautious in taking action on an issue that will directly affect his or her career.

In addition, people process information in different ways. Presenting a highly detailed and analytical document to a person who prefers the "big picture" will complicate the persuasion process. Presenting information at a technical level that is too difficult for the audience to grasp will also damage the effort. After all, most people tend to say "No" when they are confused or uncertain about the information they're receiving.

In Chapter 6 we'll talk about the best ways to adjust the delivery of your message to match the audience's expectations, preferences, and capabilities.

Source

The *source* is the person or thing doing the persuading—the politician making a speech, the sales representative trying to close a sale, the company submitting a proposal, the foundation running a public service announcement.

To be effective, the source must be both *credible* and *appealing*. People believe in people they trust, and trust is based on a combination of credibility and appeal ("rapport" is another way of defining the quality I have in mind here).

The audience must like the person delivering the message. They must feel comfortable with the source. They must believe that the person cares about them and understands them. They must respect or admire the company submitting the proposal. These are all components of appeal. If you don't establish a measure of rapport or appeal at the outset of your presentation or document, the audience may tune out and never look carefully at whether you are credible.

However, if there is an element of appeal, then listeners and readers will also look for evidence of credibility. The person doing the communicating must appear to know what he or she is talking about, must provide accurate information, must assemble relevant evidence, and must indicate that he or she understands the audience. These are all credibility factors.

If you think about advertising, you can see how companies choose representatives on the basis of these qualities. As a spokesperson for athletic shoes or sports drinks, Michael Jordan is both credible—he certainly knows something about sports—and appealing—he's good looking, successful, and apparently a friendly guy. He probably wouldn't be as effective in commercials for lawn fertilizer or dump trucks. He'd still be an appealing personality, but we'd have to question the credibility of his endorsement.

In Chapter 7 we'll discuss how you can establish credibility in your proposals.

Channel

The *channel* is the medium by which your message is delivered to the receiver. Traditionally, proposals have been delivered on paper in print, but there are now other options, and they are becoming increasingly popular.

For example, your proposal might be accompanied by a digital video of your equipment in action. Including a CD or videotape with your document expands the range of channels you are using to get your message home. Or you might present your proposal orally before handing over the document itself, using some form of multimedia presentation graphics. Combining an audiovisual channel with print is a good idea, because research indicates that for relatively simple messages an audiovisual presentation is actually more persuasive than print alone.

Remember that different receivers will respond differently to the same message presented in a particular medium. A decision maker who likes to study information in detail and who tends to be an introvert will prefer to base decisions on a written proposal. A more intuitive decision maker, by contrast, would probably glance through the details in a written proposal but rely heavily on any accompanying presentation and the overview elements.

The growth of the Internet and the widespread use of e-mail have spawned a trend for electronic submissions. Vendors are invited to send in their proposals by posting them to a Web site, e-mailing them, or responding in forms posted on the Web. To the extent that companies are using this kind of technology to save time and money, it's helpful. But when they post a spreadsheet or a rigid form, asking potential vendors to fill in the blanks, they are actually doing both themselves and the potential vendors a disservice. By reducing the buying process to spreadsheet comparisons, a company treats all products and services as commodities and limits the ability of providers to offer anything creative. Differentiators disappear and calculations of ROI or value become very difficult. All the same, you may still have an opportunity to use the principles we discuss in this book. For example, if you're allowed to submit a cover letter with your form, turn it into an executive summary. If you're allowed to provide a substantive answer, use the persuasive structural pattern for RFP responses (presented in Chapter 12). It's not an ideal situation, but if you're forced to respond in a spreadsheet, don't abandon your commitment to communicating persuasively.

5 Developing a Client-Centered Message Every Time You Write

Y ou've probably had an experience similar to the one I had recently when I was in Scottsdale for a conference. I separately asked three of the friendly people working at the Mountain Shadows Resort which was the best Mexican restaurant in Scottsdale. All three of them gave me the same answer. Hopeful that I was about to enjoy a great meal, I drove to the restaurant they recommended.

After waiting awhile to be seated, I looked at the menu and saw what I wanted, although I wanted a small change to the way it was prepared. Unfortunately, the woman who took my order was much more interested in yelling at a busboy ("Jose! I told you don't put that table over there. No! You put it in the wrong place, now you go move it!") than she was in taking my order. So when the food came, it wasn't what I had asked for. When I pointed that out, she argued with me. "Everybody orders it like this. That's what you want. You didn't say anything different." It got unpleasant pretty rapidly.

So here's the test question: Do you think I will go back to that restaurant?

Not likely, you're thinking, and you're right. In spite of the testimony of three separate people who assured me that it was a great place for dinner, the actual first experience I had there was negative enough that I'll never go back. Some research indicates that it will take seven or more positive experiences before we believe that our negative first impression was a mistake.

How does all of this apply to our proposals? Well, the "principle of first impressions" works in documents just as it does in interpersonal relations. What kind of first impression do you think proposals like these create?

A manufacturer of material handling systems developed a standard proposal, the first twenty pages of which consisted of a history of the company. Why? It's a Fortune 500 company, so it certainly didn't need to work that hard to introduce itself. What's worse, the history was boring. It was a litany of mergers and acquisitions, financial maneuvers, and so forth.

A notable research laboratory typically wrote proposals for grants that read like articles for technical journals. Each one plunged right in, discussing obscure technical issues, but never connecting the research being proposed to the granting foundation's mission or interests.

Account representatives for a major telecommunications vendor were constantly being pounded on the issue of price. The other guys were always cheaper—

or so it was claimed. Soon this vendor's proposals began to focus exclusively on issues of cost and value, almost completely ignoring the client's needs and the vendor's uniqueness factors.

The problem with all of these proposals was that they addressed what the writer was interested in long before they addressed the prospective client's needs and objectives. And in some cases, they never did address what the client cared about. These proposal writers had failed to get out of their own heads and into the heads of their customers.

Seven Questions to Keep You Client Focused

Before you ever set pencil to paper, before your fingertips caress a single key, you should answer the following seven questions. They'll force you to develop a client-centered perspective.

If you are a proposal writer who supports a field sales organization, you should ask these questions of your colleagues in sales when they submit a request for proposal that they want you to work on. Without knowing these basic aspects of the opportunity, you can't give them the best possible support. If they resist, point out to them that you don't want to undercut the work they've done during the sales process by delivering a boilerplate proposal. (If they still resist, maybe they haven't done any work during the sales process and don't know the answers. When that's the case, you should question whether or not the opportunity is "real.")

Seven Questions for a Client-Centered Proposal

1. What is the client's problem or need?
2. What makes this problem worth solving? What makes this need worth addressing?
3. What goals must be served by whatever action is taken?
4. Which goal has the highest priority?
5. What products/applications/services can I offer that will solve the problem or meet the need?
6. What results are likely to follow from each of my potential recommendations?
7. Comparing these results to the customer's desired outcomes or goals, which recommendation is best?

---

1. What is the client's problem or need?

Sometimes the client issues a request for proposal that specifically states what is wanted:

The FAA needs a course that will teach customer service and total quality principles to its management staff and hourly employees.

Smith, Goldblatt, and Wong, attorneys at law, are hereby soliciting bids for an office telecommunications system to be installed in the firm's new quarters no later than May 15 of this year. The system must provide the following features: . . .

The trustees of the Kallaher Group of Homes for the Aged solicit bids for an audit of all of the properties for the fiscal years 2002 and 2003.

Tom's Auto Parts seeks a system to manage the inventory of parts and equipment at all thirteen store locations. The desired system will use bar code data to maintain a current inventory of parts and will integrate with our existing MAS 90 accounting system to automatically update inventory as parts are sold.

These are all pretty clear. But it's not a good idea to assume that the problem or need as stated in the RFP is necessarily complete or correct. Read it, understand it, but keep an open mind. There may be more left unsaid that pertains to why the client is looking for help than has been included in the RFP.

In addition, bear in mind that the client isn't always right. Sometimes the client thinks he or she knows what the problem is, but when you begin to look at the situation, you may find that the client is wrong or has only part of the problem defined.

Use the RFP, if there is one, as a springboard for understanding the client's situation, but don't stop there. The RFP is telling you that there's a gap between what the issuing organization has or knows and what it thinks it needs in order to function effectively.

Here are a couple of examples of the kinds of statements of need that might appear in an RFP. The question you have to answer is, what are the likely business drivers that lie behind them?

■ **The client needs a detailed inspection of all cabling and wiring in the Blue River Nuclear Generating Station.**

The business driver that makes this need important: The utility company faces potential liability issues if they are found to have defective or non-compliant cabling in their nuclear power plant. Failure to comply can result in significant financial penalties.

■ **The client requests proposals for nondestructive evaluation or other advanced testing processes that can be used to guide life management practices in the maintenance and repair of turbine blades.**

The reason this problem or issue is important: The entire aviation industry is under tremendous financial pressure. Reducing maintenance costs on engine turbine blades will lower overall operating costs, easing some of the pressure on airlines and other operators. That will make this vendor's engines more competitive from a total cost of ownership standpoint.

In many sales situations, there is no RFP. You are working with a client who has expressed interest, and you have uncovered a need as part of your sales process. The client agrees that it's worth looking at in detail, requesting that you address it in a proactive proposal. This is actually a better situation for you, because you now have the opportunity to offer an unsolicited proposal without facing any direct competition. But you still need to probe that situation carefully to make sure you understand its implications and consequences fully.

In fact, one of the most frequent mistakes salespeople make in a proactive situation, one where there is no formal RFP to define the customer need, is to confuse the solution they are offering with the customer's need. I was working with a large bank, developing the basic outline for a proposal for treasury services with the account team. As part of that process, we were answering the seven questions to make sure we were client centered.

When I asked them, "What is the client's need or problem?" the senior account executive said, "Well, they need real-time verification of credit cards on their Web site."

"So if they can process credit cards online, they'll be happy?" I asked.

"Right."

Somehow that just didn't click for me. It seemed more likely that online payment verification was the bank's way of meeting a broader need of the business. So I asked the account manager the obvious question:

"Why do they need to improve their e-commerce capabilities on their Web site?"

"Their competitors have better Web sites, so these guys are losing market share to them. They're used to selling from their retail locations, and they've been slow to adapt to online selling, I guess. But now they can see it's hurting them not to have a good system."

After further discussion, we decided that the client's main problem or need was to regain market share and become more competitive by improving its ability to provide secure, fast transactions online. The ability to verify credit cards on the Web site was an enabling technology to help them achieve their broader business goal. It was, in fact, a key part of the solution. It wasn't the problem.

Try to find out who is feeling the "pain" associated with this problem. Who is having a difficult time achieving their objectives because of it? If you are unable to get better definition of the problem, you might consider doing some research into the company. A Web search might turn up press releases and news stories that suggest what the problem is. Sometimes a

visit to Web sites run by your prospective client's competitors will be revealing. The competitors may be hinting at weaknesses or problems that your
proposal is intended to fix.

How else can you find out what the customer's needs are? One way to
start recognizing customer needs is to work backwards from existing projects or contracts you have with similar companies for similar products or
services. In other words, if you have written this kind of proposal before,
perhaps the reasons that drove that opportunity are relevant in this new
opportunity. Ask yourself:

■ **What did we sell or propose to provide?**

*Starting from your own products and services is usually comfortable and
easy. Just don't stay there.*

■ **Why did the customer need that service, product, or expertise?**

*Looking back at previous opportunities, you probably have a better insight
into what was going on than you did at the time you wrote the proposal. What
was the real reason they were looking for the particular solution you provided?*

■ **Why couldn't the customer wait?**

*What made this need urgent? Was there a compelling event looming in
this customer's business life cycle that had to be addressed? Was there a competitive situation which the company could not endure? Was there a market
opportunity?*

■ **Why couldn't the customer solve the problem internally?**

*And what was it about the solution that made it necessary to go outside
the company to contract with your firm to get it? Specialized expertise? Speed
of delivery? Equipment? Perhaps this isn't part of the customer's core business
competency?*

The goal here is to understand the problem, define it accurately, and use
it as the starting point for what you bid.

2. What makes this problem worth solving?
What makes this need one that is worth addressing?

Try to look below the surface. Ask yourself *why*? *Why now?* As we said previously, there are all kinds of problems and needs that every business con-
fronts almost daily. Most of them will never get fixed, because they're just
not important enough. So what makes this situation one that can't be ignored? What makes this the right time to take action? Who in the organization is being affected by the problem? What corporate objectives are being
blocked? What outside pressures are making this problem something that
cannot be ignored? For example, if we go back to our sample problem statements from above, here are some questions we might ask:

Why does the FAA need a course on customer service and total quality principles? Why do they need it now? Why do they want to combine those two topics in the same course? Why is the course intended for both hourly and management staff? To what extent have recent changes in the aviation industry contributed to the need for this training?

Why is the law firm moving? How do they use their telecommunications system? What functions and capabilities do they include under the heading of "office telecommunications system"? Why have they specified the group of features they list in their RFP? Are there other features that could benefit them that they may not know about?

The Kallaher Group of Homes for the Aged is insolvent. Why do the trustees need an audit now? How will they use the information? Are they looking for more than just the financial statements? For example, are they seeking an opinion, a restructuring plan, or documentation prefatory to filing bankruptcy?

Tom's Auto Parts has announced expansion plans. They plan to grow from thirteen stores to fifty over the next two years. Is that a driving factor in their desire to update the inventory management system? Will scalability be a critical factor for them? And what about shrink?

3. What goals must be served by whatever action is taken?

Before you can figure out what to propose, you must know how the client will judge success. What is the client trying to accomplish and what is he or she trying to avoid?

> Delivering the right results through your solution is usually more important than quoting the lowest price. In fact, it's the definition of value.

Compelling value usually comes from a solution that goes beyond merely solving the problem to deliver important improvements. Understood in this sense, results are improvements in an organization's ability to achieve its objectives and function efficiently and profitably.

Ultimately, you have to ask the customer what he or she values. When you look back on this project, what do you hope to see as a consequence? How will the organization be better than it is now? What measures will you use to determine whether or not you got good value for the money?

As you question your customer about how he or she will measure success, make sure the results and outcomes you are noting meet three criteria:

■ **They must be measurable or quantifiable**

"Improved efficiency" is not an outcome or a meaningful goal, because you can't measure it. "Reducing system downtime by 20 percent" is a measurable result, assuming there are reliable baseline statistics available.

■ **They must be organizational in nature**

Personal or political goals are not the kinds of outcomes that can be quantified or used in a proposal. Results and outcomes are important and defensible if they benefit many people across the organization, not merely one decision maker.

■ **The results must come as a direct consequence of the impact your services or solutions have on the customer's business operations**

There must be linkage between what you specifically are offering (not what everyone who is submitting a proposal is offering, but rather the specific elements of your recommendation that differentiate you from your competition) and the specific outcomes the customer seeks. If you "own" the outcomes in the buyer's mind, you probably own the deal.

As you gain insight into the customer's desired outcomes, resist the temptation to take the first thing your customer contact says as the one, true goal for this opportunity. Sometimes this contact is thinking about personal parochial interests and not looking at the larger, organizational objectives.

For example, suppose you are talking to the I.T. manager and you are learning more about the reasons why this person's company wants to develop an in-house test bed for monitoring engine performance. You ask question #3: "What are the goals that the monitoring system must deliver? How will you know that the system you purchase is the right one for this application?" And the I.T. manager says, "The system must be compatible with our Microsoft infrastructure. That's the main thing. If it's not compatible, it won't work here."

Now, do you think that's the most important goal for the entire company? Or does it perhaps reflect the I.T. manager's anxiety about not being able to support an application that doesn't work in the corporate-approved platform and doesn't match the skill sets of his or her employees?

Always push for deeper insight into the goals. In fact, I urge you to analyze the situation in terms of four overlapping areas: *business, technical, social,* and *personal.*

Business goals might include such issues as increasing market share, increasing net profitability, reducing overhead, creating differentiation in the marketplace, or reducing unit cost of manufacturing. Business goals can often be translated into financial measures, although not always. If you are proposing to a government agency, replace the concept of *business goals* with *mission objectives.* Most government agencies or departments have a clearly defined mission, and your recommendations should be focused on helping them achieve that mission faster, safer, more completely, or more economically.

Technical goals typically address problems in the infrastructure. For example, a technical goal might be to automate a labor-intensive process, to provide greater flexibility or modularity in system design, or to enhance quality through the use of automated inspection technology. Our I.T. manager who wants the solution to be Microsoft compatible is looking for a technical outcome. It's possible, of course, that a "technical" goal may have nothing to do with technology. Instead, it might involve implementing quality management methodologies or achieving standards of compliance. For example, a factory might need to reduce emissions of volatile nitrous oxides in order to meet regulatory standards. How they achieve compliance may not matter to them, so long as they can avoid having their plant shut down and fined.

Social goals can be directed either internally or externally. Internal social goals might involve enhancing employee morale, reducing turnover, increasing the professionalism of the company's sales representatives, raising awareness among all employees on issues of diversity, and so forth. External social goals may focus on relationships with customers or on relationships with suppliers. For example, a company may want to increase brand recognition, change consumer attitudes, reduce the number of calls to customer support, increase the company's share of the customer's total spending, or capture a greater share of existing markets, among other customer-focused goals. Social goals involving suppliers might include supplier certification, integration of data systems, or development of long-term contracts.

Personal goals, finally, include all the outcomes that affect the decision maker's own career, income, or prestige. If the decision maker owns the company, there may not be much difference between personal goals and business goals. But in a typical situation, the decision maker may be looking for an opportunity to be a hero, to climb the corporate ladder, or simply to avoid making a career-damaging mistake. As we noted above, the most defensible goals are those that are organizational in nature, so be wary of making somebody's personal agenda the basis for your proposal.

4. Which goal has the highest priority?

You've identified the client's desired outcomes. Now which one matters the most? You need to know what's most important to the decision maker for two reasons.

First, you want to present your ideas in the same order that they matter to the reader, because seeing them presented from most important to least important will create the impression in that reader's mind that you think the way they do. This is the primacy principle all over again: they assume

Figure 5-1. Types of Outcomes Clients Typically Seek.

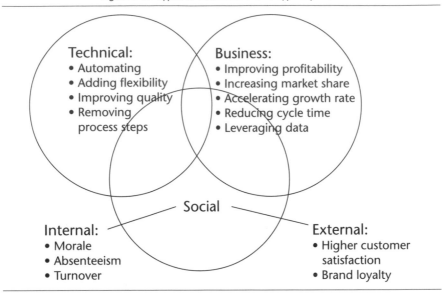

that what you say first is what is most important to you and an indication of where the proposal as a whole is headed.

Second, you want to know which goal is most important so that you can use it as the basis for developing your value proposition. Presenting an ROI based on improving quality in a production environment may be easy, given the features and functions of the nondestructive test system you sell, but if the customer is primarily looking for a way to increase market share, it may not be very convincing.

In my experience, proposal writers often attribute their own values to the customer. For example, in working with one of the world's largest professional services firms, I found that virtually every proposal contained the same value proposition. "We offer a greater breadth of services than any other firm," it went. "We can do it all. No matter what kind of analysis, implementation, or outsourcing service you may need, we can handle it." The problem was, as research into the values of their customer base revealed, customers didn't care about breadth of services as a differentiator. What they wanted was much more task specific: Speed of delivery. Risk minimization. Performance guarantees. Relevant prior experience. Introduction of new technologies that will improve productivity. Breadth of services was strictly an internal focus, something the partners in this firm were proud of but which had little meaning for customers.

5. What products/applications/services can I offer that will solve the problem or meet the need?

Usually there are several ways to solve a problem or meet a need. Brainstorm. Look at all of the approaches as uncritically as possible. At this stage, consider anything. For example, you might be able to meet the needs of a client who is seeking a training program by offering a one-day seminar at the client's site. Or you might be able to do it via the Web. Or you might propose developing a computer simulation that can be issued on a CD and reused throughout the organization. Or maybe you could just give the trainees a book to read, followed by a test.

The more creative you can be in combining what you know about the client's needs and goals and what you have to offer, the more likely you are to separate yourself from the pack and develop a truly client-centered solution.

6. What results are likely to follow from each of my potential recommendations?

Make an educated guess, perhaps based on prior experience with other customers, about the probable results of each possible course of action. Will they lead to the client's most important goal? Will they provide competitive advantage? What will they cost? How long will they take? Are cost and timing important issues? Will they require the client to commit employees to the task?

7. What should I recommend?

Choose the best option from the client's point of view, and use that as the basis of your proposal. Even though it can be tough sometimes, try to resist the temptation of recommending the solution that offers you the highest profit margin or the biggest commission check. Manage your proposals and your business for the long term.

Redefining the Customer's Need

Sometimes the client tells you his or her need explicitly, either by explaining it in conversation during your sales process or by defining it in the statement of work of the RFP the client issues. The trouble is, sometimes the client is wrong.

For example, suppose the manager of a telemarketing operation contacts you because she's unhappy with the sales volume her group is producing. "We need a course on closing techniques," she tells you. "Can you do that for us?"

Well, you can do it, but after observing the company's salespeople in action, you realize that what they really need is a course on telephone courtesy. These people are so aggressive that they cross the line into rudeness. The question is, what do you propose?

The best course is to communicate with the potential client, discuss your concerns or your observations, and try to educate and inform the decision makers before you write your proposal. But sometimes you can't. Sometimes, when you're dealing with a formal RFP released in quantity to many potential vendors, or when you're dealing with a consultant who has written the RFP, or when ego or politics or governmentally mandated procurement rules get in the way, you have to respond to the client's need as it's stated, even if that's not appropriate. And sometimes you must be sensitive to the client's or consultant's need to save face.

You have three basic options in this situation:

1. **Accept the need as defined in the RFP and study the various ways in which you or your company can satisfy that need, identify the best among them, and propose a solution in terms of that approach.** In the short term, this is the safest approach to take. Bid on the job as it's been described, try to win it, and then hope you can convince the client to alter the statement of work after you have the contract in your pocket. Unfortunately, what's safe in the short term is risky in the long. You're basing the business relationship from the outset on less than full honesty, and a tough customer who is looking for performance guarantees or service-level commitments may not be willing to approve change documents or authorize additional funding to get a solution that works.

2. **Study the client's situation as accurately as you can, independent of what the proposal may tell you, and redefine the client's need based on your analysis.** Use your own definition of the client's need as the basis for the proposal you submit.

   Redefining the need is a high-risk approach, particularly when the client has provided the original analysis or has paid a consultant to develop it. Sometimes, though, you really have nothing to lose. For instance, when the analysis has been provided by an outside consultant or a competitor, redefinition may be necessary in order to position your company more competitively. If your competitor has written the RFP, you can assume that there will be nothing in it that favors you.

3. **Do both of the above.** Respond to the client's definition of the need, but also offer an alternative perspective. You could discuss the situation frankly in the executive summary as a way of introducing your proposal. State that while you're fully prepared to respond to the statement of work as written in the original RFP, and have included a response that proves you can do exactly what the client has asked for, your analysis has led you to develop another approach to solving the client's problem. In addition, because this alternative approach will be less costly or more effective (or both), you feel obliged to at least present it as an option.

   One other technique is to offer a phased approach to solving the total problem. This is a reasonably safe approach to take, particularly when the client hasn't misdefined the need but simply hasn't requested the total solution that he or she needs. By structuring your proposed solution in terms of phases, with each phase priced separately and each phase requiring a joint review of progress and commitment to the next phase, you provide a structure in which the client can change direction without scrambling the budget or losing face.

Twelve Questions for Developing a Consultative Proposal

As you start developing your consultative proposal, answering these questions may help you:

1. What must I establish about myself and my company so that the client will believe what I say?

2. What is the key recommendation I am making? How does this recommendation address the client's needs? Have I substituted my own sense of what the client ought to do for what it thinks it needs?

3. What specific opportunities for improving the client's productivity or profitability am I presenting in this proposal? Have I demonstrated these opportunities in enough detail that the decision maker will find them credible?

4. What are the meanings of the key words I am using? Will the client understand them? Have I minimized the use of jargon?

5. How can I contrast my proposal with other, similar proposals? (Try to anticipate how the competition may bid and—preferably without disparaging or naming names—ghost the competition by showing the weaknesses of those approaches and superiority of yours.)

6. How inclusive (or limited) is this proposal? Could it be focused more narrowly or expanded to include more? Should it be?

7. How can I prove my claims, particularly regarding potential ROI or competitive superiority for my products or services? What kinds of evidence will this client find convincing? How can I illustrate or support my claims?

8. What might an opponent say against my proposal? What aspects of my recommendations might provoke resistance or disbelief?

9. Does this proposal clearly suggest that some sort of action must be taken? Does it indicate the consequences of inaction?

10. If the proposal includes a prediction or estimation of results, how accurate is this likely to be? What is it based on—factual

data, observed trends, comparisons to other situations, intuition, or what? Am I guaranteeing results?

11. What are the total costs for this client to undertake the course of action the proposal recommends? Does this include both time and money costs? Are these costs linked to a calculation of return on investment, payback period, total cost of ownership, or some other measure of value?

12. Does my proposal involve the coordination of large numbers of people or resources? If so, does the proposal make clear how this coordination effort will be managed?

Where to Put Your Client-Centered Insights

The whole proposal should be oriented toward the client, but it's particularly important to put as much of your client-centered insight up front as possible. That means including the client in your cover letter, title page, and executive summary.

One simple way to check whether your proposals are client centered or self centered is to count how many times your company's name appears in the executive summary compared to the customer's name. The customer should appear at least three times more often, because a good executive summary will focus primarily on the customer's business situation, their needs, their desired outcomes, and how your solution will match up against their expectations. If it's all about you, it's a bad executive summary.

6 *Understanding the Customer:*

The Cicero Principle

The essence of client-based persuasion can be summarized in the words of the Roman orator and statesman Cicero: "If you wish to persuade me, you must think my thoughts, feel my feelings, and speak my words." This is great advice, so excellent that it is the basis for this entire chapter. When we break it down, phrase by phrase, we can see just how profound it is.

If you wish to persuade me . . .

Why do you wish to persuade anybody of anything? Basically, you're hoping to influence their behavior, thinking, or attitude. If the context of the persuasion is sales, you're trying to motivate the audience to purchase your product or service.

. . . you must . . .

Old Cicero doesn't cut us any slack here. This is mandatory. Not "it would be a good idea if" or "beneficial results may derive from . . ." No. *You must.* And he's right, because what he goes on to emphasize is the necessity of developing your persuasive arguments from the client's perspective.

. . . think my thoughts . . .

One of the keys to thinking like the client is to try to see things from his or her point of view. In fact, that may be the fundamental key to all persuasion: getting outside your own head and away from your own interests and trying to get inside the decision maker's head.

To think the thoughts of your client, you need to watch for clues regarding his or her preferences in terms of receiving and processing information. The challenge you face as a proposal writer is twofold: you need to know what your own preferences are, since you will tend to write a proposal that you would like to receive; and you need to know what your customer's preferences for receiving and processing information are, since you want to adapt your own style to match his or hers more closely. We'll look at specific ways to do this shortly.

. . . feel my feelings . . .

What does your customer care about? What matters? If your proposal is being reviewed by a gatekeeper, someone who performs a quick, initial screen of all submissions with the goal of eliminating those that are not appropriate, that person is looking for reasons to disqualify or reject proposals. Of course, the reasons have to be "safe" and defensible, so gatekeepers typically look for a failure to comply with requirements, or for a lack of fit with engineering, legal, or contractual specifications.

If the decision maker or recommender is a hands-on user of your product or service, that person is probably most concerned with the reliability, user-friendliness, and productivity of what you're offering. The person wants to know if it will make life easier or harder. Will it work with existing systems or equipment? Will it require changing familiar and comfortable habits of work?

Finally, if the decision maker is the ultimate authority, the one who controls the checkbook, the one who says yes or no and who can overrule the recommendations of other members of the decision team, that person is probably looking at bottom-line issues of cost, productivity, return on investment, or other measures of business performance.

. . . speak my words

The last element of Cicero's formula is vital. You need to use words the customer will understand. And if there's a discrepancy between the language your audience uses and what you use, you should drop your own usage and mimic the audience. Your readers will understand more, feel more comfortable with your proposal, and be more likely to adopt your recommendations.

Analyzing the Audience

Cicero has given us the word: You must consider your audience when writing proposals. It's crucial. Ignoring or misunderstanding the audience dooms hundreds, probably thousands, of proposals to failure every year, proposals that otherwise answer the needs or solve the problems of the corporations soliciting them.

The problem is that most people write proposals under duress. And most of us, when we're feeling stressed, will do something we're confident we can do well. In the case of proposal writing, we'll create the kind of proposal that we would like to receive and we'll include the kind of content we're confident we can do pretty well. If we are technical and detail-oriented by nature, we will create proposals that are technical and detailed. But how likely is it that the client will have the same attitudes and personality traits that we have? And even if the client does have a similar personality to ours, how likely is that he or she will be comfortable with the same language we are?

As Cicero has indicated, then, to write a winning proposal, you need to consider three key factors about the audience:

1. Personality type ("think my thoughts")

   - Detail-oriented

   - Pragmatic

   - Consensus-oriented

   - Visionary

2. Level of expertise ("speak my words")

   - Expert

   - Informed

   - Familiar

   - Unfamiliar

3. Role in the decision process ("feel my feelings")

   - Ultimate authority

   - User

   - Gatekeeper

To appeal to and hold the interest of this broad spectrum of readers, you must balance many presentation skills, providing enough technical data to please the highly informed, detail-oriented customer, but not so much that visionaries will be bored or the uninformed audience intimidated.

Adjusting for Personality Type

The first factor about your decision maker is his or her personality type, by which I mean the individual's preferences regarding information gathering, information analysis, and communication styles. In fact, there are two questions to ask: What kind of personality type does my decision maker have? And what kind do I have? I guarantee that if you don't consciously think about the customer's personality, you will inevitably create a proposal that is exactly the kind you would like to receive.

Among the various tools available for analyzing and categorizing personalities, one of the most useful is the Myers-Briggs [Personality] Type Indicator. It is used by career counselors, family and marital therapists, educators, and many others to help people understand themselves and others better. The Myers-Briggs Type Indicator (MBTI) is a self-reporting test that indicates an individual's likely preferences on four pairs of opposing personality tendencies: introversion/extraversion, sensing/intuitive, thinking/feeling, and judging/perceiving.

The first pair has to do with the way people prefer to interact with the world. When you're on a plane, do you hope that no one sits next to you, or do you welcome a bit of interaction? Would you rather read a proposal or watch a presentation?

The second pair indicates the two general ways people prefer to gather data. Some people, the "sensors," are oriented toward facts by their nature. They tend to be very literal in their use of words. They need to look at all the details before reaching a conclusion. Their opposites, the "intuitives," find details boring and distracting. They prefer the big picture and appreciate the value of the generalist in an organization. Intuitives are often keen interpreters of nonverbal messages.

The third pairing, the thinking/feeling dichotomy, focuses on how people prefer to make decisions. Thinkers look at issues objectively, reaching conclusions based on what is logical and fair rather than on what makes people happy. They find logic, facts, and technical detail more credible and appealing than emotion. Feelers, by contrast, consider a good decision to be one that builds consensus and harmony. They often make decisions by asking how any given course of action will affect the people involved. They would consider service and quality issues to be as important as price.

The final pairing, judging/perceiving, indicates how a person prefers to organize his or her time. Judgers prefer punctuality, structure, order, and closure. As a result, they are more likely to reach decisions quickly, to adhere to a schedule, and to be decisive. Perceivers prefer to "go with the flow." Spontaneity and flexibility are more important to them than organization or structure. They do not feel much inner pressure to reach closure or make decisions.

This brief summary of the Myers-Briggs approach does a disservice to a subtle, nonjudgmental, and extremely rich method of discussing personalities. Combining the various traits outlined above yields sixteen different personality types. For a proposal writer, sixteen different types is a bit unwieldy, however, and it's pretty difficult to get your customer to take the Myers-Briggs test anyway. The point I want to make is that the various combinations of these tendencies do identify useful distinctions that we can use to help us modify the way we deliver our message. And we can reach conclusions about our customer's preferences without obtaining a detailed, clinical picture.

The kind of information you need is the kind you can garner from commonsense observation. What is the person's manner of speaking? Curt? Detailed? Emotional? Look at his or her office. How is it decorated? Are there schematics of jet engines on the wall or pictures of the kids? Golf and tennis trophies or Sierra Club posters? In your conversations, what really seems to matter to this person? If you had to list the ten things your customer is most passionate about, could you? If not, start paying attention and asking. Learn about your decision maker as a person so you can communicate with that person as effectively and comfortably as possible.

The crucial personality characteristics that you need to consider when looking at your decision makers are (1) how they prefer to gather data and (2) how they prefer to make decisions. You might find it useful to set up a matrix based on those variables and position your key decision makers as accurately as you can within one of the four quadrants. (See Figure 6-1.) For example, some decision makers prefer for the information they receive to be factual, logical, empirical, or sensory in nature. Others are more prone to receiving information emotionally. In MBTI terms, this is a difference between thinkers and feelers. In terms of the second characteristic, how they prefer to make decisions, a useful distinction can be made between people who are prone to take action quickly and who want you to be brief (judgers), and people who are more passive and want you to be thorough (perceivers). When we combine these two characteristics, we get four types of decision makers.

Analytical or **detail-oriented** decision makers approach experience rationally and logically. They tend to dislike emotional terms and inexact language. They value accuracy and thoroughness. They want a lot of detail and substantiation. "How can I decide anything until I know everything?" they might ask. For them, truth resides in facts, procedures, evidence, or formulas, and they want to know how things work and how a decision

Figure 6-1. Four Personality Types and Their Preferences.

Analytical	Pragmatic
• Facts, accuracy	• Bottom-line driven
• Detail oriented	• Values brevity
• Charts, schematics	• Prefers graphics to words
Concensus seeker	Visionary
• Feelings, values	• Concepts, big ideas
• Concerned about people	• Long-term view
• Responds to color	• Loves "splash"

can be logically justified. When they read your proposal (or watch your presentation), they constantly evaluate it even while they are in the act of perceiving it. If you are more of a bottom-line, pragmatic kind of decision maker, you may find their methodical approach frustrating, even irritating. That's a mistake. Be patient with their careful approach, demonstrate competence, back up everything you say with solid, factual evidence, avoid the use of hype or marketing fluff, base your persuasion on accuracy and logic, and to the extent possible minimize their sense of risk by offering guarantees. Use words and phrases that are likely to trigger a quick, positive response from an analytical decision maker, such as *factual, proven, demonstrated, tested, detailed, criteria, objective, analysis, principles, methodology,* and *experienced*. Remember, though, that words alone won't cut it with these customers. They will want the words to be backed up with proof. Thus, merely saying that "we offer a wide selection of precise gas mixtures" may not be enough. Instead, get more specific: "We offer seven classes of calibration mixtures, ranging from EPA protocol certified mixes designed to meet the most stringent monitoring requirements to instrument calibration mixtures intended for the laboratory."

Pragmatic types are results oriented. They focus on bottom-line issues. They want action. For them, the dominant issue isn't accuracy or thoroughness, it's impact. They want to know, "What have you got? What'll it do for me? How soon? At what price and at what payback?" They may become impatient with detail and want you to be concise, focused, and businesslike. (Can you see how a proposal written by an analytical person might alienate a pragmatic customer?) Like the analytical, they tend to be suspicious of emotional appeals. They want you to focus on facts, ideas, and evidence, not feelings or people. They admire precision, efficiency, and a well-organized delivery in both written and oral communications. Words and phrases that are likely to have positive connotations for the pragmatic decision maker include *planned, completed, mission, core competency, return on investment, competitive advantage, fixed, productive, total cost of ownership,* and *guaranteed*.

Consensus seekers sincerely want to understand your message. They listen carefully, but in the process they are likely to focus on how everyone else is likely to feel about the decision rather than the details or facts. They value close working relationships, and want you to be dependable and reliable. They need to feel comfortable with you, your ideas, and the level of acceptance from the rest of the team before they will make a decision, and hate feeling pressured or rushed. Your personal interest and commitment to successful outcomes are an important part of your overall persuasive message, so back up your recommendations with your own assurances of support and follow through. Consensus seekers typically have a low tolerance for risk, so provide brief but compelling evidence and offer guarantees where possible. (Social proof is more likely to be convincing to this kind of decision maker than technical proof, so great references and testimonials are important.) Consensus seekers often have flashes of insight into you as an individual and into your meaning, and they're likely to pick up inconsistencies between your apparent message and your hidden intentions. Unfortunately, they're also likely to garble technical or factual data, make erroneous assumptions, or introduce unwanted emotional messages. Trigger words and phrases for this type of decision maker include *reliable, flexible, consensus, adaptable, easy to use, widely accepted, loyal,* and *adaptable*.

Visionaries are the entrepreneurial types. They manage their lives, their responsibilities, and others on the basis of instinct and intuition. They tend to have strong egos and to believe that their ideas are fundamentally sound. They're the opposite of the detail-oriented types, in that they leap over logic and facts in quest of transformation and action. They're easily bored with technical data, but they love to be involved. On the downside, they have a hard time hearing or giving credence to any message that goes counter to their own assumptions or biases. They really aren't that interested in your product or service. What they're interested in is whether your product or service can help them accomplish their plans. They want you to be excited about their ideas, too, and to show that you are committed to them. Detail, routine, procedure, and process are not what they're about. Keep your proposal brief; make it interesting, colorful, and professional. Visionary decision makers want to know how your recommendations will move them closer to achieving their dreams. They also want to know who else is using your product or service, since they like to be associated with leaders, innovators, and winners. Visionaries fall into the category of customer that Geoffrey Moore has called the "early adopter," and they can be very helpful to you if you are going to market with something new, because they often will make a decision quickly even if there is little in the way of evidence that what you have actually works. Words and phrases that may work well in proposals aimed at a visionary decision maker include *innovative, ingenious, creative, original, breakthrough, future, trend setting,* and even *cutting edge*.

These four broad personality types and their characteristics are summarized in Figure 6-1. Notice that the most difficult challenges will be between those personality types who are positioned on opposing corners of the diagram—a pragmatic selling to a consensus seeker; a visionary selling to an analytical; and vice versa.

Sometimes a person's job requires him or her to act like a certain type of person even when that's not in alignment with his or her genuine personality. A high-level executive almost always has to think "pragmatically" and a person with technical responsibilities may have to adopt an "analytical" approach. Should you write to the "real" person or the "role" person? The answer depends on whether you're trying to inform or persuade. Information will be most acceptable if it's structured for the role; persuasion will be most successful if it's pitched to the real.

What about situations where your proposal is going to a team or committee? What then? Write a different proposal for each member of the team? No, of course not. Instead, accommodate the different types of people who are likely to be on a team by structuring your proposal in two parts. The first part, which includes the cover letter, title page, table of contents, and executive summary, should be written for a pragmatic decision maker. Keep it short, focus on business issues, emphasize payback or ROI, and minimize the amount of jargon or technical detail. The second part, which consists of your substantiation, will contain technical details about your product or service, detailed timelines and project plans, and your "proof statements"—case studies, references, testimonials, and awards, your answers to the RFP's questions, and other detailed content. This part should be written to appeal to the analytical decision maker. What about the other two types? Consensus seekers tend to get overrun in team processes by pragmatics, and visionaries are lousy team players by definition. So unless you have very strong evidence to the contrary, you don't need to worry much about those two when you are proposing to a team.

Adjusting for Levels of Expertise

Another element of Cicero's formula has to do with the audience's level of expertise: "speak my words" means to use language or, more generally, content, that the audience understands. That applies to our use of jargon and acronyms, to the assumptions we explain and those we take for granted, and to the actual details we include.

If you stay consciously aware of your audience as you write your proposal, you are much more likely to communicate at the right level. And if you don't stay aware, you'll probably end up writing to yourself. You'll use the words and make the assumptions that seem appropriate to you. But how many customers and prospects do you have who know as much as you do about your topic? How many of them use the same words, understand the same jargon, recognize the internal acronyms the way you do?

In my experience, proposal writers almost always overestimate the level of understanding of their clients. One reason for that is our own material—our products, our services, our technology, our methodology—becomes so familiar to us that it seems easy to understand. Another reason is that clients seldom tell us when they don't understand something. They may be worried that it's something they "should" understand, so they keep quiet. Or, in the context of a government bid, they may be forbidden by rules of procurement from asking for clarification.

Instead, when clients are not sure what you're talking about, they typically withdraw from the process and make noncommittal statements, such as, "We need to review this further internally." Or, "We may want to schedule another meeting before we reach a conclusion." Or, "We have some additional homework to do internally and then we'll get back to you." If you are hearing messages like these from prospects, it's possible they don't understand your proposal well enough to reach any kind of buying decision. And one thing you can count on is that when people feel confused, they don't buy.

Unfortunately, there's another reason why proposal writers communicate at a technical level that's over their clients' head: laziness. Simplifying your content can be hard work. Once when I was working with a team at a major technology firm, I guess I began to annoy one of the technical sales specialists by my constant harping about simplifying. Finally, he turned to me and said, "Look, Tom, if the client doesn't understand this, he shouldn't be buying it."

"Don't worry," I said. "He won't."

It's better to aim too low than too high. If the audience actually understands more than you thought they did, they may find your presentation a bit slow moving. As a result, they may skip over parts that they already understand. But if the audience understands less than you thought, they're stuck. Your proposal content will go sailing over their head, and there isn't a thing they can do to make it more intelligible. So if you have to guess, err on the side of keeping things too simple, not too complex.

Level One: The Uninformed Audience

Uninformed readers have virtually no background in your industry or area of expertise. They may be very bright and highly educated, but not in areas that pertain to what you are proposing. Categorizing someone at this level does not mean we think little of his or her skills or intellect. The fact is we're all at this level for a lot more topics than not. As Will Rogers once said, "Everybody's ignorant, just on different stuff."

The level one audience is most likely to be a person who reads your cover letter and executive summary carefully, then skims the rest of your proposal, relying on colleagues or employees who are more technical to evaluate the details. It's a good idea to try to keep your cover letter and executive summary short, businesslike, and focused on bottom-line issues.

Here are some guidelines to help you slant your writing toward level one audiences, people who are uninformed or unfamiliar with your field:

1. **Provide only the information the reader truly needs to know.** Avoid digressions into technical details or options, no matter how interesting they may be to you. Keep your proposal focused on the specific functionality that will be of interest to this client. Avoid giving the level one audience "extra" information—it is more likely to confuse than to impress.

2. **Keep the presentation basic.** Short is better than long; simple is better than complex. Focus on what your solution will do for the customer, not on how it works.

3. **Use clear, simple illustrations and lots of them.** There are two kinds of illustrations that can help the uninformed reader understand your message. *Visual illustrations* (bar and pie charts, uncomplicated graphs, simple flow charts, photos, maps, organization charts) communicate to many people more clearly than words. Even better, adding a graphic can actually increase the persuasiveness of your message. (One study found that adding a simple graphic increased the persuasiveness of a piece of text by 47 percent!) *Verbal illustrations* (comparisons, analogies, examples, metaphors, anecdotes) help the level one audience understand your point by making it more concrete. In explaining how a new router can alleviate slow performance on a virtual private network, you might cut through a lot of confusion by comparing the hardware to an air traffic control tower.

4. **Avoid using in-house jargon and keep acronyms to a minimum.** And don't forget that for this level of audience, your product and service names are jargon, too.

    You may have been taught that the first time you use an acronym, you should present it in words and then put the acronym in parentheses immediately after the words. You might write something like this: "We have sales and support offices through Europe, the Middle East, and Africa (EMEA) to support clients of Abecedarian Avionics." But often that is not enough, because the words themselves may not make any sense to a level one reader. For example, one of the regional telephone companies was issuing letter proposals to small business owners for "ADSL service." When asked if the use of that acronym was appropriate for a level one audience, the proposal writers decided to make it clearer by spelling out the acronym the first time they used it. But ADSL stands for "asymmetric digital subscriber line," which isn't any clearer for a level one reader than the acronym itself. In fact, it might be worse. After some debate, they decided to communicate the concept in ordinary language:

    You need high-speed access to the Internet. You can't afford to waste time while large file transfers crawl across your phone system to your computer. But you can't afford to replace your existing phone system or rewire your office, either. The answer? Our new Asymmetric Digital Subscriber Line, or ADSL service, which uses your existing phone lines but runs at speeds up to 125 times faster than traditional analog modems.

    Now the client understands the concept and the proposal writer can use the acronym in the rest of the proposal. Would it be necessary to define DSL service that thoroughly today? Probably not, since it has become a widely used application, but isn't it better to be too clear than too obscure?

5. **Keep both the words and the sentences simple and short.** Use everyday language. Choose words of one and two syllables mainly. Try to keep your sentences to an average length of fifteen to eighteen words.

6. **Avoid references to specialized reports, manuals, or sources.** This level of reader won't look for them, probably wouldn't understand them, and perhaps doesn't care. Your proposal needs to stand alone as a clear, self-contained document.

7. **Describe procedures or processes in a simple, step-by-step fashion.** When describing a project plan or explaining how something works, you will communicate more successfully if you use a simple chronological structure rather than a series of complex options. Flow charts and similar diagrams can be a great help, too, as long as they're clear. A complex, multilevel Gantt chart would not be a useful tool for the level one reader.

8. **Highlight your main points, make the transitions obvious, and reinforce your message with design and typography.** Most business readers skim, but none more so than the senior executives who are likely to make up a large portion of your level one audience. So make your proposal easy to skim. Use boldface type, headings, bullet points, color, white space, tint blocks, borders, and anything else that makes your key points jump off the page. (Just be careful not to produce a document that looks like a circus poster.)

Level Two: The Acquainted Audience

An audience who is somewhat acquainted with your recommendations may have considerable education or experience, perhaps even in your general field (business management, electrical engineering, marketing, accounting, whatever), but may still lack detailed, in-depth knowledge of your specific area of expertise. Many of the decision makers to whom you write proposals will be at this level.

All of the guidelines we just discussed for level one are appropriate for level two, because they enhance the simplicity and clarity of the writing. For the most part, you will make slightly different judgment calls regarding the jargon to be defined, the acronyms to be left unexplained, and the examples to be included. You won't offend anybody by producing a proposal that is too easy to understand, but for this audience you can make more assumptions and skip over the basics a little quicker.

Here are some guidelines to follow:

1. **Present your proposal in a larger context—a frame of reference within which your proposal can be positioned and categorized.** For

example, if you are recommending an online inventory control system that provides remote access to real-time inventory data for field sales-people, start by discussing the client's current sales model, or the client's move to an e-commerce approach, or changes in the way supply chains are being managed. The point is to show that what you will describe (your product or service) is relevant to the reader's concerns and has a place within the reader's worldview. This positioning statement can be the springboard for your discussion of the client's problem, of course, but even in the more specifically technical sections of your proposal, you should move from general and familiar to specific and new.

2. **Use more complex graphics, tables, and figures.** This audience will look at and understand visual material that is more complicated and that contains more data. However, you should still avoid equations, pro-gramming statements, schematics, complex decision trees, and other specialized examples or illustrations. You should definitely resist the urge to include illustrations from user documentation or technical man-uals.

3. **Use the accepted jargon of the field, but avoid in-house jargon.** If you are writing a proposal for telecommunications services to a level two audience, you can use terms such as "DSL," "voice over IP," or "ISDN lines" without worry.

Level Three: The Informed Audience

This audience has extensive knowledge of your field, but less knowledge of the specialized project, product, or service you are proposing. For example, a long-time client may know a lot about your material handling systems, but may not possess any details about the new photoelectric measurement tools you are introducing. An MIS or I.T. manager may be very knowledge-able about LANs, WANs, and corporate database administration, but may not be aware of the specific features of the software you provide to locate duplicate entries in a database.

The guidelines:

1. **Establish immediate links between the familiar and the new.** Sup-pose you are proposing that your client outsource all facility manage-ment services to your firm. If you know that they already contract for cleaning and landscaping services, you can draw a parallel between those specific niches and the idea of turning over complete manage-ment of the property to your firm.

2. **Focus on the new or unique aspects of what you are offering.** You can assume with a level three audience that they are familiar with the basics of your product or service. What they need to know is what differ-

entiates your new offering from what they already know and how will those differences benefit their organization.

3. **Stay client centered as you write your proposal.** The temptation when writing to a more knowledgeable audience is to lapse into informative writing, to use jargon, to focus on technology for its own sake. But that won't work. Even though this decision maker is very well informed, you must show how your recommendations help solve the prospect's problems or meet the organization's needs. No one buys a new product just to get cool new features. Instead, people buy products that have features that will deliver important outcomes for their organizations that aren't otherwise available.

Level 4: The Expert Audience

The expert audience knows as much (or more) about the products and services you are offering as you do. The expert not only has extensive knowledge of your field, but has detailed familiarity with the latest work in that field, the various products and options offered by your company and your competitors, and the industry trends.

The good news is that it's very easy to communicate with the expert audience, because it's not much different from talking with your own colleagues. The bad news is that true experts in your customer base are extremely rare.

If you do encounter a true expert among your prospects or customers, here are some guidelines to follow when you write your proposal:

1. **Summarize technical background information or indicate where it can be obtained.** The expert decision maker is more likely to be an analytical personality type, so he or she will want to have access to as much detail as possible. If you provide it by reference or attachment, you are giving them a "complete" proposal.

2. **Use jargon (but be judicious).** Even for an expert, encountering a slew of acronyms and jargon makes for a distasteful reading experience.

3. **Use math, equations, programming statements, or technical explanations if they're needed.** Almost without exception, this kind of technical content will appear in the body of a proposal, not in the executive summary.

4. **Maintain your objectivity, use a professional tone, but remember that your most important job is to persuade.** Even for the expert audience, your proposal must constantly answer the question, "So what?" In providing details, link them to benefits the decision maker cares about.

The Decision Maker's Role and Values

The third aspect of your reader that you must evaluate as you prepare your proposal is the reader's role in his or her organization. This is important, because people tend to apply the same standards in evaluating others that are applied to them. If my bonus depends on increasing net profitability, you can bet that I'll be looking at your proposal in terms of its impact on net profitability. Thus, if you understand the decision maker's role in the organization, you are more likely to understand the values, or "feelings," to use Cicero's term, that he or she brings to each decision.

Ideally, every proposal you write will go directly into the hands of the final authority, the one person charged with responsibility for signing the contract or issuing the purchase order. But in this imperfect world of ours, you will probably have to deal with intermediaries, advisors, influencers, and others in the client organization, winning their approval as you inch your deal forward toward the final throne of power. Understanding how the concerns of a decision maker change depending on his or her role can help you position your proposal as effectively as possible.

Often a proposal must go through a series of evaluations (see Figure 6-2).

Figure 6-2. Levels of Evaluation.

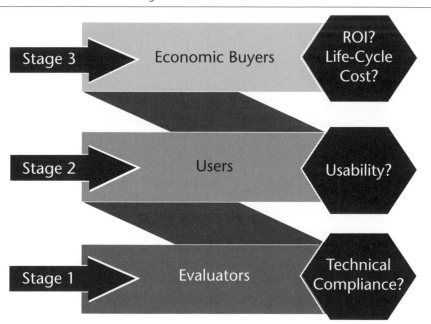

These evaluations may be sequential, with the number of candidate proposals decreasing as weak offerings are eliminated at each stage. Thus, the gatekeeper may initially review a dozen submissions, eliminating half of them very quickly on narrow grounds. The user community may then look at that half dozen, reducing the candidates down to just two or three. From this crop of survivors, the economic decision maker will attempt to select the proposal that offers the best return on investment, the lowest total cost of ownership, or some other measure of payback.

In other cases, the evaluations may occur simultaneously, with the entire team offering critiques and comments. However, because the team members will come from different areas of the company where they perform different roles, their values will also be different.

The Gatekeeper

The gatekeeper's job is to filter out solutions that are inappropriate in terms of some set of clearly defined criteria. As a result, the gatekeeper is looking for a reason to reject rather than for a reason to recommend. In addition, gatekeepers often feel that they're in a vulnerable position, since their recommendation could come back to haunt them if it proves to be a bad one. It's easier to justify rejecting what would have been a good choice than it is to explain why you recommended what proved to be a terrible one. Their tendency, therefore, is to be extremely critical and to assume the worst whenever they have doubts. Finally, gatekeepers are often drawn from that category of personalities who love details. As a result, you must provide the gatekeeper with clear, specific evidence that you meet the requirements of the RFP.

In an informal research study, we interviewed gatekeepers. We asked them to share their biggest complaints regarding the proposals they receive. Boy, did they vent! Their answers should give you an idea of what to avoid when submitting your proposal for review by a gatekeeper.

Evaluators' Complaints

1. The author did not follow the "instructions."

2. The proposal contains no compliance matrix. As a result, evaluators spend a lot of time trying to figure out if the response is compliant or not.

3. Emphasis is placed on the "wrong" portions of the solicitation (failure to understand the award criteria).

4. Lack of meaningful proposal theme(s). No story is told to the evaluator.

5. Poorly structured response, illogical TOC, misuse of appendices.

6. Differentiators are not used at all or are not clear.

7. Many requirements not addressed at all. (Silence on the SOW requirements means the proposal is noncompliant or deficient.)

8. SOW requirements not addressed with respect to the business.

9. Technical claims not substantiated with tangible, real data.

10. Difficult to read: straight text, no bullets, poor graphics, no white space.

11. Lack of section summaries. Points are buried in long text.

12. Overuse of boilerplate. The response is not tailored to the business needs of the client or agency issuing the RFP.

13. Graphics not readable after copying.

14. Volume emphasized over content: not concise, no focus, no compelling argument.

15. Writers propose solutions contrary to what is asked for in the SOW.

16. No page numbers.

17. Complex section headers and section numbering (e.g., 3.2.1a.1.3).

18. ROI and risk not addressed.

19. Misuse of supporting documentation (corporate manuals, marketing literature, etc.).

20. No ghosting of the competition.

21. Incumbents leave out details or experience, assuming evaluators "know" their history.

22. Prime contractors and subcontractors do not convey a team concept, do not appear well integrated.

23. Highly technical proposals without a substantiated management plan.

24. Flowery language, useless adjectives. Writing not simple enough.

25. Bad grammar, poor proofreading, spelling errors, bad figure references, missing pages, and so forth.

26. Lack of cost realism. Typically, too aggressive or unrealistic on costs.

The User

The user evaluates the probable impact of your solution on performance: Will this work? Will it actually make things better around here? Does it look easy? Reliable? Simple to maintain? Quick to learn? Does it meet our needs?

The user knows that lots of solutions that meet the technical specs established in an RFP don't actually do the job when they're installed or implemented.

The Ultimate Authority

The person who makes the final decision, who has veto power over the project, usually derives his or her power from direct access to or control over the money. The ultimate authority is the boss, the owner, the CEO. And the ultimate authority's criteria are usually the needs of the business. What will be the bottom-line impact of this solution? What kind of return will this investment provide?

7 Establishing Your Credibility

There are four indispensable categories of information that every proposal should contain in order to be fully credible. Over the years we have found that these four kinds of content correlate highly with winning proposals, but that when one or more of them is missing, win ratios go down significantly. To some extent, the four kinds of content are a matter of common sense. They grow naturally out of your sales process, your client-centered analysis.

The four kinds of content you must include in every proposal are:

1. **Evidence that you understand the client's problem or need.** The reason for this one is obvious, based on our earlier discussion of the persuasive paradigm and of the process for developing a client-centered message.

2. **A recommendation for a specific solution that will solve the problem and produce positive business results.** Again, an obvious kind of content. Please remember, though, that most proposals don't recommend anything. Instead, they describe products and services. Simply writing in generalities about how good your stuff is won't do the job. And providing customers with a couple of pages of bullet points, listing all of your product's features whether they apply to this customer or not, is a great way to bore people.

3. **Evidence of your qualifications and competence to do the job on time and on budget.** The kinds of evidence that work include references, testimonials, case studies and success stories, third-party validation (awards, recognition, published reviews, analyst reports), resumes of key team members, project plans, management approaches, even the company history. The kind of evidence you include should be dictated by what the customer wants to see. Less is more in this area. One good case study, from the same industry, showing the same kinds of results that your customer is seeking, is much better than three or four generic case studies from companies that aren't even similar to the prospective customer.

4. **A convincing reason why the decision maker should choose your recommendation.** Your proposal must contain a clear, explicit value proposition. It must show that the customer gets more by buying from

you than he or she can get from choosing any other option. We'll look later, in Chapter 11, at how to create a compelling win theme, but for now it's important for you to realize that if you provide the first three kinds of content, but fail to include the fourth, you have a very low probability of winning.

Why are these four essentials so important? Because they provide the decision maker with the information he or she needs to evaluate your proposal successfully and recommend it to others. Specifically, the decision maker wants to know three things:

1. **Am I getting what I need?** This question is about the responsiveness of your submission. It addresses the customer's concerns about whether you actually understand his or her business, whether you are addressing the important needs. The customer wonders, "Are they proposing what I need, or are they proposing what they have? Worse yet, are they proposing what will generate the biggest commission for them regardless of whether it really meets my needs?"

2. **Can they do it?** Can this vendor live up to the promises made in this proposal? Does the vendor have the competence to deliver the solution in a professional manner? Have they handled similar projects, built similar equipment, handled similar installations before? Do they have the resources to do the job? Do they have a quality-control program? A change management procedure? Do they know what they're talking about?

3. **Is it a fair value?** Customers are savvy enough to know that some vendors may lowball a bid, submitting an unrealistic price with the intention of making their profit on change orders. What they want is a fair price with no hidden costs, no misleading analyses, and no underestimating of the level of effort involved. They want to see what kind of return on investment they can expect, and they want to know if you are offering any value-added factors that make your pricing structure more appealing.

Generally, the decision maker's evaluation is weighted in that order: appropriateness to the needs, competence to deliver, attractiveness of the value proposition. In complex opportunities, where proposals are evaluated by committees or where the initial set of submissions is winnowed down to a manageable few, the criteria applied first are almost always about compliance and capabilities. It's not until the final stage that the customer attempts to compare on value.

Going Deeper Into the Issue of Credibility

As you get ready to write your proposal, you can gain deeper insight into the kinds of details you should provide by asking yourself:

■ **What does the decision maker think of me and/or my company?** The decision maker may have certain assumptions about you and your company that will color the review of your proposal. Perhaps your company is well known in a particular niche, but is now trying to penetrate a new market. The customer may have assumptions about your firm and its capabilities based on the past. If you can identify those assumptions and address them, you have a better chance of appearing credible and appealing.

■ **What prior experience does the client have with us?** Was it good or bad? Either way, it will influence whether you come across as credible and appealing. If it was good, you should remind the client of that fact in your proposal. If it was bad, you should directly address changes your firm has put in place to prevent bad things from happening in the future. Past performance is particularly important when you are writing proposals for government contracts.

■ **Is the client currently using our products or services? Is the client using our competitors'?** If you are the incumbent, you have a much better chance of winning additional business. If you are not the incumbent, you must focus on differentiating yourself from the current provider and emphasizing how much more value the client will receive from making the switch to you.

■ **What must I say or do to convince the decision maker that I am knowledgeable, reliable, experienced, honest—in a word, credible?** We will discuss this in much more detail in a few pages, but the ultimate answer to this question is: Communicate a believable message the way the audience wants to hear it.

■ **Do I understand my client's business situation and needs? Have I communicated that understanding clearly?** Credibility is usually proportional to specificity—not about your products or services, but rather about the client's business, the industry within which he or she is competing, and the operational parameters that affect your solution's implementation.

■ **Am I approaching my relationship with the client as a partnership?** "Partnership" is an overworked cliché, but it's better than acting subservient. Proposal writers often undercut their own credibility and appeal by adopting a tone of supplication rather than equality. I mentioned that trite, clichéd opening that so often shows up in cover letters: "Thank you for allowing me the opportunity to submit my proposal and for taking time from your busy schedule to review it." You can practically hear the sound of kissing up in the background, can't you? Remember that you have something important to bring to this relationship: the solution to the decision maker's problems or a way the decision maker can meet his or her needs or achieve crucial objectives. Be polite, of course. But don't come across as a sycophantic toady. You have the solution and the client has the money. That's the basis for a wonderfully equal partnership.

■ **Am I offering specific recommendations?** I'm amazed how often I read proposals that never recommend anything at all. Instead, they describe products or services in detail. They may include management resumes, implementation schedules, and cost analyses. But they never actually recommend that the client do anything. Make a specific recommendation. Say, "I recommend that you contract with Dayton Facility Management Corporation for a six-week trial project to determine the cost savings available from outsourcing your security, landscaping, and engineering services." Your specific recommendation will be a call to action. It will also communicate much greater confidence and commitment.

While we're on the point, resist the temptation to turn your proposal into a smorgasbord. If you are truly an expert in your field, you should be able to recommend the one or two best ways to solve a particular problem. Giving the customer a laundry list of options is an abdication of your function as a professional and an expert.

■ **Am I offering a fresh solution, one that focuses on what this customer needs?** Even if you're offering the same basic solution you've offered the last two dozen (or two thousand) clients, make sure your proposal doesn't sound bored and weary. It should sound like you're excited and enthusiastic about your recommendations. This is a matter of tone and attitude, and a matter of positioning what you have to offer against what the customer needs. Compare the difference in tone between these two statements:

■ Our engine system includes a fuel regulator, so-called because it controls how much fuel enters the engine at various operating conditions.

■ Your aircraft will operate more profitably, because the engines incorporate solid-state fuel regulators—an innovative technology that prevents the engine from wasting fuel at various critical points in the flight envelope.

Notice that the focus on the first one is on "our engine system," whereas the second version starts out talking about "your aircraft." It's a subtle difference, but it helps make the second one sound like a solution instead of product documentation.

■ **Am I focusing on the customer's organizational or business interests rather than technical issues?** Technology in and of itself doesn't sell.

People buy technology because it will have a positive impact on organizational concerns—profitability, productivity, staffing levels, quality, downtime, whatever.

■ **Am I writing clearly, concisely, emphatically, logically, and persuasively?** You wouldn't submit a proposal that had a coffee stain on the title page, would you? That would send the wrong message. Submitting a proposal that's wordy, difficult to understand, illogical, contradictory, wishy-washy, or unconvincing is just as bad. Along the same lines, submitting a proposal marred by misspellings, typos, grammar mistakes, the wrong client's name, and similar lapses also destroys your credibility.

Creating Credibility with Details

Another common weakness in proposals, one that undercuts your credibility, is the use of unsubstantiated claims. Marketing "fluff" is not convincing. The more specifically you can substantiate your value statements and differentiators, the more likely the customer is to believe them.

Here are some examples of marketing fluff you should avoid:

■ Best-of-breed

■ Leading edge

■ Leveraged

■ Market/industry leader

■ State-of-the-art

■ Unequaled

■ Uniquely qualified

■ World-class

If your proposal says that you "leverage world-class service and best-of-breed products into the industry leading solution" and that you are "uniquely qualified" to handle this project, your customers will probably just mutter to themselves, "Oh, please, not again . . ." and start skimming for something substantive.

Challenge the clichés of proposal writing. Force yourself to be concrete when you make your claims. For example, here are some typical statements that appeared in actual proposals along with suggested rewrites that make them more credible and persuasive by making them more specific:

Our servers are the most reliable in the industry	*Our servers have an average mean time between failures of 1800 hours, the best in the industry.*
Our installation team is composed of up to four qualified engineers who record their efforts in an Operation Log	*The installation team assigned to your project will consist of state-licensed engineers. Each completed step in the process of installing your repair depot will be documented in the Operation Log to assure compliance with your requirements and to provide a simple tool to transition ownership of the project to your own staff.*
We are anxious to work with the Tax Collection Board in establishing an Internet-based tax collection system, as evidenced by our efforts over the past ten years and by our substantial financial investment in developing a prototype of the proposed system	*We are eager to work with the Tax Collection Board as you improve tax payment compliance by putting tax collection on the Internet. For more than ten years we have worked with you successfully on projects that have improved the information management and technology infrastructure of the Board, most notably the Small Business Revenue Initiative in 1997 and the Taxpayer Information Portal in 2000. In addition, we have invested $13,500,000 of our own funds in developing the prototype of the Internet-based tax collection system we are recommending in this proposal. This investment will assure speedy delivery of a working system and will reduce the Board's capital expenditures for system development.*

As you can see, specificity in the details increases the persuasiveness of the message.

3

How to Manage the Process
and Keep Your Sanity

8   *An Overview of the Proposal Development Process*

O ne of my clients shared an embarrassing story during a workshop. It seems that after laboring on a proposal for several weeks, she found herself, accompanied by a colleague, shuffling papers in the back seat of a cab as it raced across town, desperately trying to assemble three copies of a proposal in hopes of beating a 3 p.m. deadline. Along the way, their frantic efforts so distracted the cab driver that he hit another car. At that point, my client grabbed her papers and began running, in high heels, toward the client's headquarters. Snapping one of the heels off, she hobbled the last couple of blocks. She got there too late, and her proposal was not accepted.

Sadly, most people who have done a few proposals have their own horror stories. These are the folks who know the location of every overnight delivery service, which ones have late pickups, which copy centers are open all night, how to save time by printing on multiple printers simultaneously, and other last-minute, time-saving tricks. Clearly, something has gone dreadfully wrong if this is the way proposal projects are managed.

Managing a complex proposal can become a real nightmare. It can threaten your sanity. At the end you may feel you've gained new insight into the concept of a Pyrrhic victory—your victory has cost you far more than you'll ever gain. But it doesn't have to be that way. This chapter addresses some of the key issues involved in managing a proposal project and in assembling a successful, cohesive team to put that proposal together.

Basically, the flow of activities involved in developing your proposal should look something like Figure 8-1.

Laying a Solid Foundation

Winning proposals have their roots in good sales and marketing. I have never believed that a proposal by itself was likely to win business if there was no prior relationship, no effective positioning or branding, no information gathering to provide insight into the opportunity. As a result, there are numerous pre-proposal activities that must be carried out long before you begin to work on the proposal.

However, sometimes you will have an RFP thrown on your desk, or a salesperson will call up and say, "Can you put together sort of a standard proposal for me?" Naturally, these are always terrific opportunities, can't miss, gotta go for it, just do the proposal and the rest will be easy.

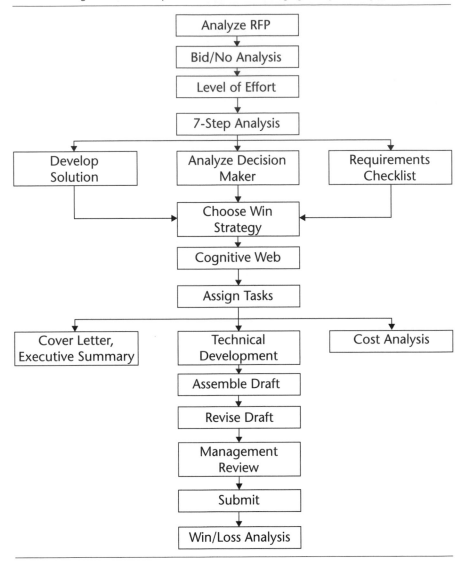

Figure 8-1. *The Sequence of Activities in Managing a Proposal Project.*

Right. In my experience and based on research we have conducted, I can tell you that you're almost surely wasting your time. If there is no prior relationship, if the buyer doesn't recognize you, if your sales team has no knowledge or insight about the opportunity, your chances of writing a winning proposal are roughly the same as winning the Super Lotto. It happens. It just isn't going to happen to you.

Suppose you have to write the proposal anyway. In that case, you need to scramble as quickly as you can to acquire any information and insight you can grab. You can get data—factual information—from public sources.

Ideally, you can supplement that with insight—the kind of information an insider possesses. It's the combination of data and insight that will give you a well-rounded understanding of the client and opportunity.

Data is usually easier to acquire than insight, so it makes sense to work first on acquiring the data. Where should you look? Start with the client's Web site. Type their name into some search engines. Look for press releases and newspaper articles. If they are publicly traded, you should be able to access their annual reports, 10-K documents, and other reports. You may be able to obtain press kits, executive bios, even marketing brochures and trade show materials if you have enough lead time.

And what are you looking for? Insight into the issues facing the firm or agency, their financial status, their objectives, the primary customer base they serve, who their chief competitors are, what kinds of values they revere in their corporate culture, the major initiatives they have launched during the past year or so, their basic organizational structure, recent events or developments among their competitors. That will do for a start.

Review the RFP Document or Opportunity

If you are responding to a formal RFP, you should immediately analyze what the RFP says and what you are being asked to do. (If there is no formal RFP document, as in the case of a proactive opportunity, it's still a very good idea to figure out what the client expects you to deliver.) As soon as you receive the RFP (or even a draft copy of the RFP), begin the analysis by reading it carefully, separating out its requirements, and performing the seven-step audience analysis to get below the surface level of technical requirements to the core issues. As with your audience, it is helpful to break the process of analyzing the RFP into several steps, in this case nine:

1. **Read** the complete RFP quickly to gain an overall sense of its scope and requirements.
2. **Note** any obvious conflicts or discrepancies in the RFP, either in the margins or on a separate sheet.
3. **Burst** (separate) the RFP contents into the following categories:
    A. *Administrative information*: information regarding logistics, the time and location of the bidders' conference, if any, your points of contact, how many copies to prepare, due dates, schedules, address to which your proposal must be sent, and so forth.
        This information will be vital in developing your timeline for getting the proposal completed.
    B. *Legal requirements:* clauses or specifications that govern contracts, including terms and conditions, subcontracting requirements, payment schedules, ownership of the work product, certifications and representations, and so on.
        This information is important in determining whether or not you can comply with the terms and conditions or other governing clauses.

C. *Format guidelines:* information regarding the required or recommended format, including page limits, font sizes, margins, restrictions on the use of color, guidelines regarding graphics, and so on.

> *This information will be important in designing and publishing your proposal and in establishing appropriate visuals, determining the length of key sections, and managing the writing.*

D. *Content requirements:* information or specifications that guide your development of a solution, including the scope of work, technical requirements, required sections, evaluation criteria, evidence required, management plan, and so on.

> *This information is vital because it shapes your actual content. Use it to develop the compliance matrix, to determine your key strategy or win theme, and to develop your cognitive web and requirements checklist.*

4. **Reorganize** the RFP if it is not clearly laid out, placing the various types of information into the categories you identified in the previous step.

> *NOTE: In reorganizing the RFP, you are simply making a document that flows more logically for your own purposes. When you respond, you should* **respond to the RFP as it was written.**

5. **Develop** a requirements checklist.

> *How do you know whether something is a requirement? Well-written RFPs will tell you what's required or mandatory and what's simply desirable. In addition, if the language states that you "shall" or "must" do something, it's a requirement. Finally, assume that issues that come up repeatedly within an RFP are so significant they constitute de facto requirements.*

6. **Define** the terminology used in the RFP
   A. Jargon
   B. Organizational names or relationships
   C. Technical terms that seem to be used in an unusual way

7. **Highlight** any requirements or instructions in the RFP that you cannot meet, including legal requirements to include proprietary or confidential information.

> *You do not have to be 100 percent compliant to win a contract. However, you must be aware of the expectations and requirements stated in the RFP and take exception to any that you can't or won't be meeting.*

8. **List** any areas of ambiguity in the RFP, any requirements that seem contradictory or incomplete, and any that seem to deviate from the functional purpose of the RFP. Some of these items may be the basis of questions you raise at the bidders' conference, if there is one. Or they might be the subject of e-mails you send back to the account team or the prospect, seeking clarification.

9. **Compile** all of the ambiguities, contradictions, inexplicable jargon, questions, and clarifications you need into a list that you can send to the client or raise at the bidders' conference.

Avoid Wasted Effort by Making Smart Pre-Proposal Decisions

Once you've analyzed the RFP, if there is one, or reviewed the customer's expectations if you're writing a proactive proposal, there are two important decisions you must make before you begin working on the proposal itself:

1. Is this job worth bidding on?

2. How much effort should I put into the proposal?

By making intelligent decisions before you start working on the opportunity, you can save yourself a lot of time and expense and you can feel confident that you are going after the deals that have the most potential value to you.

Perform a Bid/No Bid Analysis

Perhaps the most fundamental decision is whether to bid or not. Companies and individuals waste huge amounts of time and money creating proposals for opportunities they never had a chance of winning. In some companies, the phrase "no bid" is never uttered. These cockeyed optimists go after everything, perhaps on the theory that winning is unpredictable at best so you might as well give it a shot.

Good proposals are expensive. They're time consuming. They can soak up valuable resources. Before you start, why not get real? Do you really have a reasonable chance of winning? If you do win, can you fulfill the commitments you are making in the proposal? Can you do so profitably?

As my friend Tom Amrhein, who has written some of the largest winning proposals in U.S. government history, often counsels people, "The best way to improve your win ratio is to stop bidding for work you have no chance of winning." That's great advice, but it's often surprisingly hard for people to take.

In a "no win" situation, the competition is not truly open and fair. The company has solicited your proposal because they need a couple of dummy comparison points to show they did proper due diligence. Or they're hoping you'll quote a low price which they can then use to beat up their current vendor. Or they're operating under acquisition rules that require them to solicit a minimum number of bids, even though they already know who they want. The specifics may vary, but in all of these situations the decision maker's mind is already made up.

It's also smarter to pass on jobs you really don't want to win—or at least wouldn't want if you gave it some thought. Let's face it, not all business is business that's worth having. Some clients are so demanding, so high maintenance, so fundamentally unfair in their approach to doing business, that winning their business will make you wish you had lost.

To avoid these mistakes, implement a structured, flexible bid/no bid analysis. Develop your own bid/no bid analysis scheme, taking into account issues such as the following:

1. Are we the incumbent provider of the product or service being requested in this RFP?

Statistically, in government contracting incumbents win about 90 per-cent of all rebids. It's lower in the commercial sector, but the current in-cumbent vendor still has a huge advantage. Can you overcome those odds? I'm not saying you can't, but it will require a proposal that demon-strates extraordinary value to turn a decision maker away from a proven incumbent vendor.

2. Is the customer happy with the incumbent's performance?

   Even in those situations where the incumbent has done a poor job and the decision maker is unhappy, the incumbent still wins almost half the time. But common sense tells you that you have a much better chance to win if the current provider has messed up.

3. If the customer is unhappy with the current vendor's performance, was the RFP issued to deal with those problems?

   If the RFP was issued to solve problems inherent in the current ven-dor's performance, this is a good sign. You've got a chance. The client is telling you that they're really fed up. Of course, it's still possible they're just using the RFP as a stick to beat the incumbent with and aren't really committed to making a change. But it's definitely worth giving it a shot.

4. Do we have a strong relationship with the customer?

   One of the Big Four consulting firms found that the single factor most predictive of a successful proposal was the existence of a strong relation-ship with the customer. If they had a relationship, their win ratio was over 40 percent. If there was none, the win ratio was below 10 percent.

5. Does this RFP play into one of our strengths?

   Do you have provable differentiators? Can you cite compelling evi-dence of successful prior experience?

6. Does the RFP appear to be slanted toward a competitor?

   Do the requirements strongly favor a competitor? Is there language in the RFP that comes from your competitor? It's possible your competition gave the prospective client a sample RFP, parts of which ended up in the one that was issued, but the presence of content that favors one provider should be a caution signal.

7. Is this project or acquisition funded?

   Make sure there's money behind the opportunity. There are people who see nothing wrong with having you create a proposal even though they know the project isn't funded. Don't waste your time.

8. If not, are funds available within the client's budget?

   Maybe the money has been allocated for the next fiscal year's budget. This will be a judgment call, but if you can get confirmation from two or

*more executives in the client organization, particularly if they have fi-
nancial responsibility, then you have to assume the funds probably will
be there.*

9. Is the client serious about making a decision, or is this more of an
exercise in information gathering?

   *Is there a compelling, imminent event in the client's universe that's
   driving this decision?*

10. Will completing this project or deliverable require heavy investments
of time and money on our part?

    *This doesn't mean you shouldn't bid. But it could affect the potential
    profitability of the deal. And winning could preclude you from pursuing
    other opportunities for a while.*

11. Would winning this contract further our own goals?

    *Where do you want to move your company? What kinds of markets
    do you want to be in?*

12. Is this client likely to be a strong partner or reference account in the
future?

    *Landing a trophy account who is willing to be a reference or a case
    study may be invaluable to you downstream.*

13. Would winning this opportunity be particularly damaging to our competitors?

    *Do you have the chance to steal away one of your competitor's most
    important accounts? Can you shut them out of a region or a market?*

14. Are there strong political considerations affecting our decision to bid?

    *If you "no bid" an opportunity, will you be removed from the approved
    bidders list? Is the key executive at the client organization a close friend
    of your firm's CEO?*

How to Say No Nicely

As the last question above suggests, when you consider whether or not to
"no bid" an RFP, you must ask yourself what consequences that action may
have downstream. Will a "no bid" decision limit future opportunities to
bid on this customer's business? If a consultant is involved, will a "no bid"
decision affect your company's relationship with that consultant in the future?

   If you decide not to go forward with an opportunity, particularly one
where you have already moved several steps down the sales cycle, you obviously need to tell the prospect. Simply cutting off contact or not submitting

a proposal will create confusion and destroy the customer's trust. So what should you do?

The short answer is that you need to tactfully walk the line between telling them you don't want their business because of something that's wrong with them (they have lousy credit, you think their management team is nuts, and so on) and telling them that you can't do the job because there is something wrong with you (you don't have the expertise, your own management team is nuts, and so on).

So the best way to position a "no" is to suggest that the details don't provide a good business fit: "We want to make sure that the money you spend on this project produces the best possible solution for you, but in reviewing the details of the opportunity we have concluded that we are probably not the partner in this case who can provide the best solution. As a result, we respectfully decline the opportunity to bid. However, we are eager to work with you in the future where our unique combination of experience and resources can provide you with an excellent outcome."

If they press, I'd focus first on their infrastructure requirements (you want Oracle, we only do Sybase; you want brick exteriors, we only do vinyl siding). Focus next on the timing issues (given the project plan you out-lined and due to other commitments, we will not have our in-house experts available to support your project when you need them). Look last at the business focus (this is an exciting opportunity, but it is not part of our core focus at this time). Those are somewhat neutral-sounding reasons.

If you can deliver the message deftly enough, you can avoid long-term commitment but still remain friends.

Determine the Appropriate Level of Effort

The second important decision you have to make, after you decide whether or not to bid in the first place, is how hard to work on the opportunity.

A decision tree, perhaps based on some of the questions listed above or others that you would normally use in a bid/no bid analysis, can help you determine how much effort to put into responding. For example, in Figure 8-2, the first question is "Are we the incumbent vendor?" If the answer is yes, that leads to a second question, which might be, "Is the customer satisfied with us?" If that answer is yes, we're moving into a realm where our probability of winning is high. However, if the answer to the first question is no, we are not the incumbent vendor, our chances are somewhat lower. The next question in that case might be, "Is the customer satisfied with the current vendor?" In this diagram, opportunities in the upper right quadrant (labeled A) have a high probability of being successful. Opportunities in quadrant D (lower left) are almost guaranteed losers. The other two quadrants have probabilities somewhere in between, with a slightly stronger

Figure 8-2. Determining the Level of Effort.

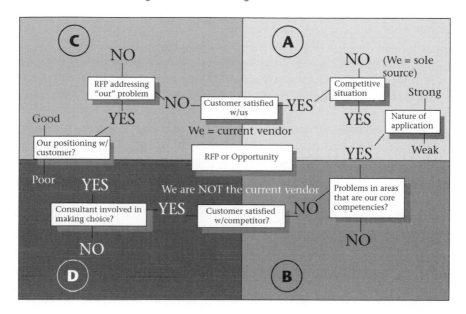

likelihood going to those opportunities where you are the incumbent (quadrant C).

If you can create this kind of decision tree, you will be able to determine how much effort to put into an opportunity. At the top level, your very best opportunities call for dedicated commitment and focused effort. You will create a formal proposal that is highly customized to the client and the opportunity.

The next level down is an opportunity where you believe the competitive playing field is open and fair, but your likelihood of winning is substantially lower. For such an opportunity, you would be wise to spend less time and effort, but still try to deliver a customized proposal. The difference is that you will rely heavily on boilerplate and spend less time during the editing process on customizing the content.

At the next level, we may be in a zone where there are lots of caution signs. We are perilously close to a "no bid," but if you decide to respond, you should consider submitting a generic proposal or one that you have generated from a proposal automation system, but not spent much time revising. Your focus should be on turning the proposal around extremely fast, in no more than a few hours, and the effort should involve the absolute minimum number of contributors.

At the lowest level, of course, we have the option of not bidding at all. In that case, we simply prepare a tactful letter explaining that this opportunity does not seem right for us.

Can You Recover the Cost of Writing a Proposal?

What about charging for a proposal? Does that ever make sense? Usually it doesn't. Your potential clients will probably refuse to consider such a request. They view the proposal as a cost of doing business that you should be willing to bear, and they assume that your pricing will include enough margin to recoup your sales and marketing costs, including proposal writing.

However, there are times when you may be tempted to attach a bill to your proposal, or to withhold detailed content until the client has agreed to pay you for it. For example, you might be justified in charging for your proposal if it:

- Required thousands of dollars worth of effort on your part, with a low probability of receiving an order because of the client's apparent indecision or lack of commitment.

- Involved R&D or design work that is highly specialized or even unique to the given opportunity, the kind of work you will not be able to use again for any other client.

- Was developed for a client who refused to sign a nondisclosure agreement.

What options do you have in such cases?

Consider seeking a preliminary letter of commitment from the client. During the pre-proposal phase of your efforts, contact the decision maker and explain that you will be making a sizable investment in gathering data, conducting tests, allocating laboratory time, or using other expensive means of preparing the content for the proposal. What you want from the client is his or her signature on a letter stating that if your proposal addresses all the key technical requirements and is within the client's budget, you will receive a contract. This kind of commitment is never easy to obtain, of course, but you have a chance if you are pursuing a proactive opportunity. If you are responding to an RFP that the client has issued to several vendors, you can probably forget it.

Another option is to break the opportunity down into manageable chunks. If you're interested in the opportunity, but unable to calculate the true costs of winning, you might be able to respond with a proposal that calls for doing the work in phases. Phase I might be a funded design study that would lay out a plan for doing the subsequent phases. To tempt the client, you might offer to deliver the subsequent phases on a fixed-price basis, to engage in revenue sharing, or to offer service-level guarantees.

A final option is to respond with a two-volume proposal. Volume one contains your executive summary, high-level information about your proposed solution, information on your management plan, case studies, references, and other general data. This volume is offered to the customer at no charge. The second volume contains your detailed design and specifications. This volume is available to the client on a fee basis, representing the amount of engineering or design effort that went into it. As an incentive, you might indicate that the fee for this volume will be deducted from the project costs if you win the contract.

Before you decide on taking this approach, be realistic about the amount of effort required and the strength of your position compared to that of your competitors. It can be an extremely tough sell. However, if you find that you are doing a lot of "free consulting work" by responding to detailed RFPs and RFIs that never result in orders—that are, in fact, used as project plans and shopping lists by the client—then this approach can serve as a wake-up call that your intellectual capital is no longer available for free.

Create a Proposal Schedule

A proposal is like any other complex project. To ensure an on-time completion, you need to establish a schedule right away and then regularly check progress against it.

To create the proposal schedule:

1. **Identify the "drop dead" date**—the absolutely last date by which the final draft must be completed and ready to go to production.

2. **Schedule printing** to be completed with plenty of time for shipping or delivery of the final document. Include at least one or two extra days to allow for emergencies and problems.

3. **Create a Gantt chart** for a large-scale project, using a tool like Microsoft Project. Identify the critical events or deliverables in your project.

4. Look for opportunities to **complete tasks in parallel, not sequentially.**

5. Don't forget to **build in time for a technical review** of the first draft **and a mock evaluation** of the final draft. The mock evaluation, or "red team review" as it's often called, should occur approximately two-thirds of the way into the schedule. (We'll discuss this process in more detail later, in Chapter 21.)

6. **Use labor-saving tools** whenever possible, including automation software, design templates, compliance checklists, and so forth.

7. **Empower your contributors to do a good job the first time** by providing them with all the information they need, including insights into the client, competitors, key issues, strategy and win theme, and so on. A kick-off meeting is an ideal place to provide this information, but you

should also build in incremental reviews to reinforce the right approach and to make sure they are heading in the right direction.

Assemble the Team

If writing proposals is your job and yours alone, assembling the team is easy. Pour yourself a cup of coffee, sit down at your desk, and the team is ready.

Complex proposals, or proposals that have extremely short deadlines, may require contributions from multiple contributors. In Chapter 16, where we discuss what's involved in setting up a dedicated proposal operation, I review the types of contributors you will want on a basic proposal team—a proposal manager, one or more writers, a graphics specialist, and one or more subject matter experts. It also makes sense to include the account manager, salesperson, or business development personnel who have uncovered the opportunity and who know the client best. Other participants, at least at the initial stage of a proposal project, might include senior management, financial analysts who can work on pricing issues, a contracts expert if there are unusual terms and conditions in the RFP, and perhaps a representative from marketing. If your solution will involve combining efforts from a number of departments, such as software development and customization, customer training, and customer support, these departments should be represented at the outset so they at least have this opportunity on their radar screens.

Hold an Effective Kick-Off Meeting

Like any complex project, writing a major proposal can be intimidating at first. You can get off to a good start if you hold an effective kick-off meeting. Your kick-off meeting process should include developing an agenda, creating checklists of requirements, gathering insight into the client, making key decisions, and generating a basic outline for the proposal quickly.

One tool that you should develop immediately if you regularly work with a team of contributors is an opportunity analysis worksheet. (See the sample in Figure 8-3.) Leave it blank before the meeting. Then work as a team to fill it in. The template should include information about who the customer is, who the decision makers are, what business relationship exists between your company and the prospective customer, and the size and focus of the opportunity. It should also cover the seven critical questions that we discussed in Chapter 5. What else? You may want additional insight into the customer's business, technical, political, economic, and social concerns; the values that will drive the selection process; the competitive landscape; the most effective strategy for positioning your firm

Figure 8-3. A Sample Worksheet.

Opportunity Analysis Worksheet
for
Trust Administration

Customer's business profile
1. Who is responsible for decisions affecting the trusts? How do they make decisions?
2. What would they change about the way the trusts are set up or administered if they could?
3. What is the main benefit they want to gain from improving the way trusts are managed?
4. What elements of the customer's business situation are driving this opportunity?
5. Is there a compelling reason why they need to move quickly in changing the administration of their trust?
6. Are we positioned with the key decision maker? Do we have access to the authorities who can make this decision? Do we have strong champions within the customer organization?

The financial issues:
1. How many trusts does the customer have? How large are the trusts?
2. Is the customer completely satisfied with the performance of the trusts?
3. Are they completely satisfied with the yield?
4. What gross return did they earn on the trusts last year?
5. Who is currently handling the trusts?
6. How are the funds invested? Certificates of deposit or stocks/bonds?
7. What is the customer's investment strategy?
8. How many different fund managers do they have? Who are they?
9. What trustee fee does their current trust administrator charge?
10. What investment management fee do they charge?
11. Does the current trust administrator offer profit sharing?

(your best value proposition and win theme); and your firm's readiness to bid. Having said all that, let me add a word of warning: don't make it too complicated. A one-page opportunity analysis will get used. Three or four pages will be ignored.

So it's time for your kick-off meeting. Here are some tips for making it go smoothly:

1. **Invite the right people,** as outlined above. Don't neglect people you may need to work with later on the project. They're less likely to feel put upon if they're included at the outset, even if they choose to skip the meeting.

2. **E-mail everyone the relevant background information,** including a copy of the RFP, and other useful data before the meeting. This information might include:

   ■ Nature and scope of the RFP

   ■ Why this has been determined to be a "bid" project

   ■ Why it's important from a strategic perspective to win

   ■ Background information on the customer and its current situation

   ■ Historical data on previous relationships, if any, with this customer

3. **Assume that no one will have looked at any of this** information when they arrive. Hey, we're all busy, you know?

4. **Create an agenda** for the meeting, but empower the attendees to modify it. That will give them some ownership in the success of the meeting.

5. **Briefly review the material you sent them in advance and then complete the opportunity analysis form.** This is also a good time to review the initial technical approach/solution that has been developed for this project, if there is one.

6. **Discuss and agree as a team on the primary value proposition** and any secondary strategies that you will use in writing the proposal.

7. **Brainstorm as a team for evidence** to support the value proposition.

8. **Assign team members their responsibilities,** along with milestones, due dates, accountability, and deliverables. Emphasize the importance of early reviews and sticking with the plan as developed in the kick-off meeting.

9. **Create a requirements checklist,** either during the kick-off meeting or very soon after, in which you list every requirement from the RFP, if there is one, or everything the customer has asked you to provide. You probably have the bones of your requirements checklist from the careful reading of the RFP you did when it first arrived. Now it has to be fleshed out, because when your proposal is done, you will use the requirements checklist to make sure nothing has been missed. Remember that the easiest way to get yourself thrown out of a bid is to miss one of the key requirements.

Create the Draft Proposal

Now that the assignments are made, contributions will start trickling in. You will need a way to keep track of them and integrate them into one master document.

In the old days, the proposal manager created a "control document" that no one was allowed to touch. The manager was the only person who could add or delete content, because multiple hands touching the document exponentially increased the chances of messing it up. If you are creating proposals using your word processor and perhaps a basic automation tool that handles the cut-and-paste function, you will still need to maintain a control document. However, there are more advanced software systems available that manage all of the various contributors' input, keep it from clashing or overwriting, and provide you with the ability to see the entire project simultaneously. This is the kind of basic productivity tool you should invest in if you typically work as a team on proposals.

Figure 8-4 shows the most efficient sequence in which to write. Start with the executive summary. Sometimes people think they should write the executive summary last, thinking that it is supposed to serve as an abstract or précis of the entire proposal. However, that isn't the function of an executive summary. Rather, it is intended to provide an overview of the business case for the top executives. It summarizes the client's key needs and desired outcomes, offers a high-level presentation of your solution, presents a couple of key differentiators, and outlines your basic value proposition. You should be able to write this content as soon as you've held your kick-off meeting. By getting it done right away, you give everyone else a model for both style and thematic positioning to which they can refer as they work on their assignments.

Next, write the introductory paragraphs to each major section of your proposal or have your contributors write them. These paragraphs contain

Figure 8-4. The Order in Which to Write.

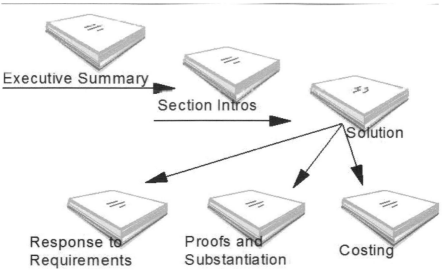

the most general information about the section and can be written even if the details of the technical solution have not been finalized. In addition, they are areas where you want to emphasize your win themes. By having your contributors write them first, you can make sure each of them is on the right path. Here's an example of what the introductory paragraphs to a section might look like:

The following section addresses the specific features of our software and how users can customize the interface to meet their own requirements or preferences. Specifically, this section discusses the tools included in the standard package that make it easy for a user to modify the view of data. These tools reduce the time it takes to locate and process data, thereby increasing productivity.

This section also discusses how a system administrator can enable users to make modifications at the desktop level or can make modifications that affect the entire enterprise. This capability allows you to match the software to your specific work environment and requirements, eliminating the need for customization and reducing the amount of time the administrator spends configuring the product for individual users.

As you probably noticed, these paragraphs are not merely descriptive. Instead, the last sentence of each paragraph states a key win theme for this particular proposal, namely that the software can improve productivity because it contains unique time-saving features.

Next, write the basic description of your solution. You may need to fill in gaps later, but get as much of it done now as you can. Once you have completed the solution description, with all of its features and benefits identified, you can move on to develop the highly detailed content—the actual response to the RFP questions or requirements, the substantiation sections, and the cost section.

Here are some additional tips on getting the first draft done quickly and efficiently:

1. Assemble all your materials, including any research you did on the client, notes from sales calls, your requirements checklist, any reusable text that might be appropriate for the proposal, and so on.

2. Review the research you did into the decision maker and evaluators, and then try to write as though you were speaking to those individuals. How would you say this if the two of you were in a conversation? That's pretty much how you ought to write it.

3. Write quickly. Don't stop to edit while you are writing. This is one of the biggest mistakes people make. It's so easy to "fix" things on a word

processor that people start fiddling with their text before they're more than a few lines into it. Soon they've lost their train of thought, perhaps even got themselves blocked.

4. Start writing on the part you find easiest or most interesting. You do not have to write the document in the same order the reader will see it.

5. For each section or major part of your proposal, try to move from general to specific, from introductory paragraphs and main ideas to supporting details.

6. If you cut and paste boilerplate or reusable text, revise it to match the win themes you are using in this proposal. Above all, make sure it doesn't contain the wrong client's name!

7. Use personal pronouns—"we," "you"—not third person or oblique references. Call the customer by name—that is, use the company's name throughout the proposal. Never refer to the customer as "they."

8. Challenge the acronyms and jargon. If in doubt, leave it out and use something simpler. (Using the customer's jargon and acronyms is permissible.)

Edit Your Draft

Editing is a vital part of creating a winning proposal. All good writers edit heavily, so please make sure you allow enough time in your project plan to do some serious editing. In fact, editing is so important, I've devoted an entire chapter to it, Chapter 21, so we won't go into a lot of detail here.

Print and Publish Your Proposal

The final steps in your proposal project are to print the document, bind it, and either ship or deliver it to the client.

Now that the proposal is gone, you can take a deep breath, catch up on some sleep, and get ready for the next one. There are some postsubmission activities you should complete, too, but you're probably exhausted at this point, so we'll talk about those tasks in Chapter 14.

9 *Writing from the Right Brain:*

Getting Your Ideas Organized

O ne of the questions I am asked most frequently in proposal writing seminars is, "How can I write my proposals faster?"

The answer to that question depends on what happens when you try to write. There may be structural or management problems in your company that impede the flow of information so that you lack the necessary facts. Or you may encounter difficulties in delegating work and then getting it back on time. Usually, though, what we are talking about is more basic. Most often, people take a long time to write because they have a hard time figuring out what they want to say and how they want to say it.

It would be interesting to know how many hours people spend in front of their computers, watching the cursor blink, trying to come up with a good opening sentence. How many drafts they create, only to discard them because they just don't sound right.

The chief engineer at one of the world's largest engineering companies told me that he hated to write proposals. "When I look at an engineering problem," he said, "I can immediately see the answer. But the answer is a totality. It's one complete thing. The problem is, I can't communicate it that way. Instead, I have to take this solid, complete answer and stuff it through a funnel so that it comes out one bit at a time. And to make it worse, the bits have to drip out in just the right order or none of it counts!" In expressing his frustration, he had concocted a perfect visual image for the process he was going through. Or, more accurately, that his brain was going through.

Nearly a quarter century ago, research into a particularly serious form of epilepsy revealed a startling fact. The two halves (or hemispheres) of the brain function quite differently from each other. The left hemisphere in most people controls most forms of sequential thinking, including language. The right hemisphere controls visualization and holistic or global thinking. (This hemispheric differentiation is sometimes reversed in left-handed people.) Equally interesting is the fact that people tend to be dominant to one hemisphere or the other. Just as you prefer to pick up a pen and sign your name with one hand over the other, you prefer to process information and "think" using the cognitive patterns of one hemisphere over the other.

What does this have to do with writing proposals? Just this: If you are a right-brain thinker, you may be able to conceptualize quickly and creatively but then have an excruciatingly difficult time communicating your thoughts because putting those thoughts into language requires sequential processing. You have to put one word in front of another, one sentence ahead of the next, and it all has to flow logically and make sense. For the right-brain thinker that's a two-step process, whereas for the left-brain thinker, it's an integral part of the thinking process itself.

No one would say that chief engineer I mentioned was anything less than brilliant. But he was strongly oriented toward right-brain thinking. And if you have trouble getting your ideas organized and on the page, maybe you are, too.

Cognitive Webbing

After witnessing people struggle to present their thoughts in clearly written form, I finally figured out a way to help right-brain people get their ideas onto the page quickly. I call it "cognitive webbing." It's a nonlinear process of capturing what you know, what you believe, key points you want to emphasize, examples and illustrations you want to include, so that you have a writing plan.

Cognitive webbing is different from another process often used to develop proposals, called storyboarding. Storyboarding is a technique borrowed from the film industry, in which each scene in a movie is represented by an image with the key points of action or dialogue noted below the image. Directors use storyboards to lay out a film (or TV ad or music video) so that they don't waste a lot of time and tape shooting footage they won't need or can't use. Some proposal processes have adapted the storyboarding approach to laying out a complex proposal document. Key sections or subsections of the proposal are represented by an image or two, with the critical content in bullet point format below those images. Often the pages containing these sketches and notes are taped to a long wall so that everyone can "see" the flow of the document.

Personally, I've never been a fan of storyboarding for proposals. The reason it works for a movie is that you already have a script before you start creating the storyboard. The storyboard is an integral step in moving from text to visualization, an obviously important process since movies are visual media.

But when it is used to create a proposal, the storyboarding process actually precedes the creation of the text. So the proposal team spends a lot of time putting pages up and taking them down, rearranging the sequence, adding and deleting content points, and so on. What seems even odder to me is the fact that in trying to use storyboarding processes to create the proposal outline, the team is using a technique designed for visualization to produce what is primarily textual output. Every time I've been involved in a storyboarding conference for a major proposal, I felt that we were trying to hammer nails with a shovel—in other words, using a perfectly good tool to do a job it was basically unsuited for.

The goal of the cognitive webbing process is to create a writing plan as quickly as possible. It can jump start the process, leaping over the writer's block that is so often characteristic of the first stages of a writing task.

A couple of other advantages of cognitive webbing: First, you can do it by yourself or you can do it as a team exercise. It's particularly effective when the entire proposal team participates in building the web, so I recommend doing it during the kick-off meeting.

Second, you can use the process to create a writing plan for the entire proposal or just for a section, such as the executive summary.

How to Create a Cognitive Web

To create a cognitive web, you need to follow three steps. The first time you do it, the process may seem a little awkward, but after you've done it three or four times, it will seem like second nature to you. The three steps of the process are:

1. Write down the **end result** the customer seeks.

2. **Brainstorm**, writing down every point, idea, example, and detail you can think of supporting the basic notion that you will help the customer achieve that desired end result.

3. **Organize** the points, using two principles:
   a. The persuasive paradigm.
   b. The customer's own priorities.

We'll go through each step in detail so you can see how it works.

Step 1: *Identify the End Result the Customer Seeks*

Ask yourself what outcome or end result this customer wants to achieve. Write that end result in the form of a phrase or brief sentence in the center of a sheet of paper, on a whiteboard, or on a flip chart. Circle it. That's your starting point.

Remember our warning from earlier. You must be careful about mistaking your own goals or outcomes or products for the customer's desired end result. If you get the first step wrong, you'll march down the wrong path. You'll find you have made a convincing argument about something the customer doesn't want.

Let's pretend that you're proposing a system integration project for Urban Bank Corporation. After careful consideration, you create the following end result statement:

> Urban Bank Corp will maintain market share and reduce operating costs by providing secure, online banking for consumer and retail customers.

Step 2: *Brainstorm*

The next step is fun. You get to be creative, you get to generate ideas at random, and there are no wrong answers. Let your mind roam freely over the end result, asking yourself or your team questions and recording any thoughts, facts, insights, or observations.

The seven questions are a good starting point. Also, sometimes it's helpful to ask yourself the traditional journalistic questions: Who? What? When? Where? Why? How? Who on our staff has done this kind of work before? What exactly will we implement? What is excluded from our scope? When does the client want this work finished? Where will the work be done? How does the desired implementation date affect our project plan? Is this date tied to some other critical event?

You can see why working in a group can be so productive. The more stuff you come up with during the brainstorming phase, the better. If you're facilitating this process, resist judging contributions at this point. You're better off not excluding or rejecting any contributions now.

As you come up with all of this material, you link the entries to the end result and to each other, grouping them into clusters of related points. Draw lines connecting related ideas or facts. Connect the key points or content groupings to the end result you wrote down first. These are the main spokes of your cognitive web. That's where the "webbing" element comes in. Your output will now look something like this (although yours will have many more elements and a lot more detail):

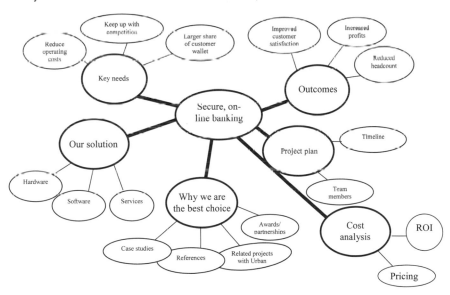

At this point, you may want to combine some elements, discard some, redraw the connections so that what was an element of the solution becomes part of the project plan, and so on.

Step 3: *Prioritize*

Generating all of this potential content was a nonlinear process. It didn't matter if the first thing you thought of was the hardware specifications, the change management process, or a really good case study. But the order in which the customer sees the content does matter. So we need to prioritize it.

First, look for the four components of the persuasive paradigm: needs, outcomes, solution, and evidence. Use those for your main groupings of content and label them in that order. Is one of them missing? Add it now. Is it hard to fit some of the points in your web into one of those four categories of content? Perhaps they really aren't relevant to your proposal.

Once you have the main categories of content identified in terms of the persuasive paradigm, look at the details within each category. Which detail is the most important to the customer? You've done your audience analysis work already, so you should be able to put yourself in the audience's place. Enumerate the points and subpoints in terms of what matters to the audience. When the task of prioritizing is complete, you will have a cognitive web that looks something like this:

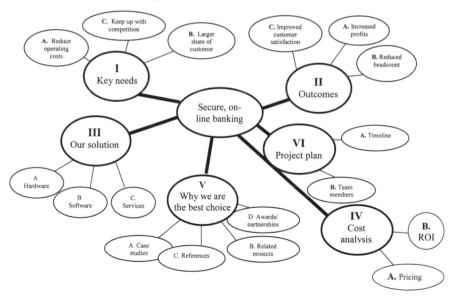

If you're working on a sheet of paper or on a whiteboard, you probably have quite a mess by now. That's good. Now you can copy this mess neatly on another sheet of paper, putting point number one first, followed by its subpoints, and so on, in nice linear fashion right down the page. Presto! You have an outline for your document. And it was fairly painless, wasn't it?

Our sample cognitive web will look like this when transformed into an outline:

I. **Urban Bank Corporation's key reasons for wanting to provide secure, online banking for both retail and commercial customers:**
   a. Reduce operating costs
   b. Gain a larger share of customers' banking business
   c. Keep up with competitors who have Internet-based banking services
II. **Key outcomes Urban will look for from a successful project**
   a. Increased profits
   b. Decreased headcount
   c. Improved customer satisfaction surveys and better service
III. **Our recommended solution**
   a. Hardware components
      (Lots of details here)
   b. Software components
      (Lots of details here, too)
   c. Services
      i. *Application development*
      ii. *Testing*
      iii. *Etc.*
IV. **Our project plan**
   a. Timeline
   b. Key personnel
V. **Cost analysis**
   a. Pricing
   b. ROI
VI. **Why we are the best choice to do this work**
   a. Case studies
   b. Recent projects with Urban Bank
   c. References
   d. Awards and partnerships

From this outline, we can write the executive summary for a formal proposal. (Take a look at the example below.) We could then repeat the process, as necessary, for each section of the proposal, focusing our cognitive web on the technical specification, functional specification, project management, and other topical areas.

Does this method work? Yes! It really does. In seminars we usually do a cognitive web based on one of the attendees' real opportunities. From the initial moment of volunteering to summarizing the executive summary, we can usually complete the exercise in twenty minutes. People have told me that it has cut their writing time on letter proposals from several hours down to thirty minutes or so. Even some left-brain writers use it, because it also helps them become more creative and do a more thorough job of analyzing the opportunity. Try it!

Executive Summary

[The following is a sample executive summary based on the outline we developed above.]

Urban Bank has identified an opportunity to use Internet-based technology to improve the bank's financial performance and deliver more value to your customers. Specifically, your research indicates that if you can provide secure, online banking services for both your retail and your commercial customer base, the bank will achieve some important objectives.

First, you will be able to reduce operating costs. The more transactional business you can move to the Internet, the fewer clerks and ATMs you will need. If you can move 5 percent of your current routine activity to the Internet, you can save in excess of $4 million annually through reduced salaries, benefits, and rental fees associated with ATMs.

Second, you will have the opportunity to gain a larger share of your best customers' banking business. The transactional records that you can store from Internet-based banking services are more extensive and easier to consolidate and mine than other records. By tracking activity online, you will be able to identify opportunities to cross-market other services to your best customers. For example, if you have a high net worth individual with a home loan through Urban, you can market investment opportunities, checking plans, or auto loans via e-mail.

Third, you will stay competitive with other banks in the region who have introduced Internet-based banking services. Customers do not usually switch banks because of differences in basic service delivery models, but over the next few years there is no question that Internet-based banking will become standard. Failing to develop a means of providing secure, online services could gradually erode the bank's reputation.

In summary, if you can provide secure, online banking services, Urban can increase profits (since reductions in operating expense go directly to the bottom line), can reduce headcount or relocate employees into more productive work, and can actually improve customer satisfaction and account retention. In fact, for many of your customers, banking online is much more convenient than going to a local branch or finding an ATM, so their perception of the service Urban is providing will not go down.

As we detail in this proposal, we are experienced in establishing exactly this kind of system for the financial industry. We recommend creating an online banking system built on a hardware platform of . . . The software components we recommend include . . .

Of course, choosing the right hardware and software is only part of the solution. You also need the services to execute the project on time and on budget. We are recognized as experts in the area of application development for banking systems, and have received commendation for three consecutive years from *North American Bank Technology Monthly,* the leading independent journal serving the baking industry. Our development services include development and customization of the applications you need, testing of those systems, phased introductions, and back-end support. In addition, we will train your own IT staff to manage and maintain the system so that you are completely self-sufficient. All of these services are detailed in Section 3 of our proposal.

Our project plan takes into account two factors. First, delays in cutting costs mean delays in generating more profit. Therefore, we have developed an aggressive timeline. Second, doing the job right the first time is always better than fixing the job later. Therefore, we have allowed enough room in the timeline to study your infrastructure thoroughly and to develop the right solution for Urban Bank.

The leader of our project team, David Williamson, has developed and installed online banking systems for some of the region's largest financial institutions, including . . . Williamson was a featured speaker at the recent International Conference of E-Commerce Strategists, where he presented our methodology for successfully designing and implementing online banking systems. He used five different projects that he had managed as examples of the right way to handle these projects.

We have included case studies that cover several of these projects. In them we document not only the systems we implemented for our clients, but the impact these systems had on their profitability and market share.

Over the past several years, we have had the opportunity to work with Urban Bank on a number of important and exciting projects. For example, we were the lead in developing the Urban Extranet, which has enabled you to clear funds in half the time it previously took. We also were the designers and implementers of the Urban E-Learning system, which has cut training costs for new employees by 70 percent. These projects have established our reputation for quality work. In addition, we have included references from other clients who have benefited from our pragmatic approach to innovative solutions.

As an award-winning technology provider, we have partnerships with and certifications from all the major technology firms, including Sun, Oracle, Microsoft, IBM, HP, and many others. You can trust us to provide well-trained, experienced people who can complete your project in a timely and cost-effective way.

We urge you to move forward on this important opportunity. The Internet will transform banking as we know it in this country. In the process, it will transform the nature of competition, the way banks work, and cost structures that underlie them. As a regional bank in a highly competitive market, Urban must take advantage of competitive opportunities as quickly as possible. We are ready to help.

10 *Presenting a Winning Value Proposition*

I n *The Wealth of Nations*, Adam Smith wrote,

> *It is not from the benevolence of the butcher, the brewer, or the baker, that we expect our dinner, but from their regard to their own self-interest. We address ourselves, not to their humanity but to their self-love, and never talk to them of our necessities but of their advantages.*

Not to put words in Adam's mouth, but what I think he's saying is unless you can offer your decision maker a compelling value proposition, winning is a game of chance. You must demonstrate that your solution offers the greatest rate of return to the client and his or her organization—an appeal to the so-called estimation heuristic or, in Adam Smith's terms, to the client's "own self-interest."

To be consistently successful at this, you need to approach the process of creating your value proposition in an organized, disciplined way. Your goal is to shift the focus away from cost and toward return, away from technical specs and toward operational impact, away from products and toward productivity.

That means you need to think strategically. In military terms, strategy is the grand plan by which commanders attempt to capitalize on their own strengths and exploit their enemy's weaknesses. Strategy is how you maximize your chance of winning in battle. The same basic concept applies to the competition you face in proposal writing.

What you must avoid are two mistakes that undercut the value of your strategic thinking: (1) choosing a strategy that reflects your own values and assumptions, and (2) choosing a strategy based on fear.

During an engagement with a global consulting firm, I had the opportunity to review dozens of proposals. Every proposal offered a value proposition based on the firm's "breadth of resources."

But the firm's own marketing team had undertaken a wide-ranging series of interviews with customers and prospects to find out what they valued. According to the marketing research, "breadth of resources" barely made the top ten. The proposals, it turned out, were reflecting what the partners valued. They were proud to be with an international corporation with decades of success. They assumed that customers would appreciate that, too.

The other mistake, basing a strategy on fear, usually results from a lack of competitive knowledge, anxiety that we are not likely to be successful in our efforts, or prior failures that have left us cynical.

Proposal writers who don't abandon their assumptions and their fears so they can think through the issue of strategy usually come up with no strategy at all. To avoid that kind of mistake, be specific. Choose a single, clearly focused strategy, then repeat it and support it throughout your proposal. Substantiate your claims with relevant, believable evidence. Link your examples, your references, your case studies, to a consistent value message so that it repeats and repeats through the proposal.

Major Mistakes in Offering a Value Proposition

What are the biggest mistakes people make instead of offering a true value proposition? Here are five killers:

1. Trying to be everything to everybody; taking a "shotgun" approach rather than focusing on a specific measure of value.

2. Making loud claims ("best of breed," "world class," "industry leading," "uniquely qualified," "unsurpassed," "100% customer satisfaction"), but failing to back them up with evidence or substance.

3. Offering a proposal that spends more time attacking a competitor than it does responding to the client's needs.

4. Writing a factual or technical description, explaining features of your solution without also indicating their value for the client.

5. Producing a "cost paranoia proposal," one that focuses exclusively on trying to prove that this solution is the cheapest, no matter what the numbers may look like.

When Value Matters the Most

Demonstrating value is always important, but sometimes it's *really* important. A proposal that can potentially transform the organization has to show the decision maker that, in spite of the risks inherent in changing a process or in handling a core function differently, the potential return to the organization is so great that not moving forward does not make sense. You have to put more effort into demonstrating value.

There are certain other situations where you need to spend extra time on your value proposition. For example, if you are trying to displace an accepted incumbent vendor, the decision maker must see such a big gap in value that he or she is willing to make the change. Second, if your recommendations change the way people work, expect stiff resistance. Even obviously sensible ideas can be shot down if they entail fundamental changes to work processes. Third, if your solution involves relocating control of something valuable—money, information, personnel, authority—it will be a tough sell. Control means power, prestige, and job security. The individual who is losing control will be adamantly opposed to your recommendations. Your only shot at winning is by demonstrating to senior management so much potential value to the organization that they will ignore the screams of protest from below. Finally, if the decision maker can reasonably choose to do nothing at all, you will need to demonstrate a lot of value. Most organizations are burdened with tremendous inertia. To create momentum for change, show a big return.

The Value Proposition

As an article in the *Harvard Business Review* pointed out, the basic value proposition can be expressed very simply:

$$(Value_s - Cost_s) > (Value_a - Cost_a)$$

where:

Value$_s$ = the value of your solution
Cost$_s$ = the cost of your solution
Value$_a$ = the value of the next best alternative
Cost$_a$ = the cost of the next best alternative

As you can see, you don't have to have the lowest price to have the greatest value. What matters is the difference between value obtained and price paid. If you can convince your buyer that your solution offers the biggest delta between value and cost, you have a very good chance of winning.

You probably remember that we said in Chapter 5 that a well-crafted statement of results or outcomes must meet three criteria: It must be measurable, it must be organizational in its impact, and it must be clearly attributable to your solution. The same qualities apply to your value proposition. In fact, we can be a bit more precise. To create a value proposition that will be truly compelling, make sure you keep the following four principles in mind:

1. The payback measurements must be client-focused.
   Look back at your seven-question analysis of the opportunity. What are the customer's desired outcomes? Which outcome is most important? This should tell you where to focus your demonstration of value.

2. The presentation of payback will be more credible if it's quantified.

   Numbers are more convincing than words. To be meaningful, our impact must be measurable.

3. The value proposition will be more persuasive if it's graphical.

   Adding a graphic can increase the persuasiveness of your message by 47 percent, according to one study.

4. Your value proposition must be based on your differentiators.

   If the value arises from the way you work or from other unique aspects of the solution available only from your firm, your competition will be unable to steal your value claim as their own.

One way to establish value or create a sense of urgency is to use benchmark data. For example, you might compare your prospect's level of performance in a critical, quantifiable area with industry standard performance and with the performance of a key regional competitor. This kind of comparison would demonstrate the gap between "what is" and "what needs to be." Another way to benchmark is to compare your own performance, capabilities, experience, or other value with those of a competitor or the industry average. If you choose to compare to a competitor, do not mention the competitor by name.

Varieties of Value: Understanding What Matters to the Client

Operational costs. Profits. Gross or net revenues. Transaction value. Salaries. Benefits. These are all types of value that are likely to be measured in financial terms.

But some clients are looking for other kinds of improvements. Don't restrict yourself to financial measures unless the client has indicated to you that nothing else matters. Here are some to think about, but this is by no means an exhaustive list, either:

■ **Financial**: getting the lowest price, receiving the greatest total value when services and add-ons are included, achieving the lowest total cost of ownership, reducing or eliminating operating expenses, increasing revenue, improving cash flow, reducing bad debt, increasing the average dollar value of each transaction, getting a larger portion of each customer's total business, and so forth.

■ **Social**: internal—increasing employee job satisfaction, enhancing job performance, reducing turnover among key staff members, reducing absenteeism, accelerating employee training, outsourcing to remove fixed costs from the payroll; external—increasing customer loyalty, improving brand recognition, creating a positive image in the community, addressing a societal concern, and so on.

■ **Quality**: improving reliability, enhancing maintainability, increasing ease of use, complying with regulatory standards, conforming to a specific quality methodology, reducing defect rates, reducing customer complaints, and so forth.

■ **Technology/Infrastructure**: achieving greater interoperability, improving system flexibility, implementing the most advanced technology, preserving the value of legacy systems, creating the most open solution, reducing downtime, adding new features or capabilities, automating a labor-intensive process, and so on.

■ **Risk minimization**: avoiding the risk of failure, implementing the safest, most proven approach, addressing health and safety issues, avoiding liability concerns, using a conservative approach to solve a critical business need, and so on.

■ **Industry trends**: keeping up with competition, entering new markets quickly, updating products and services to keep them competitive, changing delivery platforms, eliminating fixed costs, focusing on core business competencies, and so forth.

■ **Competitive advantage**: achieving the best total improvement in operational and financial performance, leaping past a competitor's position, dominating a market, and so on.

Your goal is to figure out which variety of value is most important or appealing to your decision maker, then use it to frame your strategy for the entire proposal.

In framing your value position, you can take either a positive or a negative approach. Positive strategies are based on **gain**. Your goal is to persuade the client that what you are recommending offers him or her the greatest amount of gain of all the available options. Negative strategies are based on **fear** or **avoidance**. In that case, your goal is to alert the client to the problems (even disasters) that are possible unless certain measures are taken. Either approach works and both approaches are ethical, as long as they are based on an honest assessment of the client's situation.

Differentiate Yourself in Ways That Matter

To create a solid value strategy, base your value proposition on your own strengths or differentiators. What is it that you do that no one else in your industry does? What is there that everyone does, but you do in a way that is clearly different? Sustainable, meaningful differentiation does not usually arise from operational advantages or product features. Rather, it's more likely to come from systems, processes, or methods of working.

I was consulting with a firm that handles pharmaceutical benefits for medical insurance providers. In the executive summary of each proposal they included a couple of paragraphs describing their new data center.

"I'm not sure I see how this delivers a benefit to your clients," I said. "Are your costs cheaper because you can process claims so much faster?"

"No."

"Are you giving better customer service by getting the claims approved quicker?"

"Not really."

"Is your accuracy higher?"

"Probably not."

"Then why is this material in the proposal?"

"I guess because we spent $15 million building a new data center and the vice president of I.T. said we had to describe it."

No.

A differentiator that doesn't benefit the customer isn't worth mentioning.

I usually recommend to my clients that they try to identify their differentiators first by thinking about specific competitors. One by one, create a list of as many differentiators per competitor as you can.

The second approach to defining differentiators is to think about the cycle of activity involved in a typical customer engagement. From the early phases of the sales process all the way through postinstallation and customer support activities, perhaps even to the decommissioning and removal of your products, think about the various moments when you interact with the customer. What do you do that's different? What do you provide as a deliverable that customers don't get from anyone else? What processes or systems have you implemented that assure satisfactory outcomes?

You don't have to have a lot of differentiators. You only need a couple as long as they matter to the client. If you think about Dell, for instance, their main differentiator for years has been the ability to build to order and ship faster than their competitors. Since computers themselves have essentially become commodities, that service differentiator has been significant enough to keep Dell at the top.

If you're delivering services, either in conjunction with products or as a solution in themselves, what kinds of differentiators matter the most? Typically, decision makers will want to see something that sets you apart in one or more of four broad areas:

1. **How you will do the work.** Explain how you will do the project, what is different or unique about your methods, and why your way is the best way.

2. **How you will manage the work.** Poor project management is the leading cause of failure in technical projects, and is a major fear for many

buyers, even when the product or service isn't particularly technical. Present a detailed management plan, emphasizing the value-added components of your management approach, particularly in areas of measurement, tracking, and reporting.

3. **The people you will provide.** Intellectual capital has to reside in somebody's intellect. Whose? Who are you providing, and what makes them particularly well suited by training or experience to do the job right?

4. **Special facilities or equipment you have available.** Are your gas analysis labs the best in the industry? Do you have a system developed in-house for handling Webcast auctions that is fully integrated into all back-office functions? If the project will benefit from special equipment or facilities that only you have, mention them.

Linking Your Differentiators with the Customer's Values

Suppose you've taken the time to develop a comprehensive list of differentiators. Let's assume your list of differentiators includes the following:

- Standard code base

- User-friendly tools for customizing the interface

- True Web-based architecture

- Awards for superior products

- Lease or buy options

- Fastest loading system

- Options to access application data via a cell phone or PDA

- Open architecture

- First to market

- End-to-end capabilities, including design, user training, and support

- ISO 9000 certified vendor

- Certified six-sigma quality operation

- Financial stability with more than twenty-five years of profitable operation

This is kind of a mixed bag. Some relate to your products, some to your policies for doing business, some to your corporate history, and so on. How can you select the ones most likely to create an impression of superior value in the mind of your decision maker?

Start by cross-indexing your differentiators to the various value strategies you have identified. Knowing which varieties of value your customers care about is a matter of knowing your customers, of course, but let's suppose that many of the types of value we discussed earlier are of interest to some of your decision makers. Some of them will be looking for a financial return. Others in your market are focused on quality. Others are looking for risk minimization. And so on.

Create a table in which you list all of your differentiators in the first column and all of the various value positions you need to address across the top row. It will look something like this:

	FINANCIAL	TECHNICAL	QUALITY	SOCIAL	MINIMAL RISK	INDUSTRY TRENDS	COMPETITIVE ADVANTAGE
STANDARD CODE BASE							
CUSTOMIZATION TOOLS							
WEB-BASED ARCHITECTURE							
AWARDS FOR PRODUCTS							
LEASE OR BUY OPTIONS							
FASTEST LOADING TIME							
PDA/CELL PHONE ACCESS							
OPEN ARCHITECTURE							
FIRST TO MARKET							
END-TO-END PROVIDER							
ISO 9000 CERTIFIED							
SIX-SIGMA METHODOLOGY							
FINANCIALLY STABLE							

Now ask yourself: Does this specific differentiator support this particular value message? If it's an excellent way of communicating to the client that he or she gets a certain kind of value, give it five points. If it's very weak, give it just one point. Something in the middle, assign a point value based on your gut instinct. Don't spend too much time on this. Your quick initial impressions are probably a good guideline. When you've completed this process, your table will contain point values, like this:

	FINANCIAL	TECHNICAL	QUALITY	SOCIAL	MINIMAL RISK	INDUSTRY TRENDS	COMPETITIVE ADVANTAGE
STANDARD CODE BASE	4	5	4	1	4	5	3
CUSTOMIZATION TOOLS	5	4	3	3	2	3	2
WEB-BASED ARCHITECTURE	2	5	2	4	1	5	3
AWARDS FOR PRODUCTS	1	5	4	2	4	1	4
LEASE OR BUY OPTIONS	5	1	1	2	4	3	3
FASTEST LOADING TIME	3	5	4	4	1	1	3
PDA/CELL PHONE ACCESS	2	5	3	4	2	5	4
OPEN ARCHITECTURE	4	5	4	3	5	5	3
FIRST TO MARKET	4	3	5	1	3	1	2
END-TO-END PROVIDER	5	2	4	3	5	4	4
ISO 9000 CERTIFIED	2	2	5	3	4	4	3
SIX-SIGMA METHODOLOGY	2	3	5	3	4	3	3
FINANCIALLY STABLE	3	1	2	4	5	3	3

What does this chart tell you? If you add up the rows, you will see which differentiator has the highest overall value, regardless of the strategic positioning. In the case above, your strongest overall differentiators are "open architecture" and "end-to-end provider." So if you had no idea what the client's value orientation was, you might want to include those two at least because they're fairly strong in general.

Similarly, if you add up the columns, you'll get an idea which value position is best for you, given the differentiators you currently have. You'll also get an idea which kind of value position is weakest, suggesting that you may need to find some additional differentiators or you may need to focus on a different strategic value position. In the example above, your best option is to base your value proposition on your technical superiority or your impact on quality.

But the best way to use this chart is to figure out how the client wants to see value presented and then to identify which differentiators are the right ones to emphasize. If you have a client whose focus is on minimizing risk, for example, your most important differentiators are those that scored a five or four: open architecture, end-to-end provider, financial stability, standard code base, awards, and lease or buy options. Next week, when you are writing a proposal to somebody whose focus is on financial return, the differentiators you emphasize will be the customization tools, lease or buy options, end-to-end provider, standard code base, open architecture, and first to market. Some are the same, some are different, but all help support your value strategy.

The worst mistake you can make with your differentiators is to just dump all of them into every proposal. If you do that, they have no focus and make no point.

Proving Your Value with Win Themes

Your strategy is your overall approach to the issue of value. It's the broad message of value that you'd like each person who evaluates your proposal to walk away with. A **win theme** is a specific, tactical message that supports your overall strategy. Win themes provide you with an opportunity for substantiation and specificity. Win themes can provide cohesion to a proposal, unifying the message and lifting it from merely providing information in response to a request to a persuasive presentation of a business case.

A proposal should have one strategy. It doesn't have to be perfect, but if you've done your homework to uncover the customer's needs and values, it'll be effective. That strategy can then be supported and substantiated by several win themes. I would recommend selecting only two or three win themes to make the process easier to manage and to keep your proposal focused.

In developing win themes, you will want to identify which value strategies a particular theme can support, which differentiators link to it, and what evidence or substantiation you can marshal to prove it. Evidence might include:

■ Case studies

■ References

■ Testimonials

■ Third-party endorsements

■ Partnerships

■ Statistics and facts about your organization (such as number of employees, worldwide locations, and so forth)

■ Tools

■ Methodologies

■ Patents

■ Contracts

■ Publications and white papers

■ Unique expertise among your employees

Evidence becomes meaningful when it is clearly aligned to a specific theme. Otherwise, it runs the risk of just being background noise.

Here are some examples of win themes. These may not be appropriate for your business, but I hope they at least get you thinking about what kind of tactical messages you can develop to support the notion that the client gets superior value if they choose you.

1. **Speed of delivery:** We can deliver the right solution for you much faster than anyone else in the industry, so you begin to reap the benefits of that solution sooner.

2. **Creativity and innovation:** We are able to think creatively about what you really need and develop innovative approaches that exactly match your requirements, instead of trying to shove your requirements into predefined solutions.

3. **Good corporate citizen:** As a member of the community, we are committed to building it and collaborating with local government and citizens to improve the quality of life.

4. **Outsourcing as a smart way to manage your business:** We can help you eliminate or reduce fixed expenses, thus giving you more financial control.

5. **Mission fulfillment:** We understand your need to fulfill the charter of responsibilities inherent in your mission statement and can help you achieve success in that area.

6. **Crossing the threshold into e-commerce:** We can help you develop the tools, strategies, security policies, and enabling technologies that open up markets for you on the Web.

7. **Public/private partnership:** We can offer you greater value and lower net investment costs by providing a creative fee structure that includes a partnership between our firm and your agency.

Supporting Your Win Themes

In your proposal, you must support your win themes (and thus your overall strategy) by providing plenty of evidence to prove that what you claim is true. You will want to provide both top-level substantiation and incremental evidence.

Top-level substantiation consists of proof statements and factual evidence included specifically to make a point about your ability to deliver value. Areas of the proposal where you can tailor the content to support or substantiate a specific theme include:

- Past performance reports
- Case studies
- Customer testimonials
- Project summaries
- Corporate capabilities
- Company history
- Management plan

Incremental evidence consists of spots where you can mention or reinforce your overall value strategy and the enabling win themes you have chosen with a phrase, a sentence, or a brief example. Look for opportunities to weave incremental evidence into your proposal in these areas:

- Cover letter
- Proposal title
- Executive summary
- Section summaries
- Headings and subheadings
- Product/service details

■ Resumes

■ Titles of figures and graphics

Final Thoughts on Value

If you don't show compelling value, winning becomes a matter of chance. Take the time to develop a clear value proposition for your proposals. In addition, try to develop reusable content and standard value messages that you can use when you create proposals for your most common products and services.

It will also help you and your colleagues compete more successfully if you develop standard approaches to quantifying impact. These may be ROI models or formulas to generate a payback analysis. The goal is to create something appropriate to your client base and markets. If you can provide your decision makers with a benchmark against which they can do their own calculations of probable return, you will have successfully shifted their attention away from price and onto value. That's a much better place to be.

11 | *The Structure of the Letter Proposal*

The letter proposal may be as brief as a single page or as long as three or four pages with attachments. The exact salutation you use, the particular format you choose (block, modified block, whatever), the complimentary close, none of that's really very important. What's important is that your letter proposal clearly address the essential elements of the persuasive paradigm as described in Chapter 4:

1. **The client's need or problem.** Get right to the point. Don't waste time with cliché openings. In fact, mark it down as an infallible rule, any sentence that begins *"Per your . . ."* is a bad sentence. Even more common is an opening sentence like this: *"I would like to take this opportunity to thank you for allowing us to submit our proposal for your consideration."* What's wrong with that? It sounds like the writer is groveling.

   What's a better opening?

   Well, you can start with a "thank you," if you want to. For example, *"Thank you for providing the information we requested so that we could complete our proposal and develop the right solution for your situation. We are committed to developing a solution that offers the right business fit as well as conforming to your key technical requirements."*

   Or you can start by referencing previous meetings, contacts, or the client's RFP:

   "Based on the meeting held at your offices the first and third weeks of June, plus several phone interviews with other members of your team, we have developed an approach to deal with the three specific challenges you identified."

   But the best opening is usually one that gets right to the point, focusing on the specific problem or need that is affecting the client's profitability or productivity:

   "Physicians and nurses working in your hospital have indicated that the current process for recording case notes is awkward, time consuming, and inaccurate. As you explained to us, it represents a legacy system, which has long been out of date, and a number of patches and additions created in-house."

   Or like this:

   "Your decision to provide an online option for those customers who prefer not to shop at one of your three retail outlets is very exciting, because it will make it possible for them to order the finest in golf equipment, balls, and clothing at any time of the day or night and from any location. But it also

means your Web site must be overhauled to be more user-friendly, more secure, more interactive, and more compatible with your e-commerce strategy."

2. **The benefits of solving the problem or meeting the need.** You arouse the client's interest by reminding them of a particular problem they have. You hold their interest and motivate them to take action by showing them there's a significant payoff that comes from fixing the problem or meeting the need.

As we said earlier, most businesses have lots of problems, but the vast majority of them will never be solved. They just aren't worth it. There's no payoff to the company, no ROI for the investment, nothing that makes this problem important enough that the client is willing to spend time and money to fix it.

If we take the example of physicians and nurses who are spending too long to enter notes in their patients' files, the benefits paragraph might read something like this:

"Simplifying the process of updating case files, entering patient care notes, and documenting treatments can save Rutherford Psychiatric Hospital hundreds of hours and thousands of dollars every week. In fact, we estimate it can save your physicians a total of 120 hours weekly and your nursing staff a weekly total of 1,650 hours! Here's how we calculated the savings:

	DICTATION/ WRITING TIME PER WEEK	REVIEW TIME	PATIENT LOAD	TOTAL TIME
PHYSICIAN	10 min./patient	5 min./patient	20 patients	5 hours
NURSE	20 min./patient	10 min./patient	30 patients	15 hours

The table above summarizes the average time a typical physician and nurse respectively spend recording and reviewing notes on patients each week. Multiply that by the number of physicians on staff (24) and the number of full-time equivalent nurses at Rutherford (110), and you're looking at a huge drain on productivity. Add in the staff of clerks who do nothing but type up physician notes because the existing system doesn't work well and you're looking at a massive expense that contributes nothing positive to patient care."

If you knew what the average charge rate was for physicians and nurses at Rutherford Hospital, you could calculate exactly what that expense is. But you can see how marshalling the numbers makes the analysis of impact more convincing, particularly compared to just offering generalities about *"dramatic improvements in productivity"* from replacing the existing system.

3. **The solution.** The presentation of your solution in a letter proposal should contain:

A high-level description of the product or service you are recommending

- Include enough detail to answer the customer's primary questions

- Tie those details to the client's needs, showing how the features of your system address the issues the customer is concerned about

- Remember to stress your company's differentiators

A specific, clear recommendation to act

- Use phrases like, *"I recommend . . ."* and *"I urge you to move forward . . ."* so there is no doubt where you stand

- Too many proposals merely describe a solution rather than actually recommending it; descriptions don't motivate anybody to do anything

You might also consider covering alternative solutions very briefly. Typically, you will cover them not to recommend them but to show why they aren't as desirable as the approach you are recommending. This creates the appearance of thoroughness on your part, something the analytical decision maker values. More importantly, by briefly considering and dismissing alternative approaches, you have the opportunity to anticipate the competition's approach and point out its weaknesses without engaging in disparagement. This technique is sometimes called "ghosting" the competition, perhaps because it raises issues that come back to haunt your competitors.

4. **The wrap-up.** The final part of your letter proposal should address three key issues:

First, articulate the cost/benefit ratio. Line item pricing, if it's even necessary, can be relegated to an attachment, but within the body of your letter itself you should graphically show that the return on investment or payback period or total cost of ownership being offered by your solution is extremely compelling. You want to show the client that the benefits of moving forward far outweigh the costs. The essence of your analysis of the cost/benefit ratio will be based on the price of your solution compared to the benefits calculated in the second section of your letter proposal. You should also include the intangible costs, such as training, necessary equipment upgrades, and so forth. Mention the intangible benefits, too, of course, such as higher employee morale, regulatory compliance, better customer service, elimination of maintenance and repair costs, and so on.

Second, provide basic information about the implementation schedule, project plan, and deliverables. If this information threatens to become lengthy or very detailed, include just the key dates and put the rest in an attachment. Mention any assumptions you have made which could affect the schedule, and indicate how the responsibilities will be shared between your firm and the client's.

Third, cover any special technical considerations. If the customer has made very specific technical demands, indicate that you will meet them. Or, if you cannot meet these technical requirements, indicate that you will be able to deliver the functional requirements and will be doing it in a way that is somewhat different from what the customer specified. You will need to judge how big a problem this will pose to winning the opportunity, but concealing the fact that you do not intend to deliver the solution in conformity to the client's technical specifications is not a good idea. If your pre-proposal research has indicated that this aspect of the bid will make or break the deal, perhaps you should consider not bidding at all. However, you can usually expect a client to take a somewhat open-minded attitude toward technical issues if other aspects of the solution are attractive. Also, if you must take exception to certain requirements or terms, or if you have reservations about the delivery schedule or implementation plan, you may want to point them out here. It's very difficult to put anything the client might construe as a negative into your proposal, but nothing good ever comes from deceiving the client or withholding information, either.

A Few Tips on Writing Winning Letter Proposals

Here are a few suggestions to improve the effectiveness of your letter proposals:

1. **Don't let the tone become too stuffy.** For some reason, people lapse into a pompous tone when writing business letters and proposals. You'll sound more sincere, maintain a level of rapport, and produce more readable proposals if you simplify the tone. Avoid long sentences and inflated language. Use the customer's name throughout the letter. Refer to the customer as "you," not "it" or "they."

2. **Similarly, don't let your legal department include language that will alarm or offend your customer.** The corporate attorneys have the mission of keeping your company out of trouble. Unfortunately, that sometimes leads them to do things that violate common sense. For example, I have seen letter proposals (and cover letters for formal proposals) that

included paragraphs saying, "Nothing in this proposal should be construed as a binding promise to deliver nor a commitment to any particular schedule or pricing, until such time as customer has executed a purchase order and/or agreed in writing to contractual terms." What an exercise in dissembling! If you read that, would you want to bother reading the rest of the proposal? No, me neither. You can find a positive way to make that kind of statement or can include it as a separate attachment of terms and conditions, but putting it on the first page of your letter proposal is a bad tactical mistake.

3. **Avoid the clichés of business writing.** Avoid the hackneyed openings and closing that your reader has probably seen a hundred times before. In particular, avoid clichéd openings such as, *"I would like to take this opportunity to thank you for considering the enclosed proposal . . . blah, blah, blah."* Other cliché openings that need to be retired:

   ■ *"Pursuant to your request, we are submitting our recommendation . . ."*

   ■ *"Attached please find . . ."*
   Get to the point.

4. **Use a strong close.** Avoid the clichéd, all-purpose closing that everybody uses: *"If you have any questions, please feel free to call."* That's been done to death. So bury it. Don't ever use it again. I know it's easy, and I know everyone does it, but think about what it says: Basically, it tells the reader, "Look, I know I don't write very well. I always confuse people. So if I've confused you, don't worry about it. Give me a call and together we'll figure out what I was trying to say." Also, notice that if you use that closing, you have turned over control of the sales process to the customer. Your job is to sit by the phone and wait until the customer comes up with a question. What a lousy way to end your proposal!

   To close effectively, ask for the business. Set a date when you will contact the customer to discuss next steps, or express eagerness to win the contract and deliver the solution. Return to your primary value proposition: financial gain, improved quality, infrastructure improvements, risk avoidance, competitive advantage, or whatever you have chosen. Tell the reader what he or she must do to gain this advantage. Return to the benefits of taking action. And make the action something that's easy to do—the easier the better.

   Finally, close with confidence. Avoid expressions like "I hope that" and "If it would be all right." When you have said what you wanted to say and have asked the customer for appropriate action—stop. Figure 11-1 shows a sample letter proposal.

Figure 11-1. Sample Letter Proposal.

[Date]

Ms. Jane Woods
Sr. Vice President
Information Systems
Diston Drugs Corporation
8333 Dairy Creek Road
San Francisco, CA 94133

Dear Ms. Woods,

Thank you for meeting with us and helping us understand the Diston Corporation security infrastructure in greater depth. Based on our meetings with you and your staff, we propose to conduct a security review of your environment, develop IS security checklists, and develop an overall information security plan. Our approach is based on our understanding of your needs and on Waugh Security's experience with similar clients in the retail industry. As you requested, we have made the project's scope and pricing scalable.

Understanding Your Security Needs
Because of numerous mergers and consolidations during the past three years, Diston's environment has become complex to manage. Although this has affected every aspect of the firm's operations, from corporate headquarters down to the store level, one of the most challenging areas has been information security:

- Because you have inherited a variety of legacy systems, Diston is currently utilizing a variety of computing platforms, including DEC, HP, IBM, and Tandem, and a variety of operating systems, including Netware, UNIX, and VM.
- In addition, the corporation communicates through an extensive network which includes external connections to wide area networks, virtual private networks, and the Internet.
- Departments throughout the corporation, regional offices, and retail outlets in widely dispersed locations currently all have different security policies, different procedures for managing each system, and different understandings of security requirements across the business units.

Key Goals and Objectives
Your goal is to standardize security within the corporation and to develop a program that will give you more proactive control of your systems and operating environments. In addition, you want to establish

(continues)

Figure 11-1. (Continued).

a blueprint for a security organization that will keep the corporation's systems as secure as possible and to develop plans for anticipating future security requirements. A related goal is to make sure your overall security environment remains current as requirements evolve.

Based on the figures you provided us and on information obtained from previous security assessments we have conducted, we estimate that Diston will see cost savings from increased efficiency of more than $500,000 a year. More significantly, through threat reduction and enhanced security procedures, the company will avoid information losses valued at more than $2 million annually and will reduce fraud by an expected 35 percent. These figures are based on estimates derived from experience with other firms in the retail space. We will calculate actual risk avoidance values for Diston Drugs as part of our deliverables.

From an execution standpoint, the key objectives of this project are to:
- Conduct a comprehensive security review of your environment
- Develop checklists to ensure consistent application of security procedures
- Develop a plan for implementing recommendations resulting from the review

Project Scope and Deliverables
Diston relies on the availability and integrity of your business application systems and network to operate more than five hundred retail outlets throughout North America. Proper measures must be taken to protect the sensitive information that is passed from these systems throughout the Diston network. Waugh Security will help Diston identify risks in the environment and then recommend controls to mitigate these security exposures.

The project will include the following activities:

I: **Conduct a Security Review**. This review will include an assessment of:
- Security processes (e.g., auditing, event escalation, user administration, etc.)
- UNIX and Novell server operating systems
- Windows and NT workstations
- Network security provisions
  - dial-up security
  - routers, intelligent hubs
  - security of network management and network monitoring systems
  - external connection security

To complete this review, Waugh Security will utilize automated security assessment tools, including special tools for NT and UNIX. Due to the short project time frame, we will not assess each system in the environment, but will look at a representative sample of high-priority systems. This will include five UNIX systems at headquarters and five Novell file servers. We will also assess points of entry into the network, including dial-up and external connections. These entry points exist at headquarters, stores, and the data center. Interviews, documentation reviews, and on-site tours will be critical to the security review. Areas that are out-of-scope of this review include the Lexington mainframe operating system, the Internet connection via QwikLink, application security controls, and the operating system of the in-store processor systems.

At the conclusion of this review, Waugh Security will provide Diston with a report detailing security strengths and weaknesses. This report will also prioritize recommendations for improving security, and will quantify to the extent possible the risks associated with not implementing the recommendations.

II: **Create a Data Inventory.** We will conduct a high-level inventory of the types of data in the Diston network and will document the current controls and risks for each data type. This inventory will help spot areas of weakness, where additional controls are necessary to protect sensitive data.

III: **Analyze Roles and Responsibilities Within the Security Organization.** As Diston begins to formalize a security organization, the entire corporation needs to understand the roles within the security organization and each member's responsibilities. This analysis will serve as a blueprint for building the security organization and assuring its effective integration into the corporation structure as a whole. We will also include a job description for an Information Security Officer, which will help ensure that you hire an individual with the correct skills.

IV: **Develop Checklists of Best Practice in Security Procedures.** Waugh Security will develop security checklists for Diston covering the following areas:
- Novell Netware
- UNIX
- External access (firewalls, gateways, dial-up, etc.)
- Network (routers, network administration, encryption, etc.)
- PCs (Windows 3.1 and NT)
- System audits

(continues)

Figure 11-1. (Continued).

- Virus control
- Security provisions appropriate for generic applications

The Diston IS team can then tailor these checklists further to bring common controls to the entire Diston environment.

Deliverables for this project will include:
- High-level data inventory detailing controls and risks
- A report itemizing current security strengths and weaknesses
- Recommendations for mitigating current weaknesses and a quantification of the risks of not taking action
- A cost/benefit matrix for implementing the security recommendations and identifying key tasks, benefits, and representative implementation costs
- Recommendations for establishing the Security Organization with an analysis of roles and responsibilities
- Security checklists for your major systems, including Novell Netware, UNIX, external access, network, PCs, system audit, virus control, application security
- A presentation to Diston management of our findings and recommendations
- Project working papers

Project Methodology, Staffing and Schedule
Methodology. Waugh Security has developed a unique methodology for managing security reviews. This methodology, which we call Professional Review of Information Security Matters (PRISM), has been recognized by independent, third-party evaluators as the most effective process of its kind in the industry. The advantage to Diston of the PRISM methodology is that it will save you time and money while assuring you of a thorough review and complete set of actionable recommendations.

Our process will begin with an assessment of Diston's current procedures and security gaps. During this phase we will interview key personnel, review current security documentation, conduct on-site assessments at headquarters and key retail stores, and use automated security assessment tools to probe the Diston environment. From this assessment, Waugh Security will document the strengths and weaknesses in each area we assess. We will then develop recommendations to improve security controls and will quantify the risks associated with not acting on the recommendations.

Staffing. To complete this project in the timeframe you indicated was necessary (i.e., before June 1), we will assign a three-person core project team. In addition, we will need the full-time participation of Charles Vincent, Diston IS quality assurance manager.

The Waugh team will be led by Richard Hsiung. Dr. Hsiung will participate on a part-time basis, providing technology oversight. Dr. Hsiung is the senior manager of Waugh Security's Infrastructure Assessment Group (IAG). He has more than twenty years' experience in developing systems solutions to real-world problems. In particular, he is recognized as an expert on information security and authentication issues and was a senior member of the U.S. government's task force on Public Key Infrastructure issues for corporate security.

H. William Jones will serve as project manager. He will provide the day-to-day supervision of the Diston security assessment project. Mr. Jones has extensive experience in strategic planning of information management systems for retail and manufacturing environments. He most recently had the lead role in developing e-commerce strategies for one of Waugh Security's largest retail clients, Heartland Clothing Inc. We have attached a case study reviewing this project.

Clark Johnson will complete the Waugh Security team. Mr. Johnson will oversee assessment activities, will gather data from the automated tools, and will conduct interviews with Diston managers and employees. Mr. Johnson is an IAG technology specialist with more than five years' experience in using security assessment tools and conducting assessment activities.

In addition to Mr. Vincent, other Diston personnel will be required to participate in this project as described in the attached description of project assumptions. Given the short timeframe of this project, timely participation of Diston personnel will be critical to its success.

Schedule. Based on the scope, approach, and staffing described above, as well as the attached Project Assumptions document, we estimate this project will require five weeks to complete. We are prepared to begin on April 13 and to complete the work no later than May 23. The chart below outlines the project phases and work. We have attached a project plan that describes the phases, tasks, and resources for this project in more detail.

(continues)

Figure 11-1. (Continued).

We propose the following project timeline:

Project Phase	Week 1	Week 2	Week 3	Week 4	Week 5
Project Organization	■				
Security Review	■	■	■	■	
• *Review Background Material*	�				
• *Document Assets*	▒	▒			
• *Identify Threats*	▒	▒			
• *Calculate Potential Loss*	▒				
• *Document Environment*		▒	▒		
• *Document Controls*		▒	▒		
• *Develop Recommendations*			▒	▒	
Prepare Data Inventory		■	■	■	
Analyze Roles and Responsibilities			■	■	
Create Checklists of Best Practices		■	■	■	
Present Project Results					■

Estimated Project Fees and Expenses

We estimate our professional fees will be $182,000. Travel and living expenses and appropriate out-of-pocket expenses will be additional. Based on our preliminary estimate of cost savings from enhanced efficiency, this project will pay for itself within the first six months. If you factor in risk minimization and avoidance of loss, the payback is even faster.

We will submit an invoice to you at the end of each month for fees and expenses incurred during that month. If circumstances suggest that the scope of our work will change from what we have described in this letter, we will obtain your written approval prior to incurring fees in excess of those noted above.

I will call you on Wednesday, March 28, to discuss the next steps. We look forward to working with you to create a more secure environment at Diston Drugs and to preserve the information assets that are such a vital part of the corporation's capital.

Very truly yours,

Jeffrey Christiansen
Vice President
Waugh Security

Attachments:
1. Project assumptions
2. Project plan and GANTT chart
3. Case study: Assessment of Information Security Vulnerabilities
   for Heartland Clothing
4. Waugh Security standard business terms

12 *The Structure of the Formal Proposal*

Sometimes it's more appropriate to write a formal proposal than to submit a letter proposal. You may decide to do so, for example, if the document is too long (that is, more than four or five pages) to fit comfortably in the letter format, if it's proposing a costly or complicated solution, or if a formal, sectioned response has been mandated by the RFP to which you are responding.

Formal proposals will vary, depending on what's appropriate for the given audience. But, as a general rule, all formal proposals will contain three broad categories of content: the business case; the detailed solution and substantiation; and any attachments.

THE BUSINESS CASE	Cover letter Title page Table of contents Executive Summary • Customer needs • Customer desired outcomes • High-level presentation of solution • Key value-added components or uniqueness factors Pricing and payback analysis	**Accessible:** by all audiences, but focused on the top-level executives and financial buyers **Content:** overview, high-level content focusing mainly on business issues, bottom-line factors **Graphics:** ROI charts, payback analysis, focus boxes to highlight key text
SOLUTIONS AND SUBSTANTIATION	Solution in significant detail, including: • Deliverables • Operational description of the equipment or system proposed • Training • Documentation • Implementation Pricing/cost analysis ROI or payback calculation Value-added components Scope of work Project plan/master schedule Timeline	**Accessible:** primarily by technical reviewers **Content:** details addressing how the system works, establishing value, differentiating your offering from competitors' **Graphics:** • Product illustrations • Flow charts • Process diagrams • Schematics • CAD drawings • Gantt chart

	Project team, resumes, organization chart	• Cost comparison table
	Subcontractors	
	References	
	Case studies	
	Testimonials	
	Uniqueness factors	
	Warranties, service-level agreements	
	RFP response	
	• Compliance matrix	
	• Question and answer section	
ATTACHMENTS AND APPENDICES	Terms and conditions	**Accessible:** varies; usually a highly specialized reviewer
	Glossary/nomenclature	
	Relevant marketing materials	**Content:** specialized information to facilitate the decision process
	Attachments (digital media, sample code, video, photo tour of prospective facility, etc.)	

The reason you want to structure your formal proposal this way is to provide the right kind of content, aimed at the right level of expertise, for all of the various evaluators who will look at it:

Senior executives will want the basics: What are they proposing? Why should we do this? What do we gain from choosing these people? What differentiates them? How much will it cost? What kind of ROI can we expect?

Technical evaluators and **gatekeepers** have more specialized interests. They want specific, detailed content that addresses their areas of responsibility and concerns.

■ A gatekeeper, who often performs the initial screen of all proposals to eliminate as many as possible, is looking for issues of compliance. Are we getting what we asked for? Has this vendor answered all of the questions? Did they follow our instructions?

■ A technical evaluator is looking at the proposed solution and all the factors surrounding it, including issues of installation, implementation, training, support, and so forth. This evaluator wants to know: What are they proposing? How does it work? What are the risk factors? Do they have sufficient experience? How will it fit into our operation?

By writing your proposal with three distinct components in mind, you satisfy the information requirements of these different audiences.

Protecting Your Proprietary Interests

Before we look at the parts of a formal proposal, let's take a minute to consider an issue that worries a lot of people. How do you write a proposal that presents a creative solution and that may contain information that is confidential or proprietary to your business without having your solution and your proprietary content taken by an unethical client, shared with a competitor, or otherwise misused?

The first and most obvious answer is to know your client. If you have concerns about their ethics, maybe you should revisit the bid/no bid analysis one more time. If you still want to go after the business, but you're worried they might steal your ideas, you have a few options:

1. Limit the amount of specific technical detail you provide. If you can describe your solution in general terms without revealing exactly how you will execute it, you may prevent someone from deciding they can do it themselves. Similarly, if you provide aggregated pricing instead of line item, detailed pricing, you make it a little more difficult for somebody to use your proposal as a shopping list. The downside to this approach, of course, is that you also lose a little credibility because of the vagueness and you may lose an opportunity to differentiate your approach.

2. Seek a nondisclosure agreement and/or a letter of understanding before you submit. Ask the client to sign a nondisclosure agreement in which they acknowledge your ownership of the content in your proposal and agree not to share it with anyone outside the evaluation team without your written consent.

3. Mark your proposal "Proprietary" or "Business Confidential." Put these warnings on the pages of your proposal that actually contain proprietary content. Don't put them on every page, because if you mark content proprietary that is actually in the public domain or that belongs to the client, you invalidate your proprietary claim in general. You can also put a statement of proprietary rights up front in your proposal. I recommend putting it on a separate page, not trying to fold it into your cover letter, title page, or executive summary.

4. Copyright your proposal. To do that, simply put "Copyright <year> <Your Company Name>" on the title page or in the footer.

5. Submit at deadline. If you submit early, who knows what will happen to your proposal while the client waits for others to arrive?

6. Build your proposal on your differentiators, so that there's no way a customer can do it itself or give it to a competitor to do. This can be

difficult if you don't have differentiators that are unique enough, but it's ultimately the best way.

Writing the Business Case

Writing a formal proposal can be a daunting task. Some of them may be hundreds, even thousands of pages long, but even if they are much shorter, they are still complex documents. As the old proverb about eating an elephant says, you can only get the job done one bite at a time.

The most important bites are the ones that appear up front—your cover letter and executive summary. Allow yourself enough time to do a good job with those parts and you'll at least create a positive first impression.

The Cover Letter

The cover letter is your firm's official transmittal message. It should be signed by an executive of sufficient rank to bind the company to a contract, ideally by someone in your organization who is the peer of the person who will make the buying decision in the client's organization. What about having the salesperson or account manager sign the cover letter? You can do it that way, but it will not have the same impact as having the president or a senior vice president sign. If you wish, you could have both the senior executive and the salesperson sign the cover letter.

The cover letter is part of the total proposal package and should help sell your solution. Think of the cover letter as a mini executive summary. Include the customer's key need or needs, one or two important outcomes from meeting those needs, your basic approach or solution in a sentence or two, and your two most important differentiators. If your proposal was written in response to an RFP, reference the RFP by name or number. Indicate in the cover letter the effective period for the pricing, staffing, and implementation schedules offered in the proposal. Just as we discussed in reference to the letter proposal, never end your cover letter with that tired old cliché, "Call me if you have any questions." End with a specific call to action.

The cover letter is also a place where you can thank individuals in the client's organization who have been helpful to you.

If your proposal is a revision, indicate that in the cover letter. You may want to point out specific sections where changes have been made.

Finally, some proposal writers include a statement of proprietary rights in the cover letter. Be careful not to lapse into legalistic language if you decide to make a statement of this sort in the cover letter. As I already mentioned, I strongly recommend that you put your proprietary claim elsewhere in the document, not in the cover letter.

Likewise, avoid making statements that undercut rapport and trust, such as this one that appeared in the cover letter of an actual proposal:

All assumptions are considered preliminary until the final proposal, SOW and vendor management responsibilities for each study are approved.

Would that sentence make you feel confident that the vendor will stand by what they are proposing? Or do they already seem to be looking for wiggle room?

Figures 12-1, 12-2, and 12-3 offer examples of effective cover letters.

Title Page

The title page should include a title for the proposal, the name of the recipient, the name of the preparer(s), and the date of submission. You can also put the client's logo and your company's logo on the title page. It's a nice way to personalize the title page, but don't do it if the client is touchy about anyone reproducing their logo.

Never title your proposal "Proposal." That doesn't say anything your clients can't figure out themselves. (It's a little like writing a book and titling it "Book," isn't it?) Also, avoid using generic titles such as "A Proposal for New American Corporation." Finally, avoid any proposal title that is basically nothing more than the name of your product or service: "Proposal to Analyze Internet Security Requirements." "Proposal for the TurboEncabulator Model 5000." All of those are losers.

You'll get better results if you create a substantive title that states a benefit to the client or focuses on the primary outcome the client desires. Try to construct a title that does the following:

■ Describes your recommendation in terms of its outcome or impact on the client organization

■ Contains a verb that expresses a beneficial state of change for the client

■ Focuses on results, not product names

■ Avoids any use of your own in-house jargon

Here are some examples:

REDUCING DATA TRANSMISSION COSTS
A Union Technology Solution for AmeriBank Corporation

IMPROVING PRODUCTIVITY THROUGH ONLINE INVENTORY ACCESS

INCREASING CUSTOMER LOYALTY THROUGH ENHANCED SERVICE OPTIONS

CUTTING COSTS IN THE ACCOUNTS PAYABLE AREA
WITH AUTOMATED WORKFLOW PROCESSES

Figure 12-1. Sample Cover Letter 1.

[date]

Mr. Samuel Taylor, CPA
Chief Financial Officer
Kallaher Financial Group
123 E. Fourth Street, 5th Floor
Redlands, California

Dear Mr. Taylor:

The enclosed proposal responds to your request for audits of the
following facilities:
  • the Patriot Center for Rehabilitative Medicine in San Luis Obispo,
    California
  • the Phoenix City Hospital in Phoenix, Arizona
  • the Moreno Valley Wellness Center in Sunnymead, California
  • the Claremont Health Care Center in Claremont, California

Our proposal addresses your need for thorough audits of all four
operations, but we have also gone a step further, taking into account
your broader objectives. We have developed an overall plan to help you
gather the necessary data to turn the properties around financially and
protect the value of your investment. We have also outlined our
services in the event that one or more of these properties cannot be
made profitable and must be sold or liquidated.

We recommend handling the audits by means of a partnership between
ourselves, through our Redlands, California, headquarters, where we
have extensive experience in real estate audits, and James J. Harrison,
CPA, & Company, a firm with offices in Phoenix, Arizona, with
recognized expertise in supporting the health care industry. This
partnership is uniquely qualified to handle the audit and provide
additional services as may be required.

We bring some distinct advantages to the process of handling your
audit:
  1. As medium-size firms, we have the flexibility and responsiveness
     to meet all deadlines, especially those imposed by third parties
     and regulators. We offer you the level of service and commitment
     that the national firms save for their largest clients.
  2. At the same time, we have the resources, specialized knowledge,
     and experience to handle complex audits of long-term-care
     facilities quickly.

(continues)

Figure 12-1. (Continued).

3. Senior partners of both firms will be personally involved in conducting your audits.
4. We provide the highest-quality services at a cost-effective price.

We seek to handle all four audits because it is important to develop a total picture of the financial situation for all four facilities. In addition, by handling all four audits, we can save you money. For these reasons, our firms would decline to participate in a split or partial award.

We are eager to work with you on this project. May we schedule a time to present our proposal to the entire management team?

Sincerely,

Donald Miller, CPA   Nancy Jamison
Partner   Business Development Manager

Some federal, state, and local government programs and some RFPs prepared by consultants specify a format for the title page or even provide a form for you to complete. In that case, do what they ask.

Figures 12-4 and 12-5 each exemplify a complete title page.

Table of Contents

One of the key principles of successful proposal writing is to make your proposal easy to use. People are more likely to view your submission positively if it seems easy to understand. The table of contents is a helpful tool for achieving that goal.

Does your proposal need a table of contents? It probably does if it contains more than four or five pages of content or if it is divided into two or more sections.

List the title of each section and the headings of each major subsection in your table of contents. If the RFP uses a numbering scheme or a particular nomenclature for sections or division of content, mirror it in your table of contents.

Make sure the table of contents includes page numbers. Number the pages consecutively through the entire proposal. Don't start renumbering the pages with each section.

Figures 12-6, 12-7, and 12-8 show the structural clarity a table of contents can lend to a proposal.

Executive Summary

The executive summary is the single most important part of your proposal. It's the only part that's likely to be read by everybody involved in making

Figure 12-2. Sample Cover Letter 2.

[date]

Mr. Fred Landers
Director, Professional Development
Canadian Micrometer
155 Lake Louise Drive
Banff, Alberta
Canada

Dear Mr. Landers:

The enclosed proposal is a response to your recent RFP #03-B433 to provide commercial management training. We believe our proposal offers you an exceptional combination of experience and resources to meet your training needs cost-effectively.

In today's fast-moving business environment, mergers and acquisitions are commonplace. Canadian Micrometer's recent acquisition and merger activity has created a need to consolidate your systems and processes, particularly those involving commercial management processes. This will maximize the benefits of your mergers and help ensure seamless transition to a centralized operation.

As the enclosed proposal shows, we specialize in the development of tailored and custom-developed management courses. Each member of the Management Performance, Inc., team is a dynamic presenter, bringing to the classroom both formal training and years of experience in commercial management functions. We have established an outstanding record for tailoring programs to meet the needs of both our clients and each individual participant.

We also offer you the flexibility of combining various training media. Besides our years of success in developing and delivering classroom instruction, we are leaders in creating self-paced learning materials, computer-based and Web-based interactive instruction, and innovative educational tools, such as games and experiential learning activities.

Please note that our proposal is exactly that: a set of proposed recommendations based on our preliminary look at your needs. To finalize the content of the training and to assure the most effective delivery media, we urge you to work with us in completing a detailed assessment of your exact requirements.

(continues)

Figure 12-2. (Continued).

We look forward to working with Canadian Micrometer and are committed to providing you with top-quality support for your training initiative at a very competitive price. The result will be enhanced skill and knowledge among your professional staff, accelerated integration of the various organizations you have acquired during the past eighteen months, and a rapid payback. I will call you next week to discuss the next steps.

Sincerely,

Ursula E. Drew
Vice President, Account Development Services

a decision. In fact, it's the *only* part of your proposal that some decision makers will read.

Calling it an "executive summary" is a bit of a misnomer, but we're stuck with it now. The name is misleading because this part of your proposal doesn't really summarize the rest of the document. Think of it as a business overview or a management case. That will help you include only the content that matters.

Here are some additional guidelines:

1. Write the executive summary so that it is accessible to anyone from the janitor to the chairman of the board.

2. Focus on organizational issues and outcomes, and keep technical content to the essential minimum.

3. Present your strategy and win themes in the executive summary. You will develop and substantiate them elsewhere in the proposal, but make sure they are clear and prominent parts of the executive summary

4. The executive summary should be about the customer, not you. Count how many times the customer's name appears and compare that to the number of times your firm's name appears—the ratio ought to be 3:1 in favor of the customer.

5. Keep your executive summary short—one to two pages for the first twenty-five pages of proposal text and an additional page for each fifty pages thereafter.

Remember that the last comment regarding length is just a guideline, not an absolute rule. Write an executive summary that tells your story clearly and persuasively, even if that takes an extra page or two.

The structure of the executive summary is almost identical to the struc-

Figure 12-3. Sample Cover Letter 3.

[date]

Ms. Mary Carpenter
U.S. Department of Housing and Urban Development
Office of Procurement and Contracts
451 7th Street SW
Washington, DC 20410

Reference: Solicitation No. EV211D1111127204

Dear Ms. Carpenter:

We are pleased to submit the enclosed proposal to provide the research, writing, editing, proofreading, text entry, manuscript preparation, and special services necessary for producing a *Handbook* for the United States Department of Housing and Urban Development.

Documentation Plus, a qualified woman-owned small business, will serve as prime contractor. As the enclosed proposal shows, we are writers foremost, specializing in legal and technical communications designed for nonspecialist audiences. Each member of the Documentation Plus team has experience writing about legal issues, particularly in the areas of housing civil rights. In addition, we are familiar with a wide variety of media, having produced Web sites, technical journals, newsletters, audio-visual presentations, videotapes, and interactive CD-ROMs.

American Legal Resource Systems, a minority-owned, qualified 8a small business, will serve as subcontractor on the project. ALRS has extensive experience in providing publication support services to commercial, federal, and other government accounts. These services include technical writing and editing, graphic development, layout, production, document design, and publishing.

We look forward to working with the Department of Housing and Urban Development and are committed to providing cost-effective, high-quality support of all your writing, editing, and other communication needs associated with the proposed *Handbook*.

Sincerely,

Jennifer McCorkle   James T. Olson
CEO   President
Documentation Plus   American Legal Resource Systems

Figure 12-4. Sample Title Page 1.

Converting More Leads to Orders

A SALES TRAINING PROPOSAL FROM TRAINING SPECIALISTS INTERNATIONAL
TO
WHITE DAIRY

Submitted in Response to RFP #A02-29

[date]

Submitted to:

Nancy Coogan, Vice President of Sales

Prepared by:

Jack Adamson, National Account Manager

ture of the letter proposal. Both are based on the persuasive paradigm, both use a minimal amount of detailed substantiation, and both are primarily concerned with defining the customer's problem or need correctly, articulating the positive outcomes that will come from solving that problem, and recommending a solution. Keep your executive summary focused on the bottom-line issues the customer cares about the most. Figures 12-9, 12-10, and 12-11 offer examples of an executive summary.

Body Copy

The actual "meat" of your proposal goes in the body. What should you address in this section? Here are some suggestions, but remember that the overriding rule should be that you provide exactly what your client wants to see in the order that he or she wants to see it. Avoid the temptation to "bulk up" your proposal by including lots of extraneous detail.

Figure 12-5. Sample Title Page 2.

Reducing Scrap and Dimensional Deviations Through Laser Measurement Systems

A RECOMMENDATION FOR GENERAL MILLING AND MACHINING CORPORATION
FROM
BRUNSWICK METROLOGY LABORATORIES

[date]

Submitted to:

P. K. Choi, Vice President of Operations

Prepared by:

Allen Michelson, Director of Business Acquisition

Samuel J. Pollick, Director of Metrology Systems

- The technical section, which may include the technical details, functional analysis, operational description, design specifications, and implementation programs associated with your recommendation

- The pricing section, which will include detailed costs and an analysis of return on investment or another form of cost justification

- Detailed response to the questions and requirements of the RFP

- Case studies, success stories, and past performance summaries

- Related applications that have been successful

- References to satisfied clients

- Testimonials

- The management plan, including project schedules, critical milestones, and the allocation of responsibilities among your firm, the customer, and other vendors, if any

Figure 12-6. Sample Table of Contents 1.

TABLE OF CONTENTS

■ Brief resumes of key personnel who will oversee or work on the project

■ Logistical and support issues

■ Warranties, service-level agreements, and risk-sharing options, if any

■ Documentation

■ Training plans

Not every proposal needs to contain all of this content. In fact, most of them won't. Include the elements that are of most interest to your customer and deal with them in their order of importance as the customer sees it. If you are responding to an RFP, use it as your guide. It may specify an order for the content in your proposal. Even if it doesn't, look at the sequencing of issues in the RFP and mirror that in your proposal.

Section Introductions

One of the most important areas of your proposal is the introduction you write to each major section. A short introductory paragraph, particularly if you highlight it with a box or shading, focuses the reader's attention, provides the reader with a transition from one major idea to the next, and gives you an opportunity to state your key themes.

Figure 12-7. Sample Table of Contents 2.

Table of *Contents*

Here's an example:

> *The following section addresses the specific features of our software and how users can customize the interface to meet their own require-ments or preferences. Specifically, this section discusses the tools in-cluded in the standard package that make it easy for a user to modify the view of data. These tools reduce the time it takes to lo-cate and process data, thereby increasing productivity.*
>
> *This section also discusses how a system administrator can en-able users to make modifications at the desktop level or can make modifications that affect the entire enterprise. This capability allows you to match the software to your specific work environment and requirements, eliminating the need for customization and re-ducing the amount of time the administrator spends configuring the product for individual users.*

Figure 12-8. Sample Table of Contents 3.

PROPOSAL CONTENTS

Recommending and Substantiating Your Solution

Of the thousands of proposals I read each year, the majority do not recommend anything. Most of them merely describe a product or service in neutral, informative prose. Descriptions are nice, but they can come across as evasive in a proposal. It may appear to the customer that you don't really believe in what you are saying. In addition, descriptions typically consist of undifferentiated verbiage that provides a general understanding of the

(text continues on page 154)

Figure 12-9. Sample Executive Summary 1.

Enhancing Communications and Increasing Productivity at North American Chemicals

THE OPPORTUNITY AND THE CHALLENGE

North American Chemicals' trial application of our competitor's voice mail system has already demonstrated a tremendous opportunity to increase employee productivity and reduce long-distance costs. But any opportunity such as this also contains an inherent challenge: maximizing the potential payoff that the opportunity offers.

To gain the greatest possible benefit from the introduction of a voice messaging system, North American Chemicals should consider four key factors:

1. *The system's ease of access and user-friendliness.* Will employees and customers actually use it?

2. *The professionalism of the image the system creates, both for individuals and for the company as a whole.* Does the system enhance the company's image or detract from it?

3. *The technical quality of the system.* Is the system technically robust enough to accommodate future needs, adaptations, modifications, or enhancements, as North American Chemicals needs them?

4. *The overall value of the system.* Will it quickly and conveniently become an everyday tool? Will it be fully supported? Will it fit into the overall telecommunications system?

The challenge for North American is to select the system that offers the biggest payoff in terms of these key factors.

EASE OF ACCESS AND USER-FRIENDLINESS

Voice messaging systems have become standard business tools, and the technology behind these systems is evolving rapidly. Most of the enhancements have focused on making the systems easy to access and easy to use. Integration with wireless networks and multiple modes of access are important, particularly for mobile employees and those who work in factory or warehouse settings.

(continues)

Figure 12-9. (Continued).

The voice mail system North American Chemicals has used for the past decade was a good system for its time and employees are relatively comfortable with it, even though they sometimes become frustrated with its limitations. Introducing a new system will inevitably produce resistance to change. By choosing a system that offers the shortest possible "learning curve," a system that is easy and quick to use, North American will enhance the success of the system and the value of your investment. Employees and customers alike will use the system, or resist it, depending on how easy it is to understand. If they don't use it, obviously it won't have a positive impact on productivity.

No system available today has a faster rate of acceptance among users than Vox Populi's voice messaging system. From the perspective of your customers, the Vox Populi is a refreshing change from systems that take them through endless menus of user prompts. In most cases, customers can reach the right person or department by entering five numbers or less. For your employees, the system will give them a double increase in productivity. With its simple, two-key forwarding function, the Vox Populi allows them to transfer calls and messages to a cell phone or another extension. Retrieving messages is just as simple, and the advanced functions, including message forwarding and broadcast forwarding, are all available through a menu of prompts. No cards, no booklets, no failure to use the system because employees can't remember what to do.

Enhancing Your Professional Image
The voice messaging system you select will often be your customers' first contact with North American. It's important to use a system that creates a professional impression. After all, first impressions are much easier to make than to undo.

The Vox Populi Message Network offers a number of features that will enhance the professional image of North American Chemicals and your employees:

- *Single-digit voice prompts that are simple to use.* Other systems sometimes require entering four to ten digits. Think about the last time you called your airline mileage club. Was it a positive experience that made you feel like a valued customer? Or did you feel like you were being imposed upon? What about trying to reach someone at a credit card company? Your customers have many choices. They will do business with the company that gives them the best combination of quality service and quality products.

- *Greetings and instructions that duplicate real human speech.* Many systems use synthesized messages. As a result, their messages sound robotic. The overall impression on callers is negative.

- *The opportunity to designate messages "Urgent" or "Private."* Good communications depends on the ability to communicate in the appropriate way.

- *Guest mailboxes.* This is particularly useful for subcontractors.

- *Support twenty-four hours a day, seven days a week.*

TECHNOLOGY TODAY: THE ISSUE IS QUALITY

In selecting your system, you need to evaluate the vendor as well as the system. Is this company a leader in the industry? Are they financially solid? Do they adhere to international standards? Will their system be open enough to accommodate future developments? Will the vendor continue to update the system technically, offering valuable enhancements without requiring you to replace the entire system?

The Vox Populi Message Network is a technically advanced system, designed to respond to the growing sophistication of voice mail users and to work with the growing range of wireless and voice-over-IP applications that are appearing on the market. It comes from one of the world's largest telecommunications companies with a solid financial standing and dedicated team of developers.

Unlike many in the market, we can provide you with equipment that resides in your facility, or can provide the same voice messaging functionality as a service, not requiring any investment in equipment on your part. We can even combine the two options, as appropriate, to support your manufacturing and operational facilities as well as your home-based employees around the world.

TOTAL VALUE: SYSTEM, SERVICE, AND SUPPORT

Vox Populi is unique in its ability to offer North American Chemicals a single source for all of your telecommunications needs. Whether you are looking for on-site equipment, voice messaging services, networking services, broadband applications, video and teleconferencing, computer/telephony integration, we can supply what you need. We have the products, services, and expertise to meet your needs now and in the future. And we have dedicated service and support available locally.

(continues)

Figure 12-9. (Continued).

Your Vox Populi support team will manage all aspects of installation for you and will customize the system to ensure that it meets your specific needs at each location. Vox Populi will provide unlimited local training and remote teletraining and e-learning to familiarize your employees with the system's features and operation. In addition, we schedule regular Webinars to provide helpful hints on how to use the system even more effectively.

THE VOX POPULI MESSAGE NETWORK: ADVANCED FEATURES, LOWER COSTS

Installing a voice messaging system will enhance the productivity and accessibility of your sales and support team. And it will lower your overall telecommunications costs. The reason you should choose a system from Vox Populi is that it offers you the highest possible payoff.

- Our system will give North American Chemicals an easy-to-use service that will be up and running in a minimum amount of time.

- It offers flexibility and an open design to integrate with your computer networks, wireless phone systems, even voice over the Internet.

- Your employees and customers will adapt to it quickly and use it eagerly because of its simple, intelligent design and advanced features.

- As we document later in this proposal, the number of calls that drop off the sales line will go down, meaning a higher percentage of customers get through to your sales staff. That will give you the opportunity to close more business.

- The Vox Populi system will enhance North American Chemicals' professionalism and will enable you to keep pace with your evolving needs.

Choosing Vox Populi's Message Network will maximize the success of voice messaging for North American. You will have the best available tool for communicating with your employees and customers.

When you consider the four key factors of user-friendliness, professionalism, technological quality, and overall value, you come to one inescapable conclusion: Vox Populi's Message Network is the best choice for North American Chemicals.

Figure 12-10. Sample Executive Summary 2.

The bottom line is this:
MidAmerican Metal Fabrications can improve productivity
and increase overall profitability by an additional $5/ton.

EXECUTIVE SUMMARY

The American steel industry has become fiercely competitive during the past decade. Recent economic conditions have added to the challenge of operating profitably. MidAmerican Metal Fabrications' decision to install a new continuous slab caster is a vital step forward. It will enhance MidAmerican's productivity and profitability. In fact, industry analysts have already applauded the move:

> Installation of a $115 million continuous slab caster at Silverman Group's MidAmerican Metal Fabrications plant has analysts bullish on the company's future. . . .

> According to Louis E. Hannen, an analyst with Wheat First Securities Inc. in Richmond, Va., ". . . the caster will increase annual capacity from 300,000 tons to about 500,000 tons." Silverman Group will also be able to produce a higher grade of product and won't have to sell as much lower-priced, substandard steel.

> *The Midwestern Business Courier,* II: 40, p. 2

The challenge you face is to manage the selection and installation of a continuous caster to make sure you wring every bit of profit and productivity improvement from the new equipment. And that means not overlooking a vital element in the process: scrap handling.

Problems with the Current Process
Unless decisive action is taken quickly, your current scrap-handling system will quickly prove to be a limiting factor, one that reduces the actual payoff from your installation of a continuous caster.

There are four problems inherent in the current scrap-handling system:

1. The current system limits the number of grades of scrap that can be used in a given blend and does not provide an effective means for controlling the blend.

(continues)

Figure 12-10. (Continued).

- This means you will miss potential opportunities to reduce blending costs.

- It also means that there will be inherent inconsistencies in the scrap mix, causing variations in melt chemistries and potential caster interruptions.

- The current system provides only limited traceability when problems do occur.

2. The current scrap-handling system is inefficient and occasionally unreliable.

    - In some instances, scrap must be handled twice for the same operation because of remote storage in Area 17.

    - The current system cannot handle barge shipments, which require double handling.

    - The current system's unreliability has resulted in melt shop downtime.

3. The current scrap yard is logistically constrained.

    - The yard has limited flexibility, which puts MidAmerican Metal Fabrications at the mercy of scrap market fluctuations.

    - The yard has limited potential for future expansion.

4. The current yard offers limited capacity, which may result in dangerously low inventory levels once the continuous caster is running.

    - Limited capacity threatens the full productivity of the new caster system.

    - MidAmerican Metal Fabrications' responsiveness to customer demands will be hampered unless you can maintain adequate inventory.

Overcoming Scrap-Handling Problems

SCJ and Company proposes a solution to these scrap-handling problems. Our solution will maximize the productivity and profitability of your new continuous caster. In addition, our approach to scrap handling will enhance product and process quality. It will eliminate problems with scrap flow, inventory control, and material handling. It will provide greater traceability and product quality than you can achieve with your current system.

In our proposal we demonstrate the return on investment you can achieve by changing your method of scrap handling. The bottom line is this: A change in scrap handling now will dramatically improve productivity and increase overall profitability of the MidAmerican operation by an additional $5/ton. This system will pay for itself and still deliver additional profits.

SCJ and Company is so confident of our ability to provide a technically sound, profitable solution for MidAmerican that we are offering you a guarantee. This guarantee is outlined in Section III.

The attached proposal also provides the technical specifications of the system, showing how scrap would flow through the process and how blending would be enhanced.

SCJ and Company proposes to provide a range of services for MidAmerican Metal Fabrications:

- Scrap procurement

- Stockpiling

- Blending

- Bucket loading

- Delivery to the melt shop

These services will enable your melt shop to run at peak productivity and will open up additional work area, because you will be able to remove the cranes currently used in the melt shop area to handle scrap. In addition, the system we will provide will include a data link between the scrap yard and the melt shop providing for immediate communications, an online status report on the buckets ready for the caster, and permanent record storage for precise traceability.

The expansion of your capabilities through continuous casting is a necessary next step in the growth of MidAmerican Metal Fabrications' business. It's a vital move to maintain cost competitiveness. But unless

(continues)

Figure 12-10. (Continued).

that step includes new processes for scrap handling as proposed by SCJ and Company, continuous casting cannot deliver its full payoff to the bottom line: increased productivity, enhanced quality, and greater profitability.

We recommend adoption of this proposal now so that the new scrap-handling process can be ready when your continuous caster goes on line.

product or service, plus lots of features, usually presented as bullet points. That's not very effective. A solution links specific features of the product or service back to the customer's needs and outcomes, constantly answering the question, "So what?" In a solution, each feature has relevance. It either solves part of the customer's problem or delivers value, or both.

In most proposals, you need to explain your solution in enough detail that the customer sees it as a plausible approach to solving his or her problem. You also need to include enough evidence to substantiate the notion that your recommendations will work and that they will produce the results the customer is looking for. Here are some guidelines to help you do that well:

1. Stay focused on the controlling strategy you established in the executive summary. Remember that your value proposition is established incrementally. Repetition is the key to making certain the client sees it, understands it, and remembers it.

2. Be objective. Don't allow your enthusiasm to carry you away into using wild superlatives or making unsupported claims.

3. Use specific, concrete language. Use details. Avoid vague words and phrases that sound like marketing fluff, such as

    - Uniquely qualified

    - World-class

    - Leading edge

    - State-of-the-art

    - Best-of-breed

Simply saying that a system is "efficient" or "ideal for these purposes" is not enough. Go into detail: "This system achieves 99.96 percent up time, the best in the industry, as documented by the independent journal *Manufacturing Monthly*." Statistics, third-party validation, test re-

(text continues on page 157)

Figure 12-11. Sample Executive Summary 3.

EXECUTIVE SUMMARY

HOW HENDERSON FINANCIAL CAN SAVE MONEY ON SOFTWARE AND HARDWARE BY WORKING WITH ABECEDARIAN TECHNOLOGY LICENSING

Henderson Financial operates over forty offices nationwide where your clients come for financial planning and investment opportunities. All of these offices use a variety of hardware and software tools to maximize employee productivity. The problem you have recognized is that purchasing has been decentralized, resulting in Henderson paying higher prices than necessary and sometimes struggling to maintain consistency in the products being used by your employees.

Your goals are to obtain (a) the lowest prices on software and add-on hardware for your offices, (b) faster delivery, (c) accurate invoicing, (d) cost reductions through volume purchasing, and (e) a wide range of value-added services, including user training.

The answer: turn to Abecedarian Technology Licensing.

THE CHALLENGES YOU FACE

Like most organizations, Henderson Financial is experiencing growing pressure to cut costs. However, you must provide your employees with the technology they need to work efficiently. Abecedarian has the experience to help you balance the business issues identified below with Henderson's need to cut costs.

CONTROLLING COSTS

Hardware and software purchases were the fourth largest expense associated with running your offices last year. If you can bring those costs down, your net profitability will go up.

MANAGING SOFTWARE LICENSES

Companies face severe penalties if they are found to be using software for which they do not own appropriate licenses. In addition, companies find that employees sometimes purchase and install software on their office computers that is not approved for use by the corporation. Henderson needs a way to document licenses and control what software is installed in your offices.

(continues)

Figure 12-11. (Continued).

SAVING MONEY ON TECHNICAL EDUCATION

Henderson Financial spends a large amount of money on technical training every year for new employees and to keep up your current employees' skills. Reducing the amount spent on training without compromising the quality of preparation your people receive will reduce your overall operating costs.

IMPLEMENTING AN EFFECTIVE PROGRAM FOR REFRESHING TECHNOLOGY

Software and hardware are constantly evolving, but not every new product is worth investing in. Which innovations are most likely to pay off for you? Where is the most effective place to implement new technology? Is there a way to roll out new hardware and transfer existing equipment to smaller offices to conserve costs? Henderson Financial needs a partner with the ability to design and manage a program of technology "refresh" so that you take advantage of new technology in a prudent, cost-effective way.

ACHIEVING YOUR GOALS

Addressing these challenges will have a number of positive results on Henderson Financial's operations. In fact, you will see positive impact in your business performance, technical infrastructure, and employee performance.

IMPROVED CONTROL AND PLANNING

Software expenses can mushroom out of control if you don't have processes in place to manage them and a plan to guide them. Working with Abecedarian will enable Henderson Financial to improve both control and planning.

IMPROVED BUDGETARY PERFORMANCE

Working with Abecedarian will enable Henderson to reduce the net amount you spend for technical resources. This will have a dramatic impact on your overall budgetary performance.

THE ABECEDARIAN SOLUTION

We are committed to helping you save money by reducing your software and hardware costs. As you know, by buying in small quantities, you typically pay the highest prices. But even if you were to consolidate all of your purchasing for the entire company, you would not be able to save as much as you will save by working with us. When dealing with the major suppliers of software and hardware, it's very difficult for a company the size of Henderson to obtain aggressive pricing. But Abecedarian can do it for you.

The answer is to use a volume leasing contract, which will assure you of the lowest possible prices. By aggregating all software and hardware requirements for all of our clients, Abecedarian is able to obtain concessions on price that you would never receive on your own.

In addition, outright purchases require significant capital outlay. By structuring your acquisition as a lease, you can cut your costs to just pennies per user.

One factor to keep in mind is that volume licensing contracts are cumbersome to evaluate and administer. However, they are our core competency. We manage the contracts for you, which keeps the entire process simple and straightforward.

We also provide you with a range of programs and supporting tools so you get the most out of the software and hardware you use. For example, we can perform a complete system audit to determine exactly what software and hardware you currently own, whether you have licenses for everything in place in your offices, and whether the versions you have are eligible for upgrades. We can also conduct security and virus audits to protect you from unauthorized access to proprietary data or from damage caused by the uncontrolled spread of malicious virus code.

Ours is a comprehensive offering. You can be assured that every element of our solution is focused on helping you achieve the lowest total cost of buying and supporting your computing infrastructure.

sults, awards, and other forms of evidence are more convincing than generic claims.

4. Support your claims with substantive evidence. Provide enclosures, if you have them, such as copies of review articles or testimonial letters. Case studies that showcase successful applications of your products or services are very effective. References to satisfied customers also help, particularly if they come from well-known firms in the same industry as your prospective client.

Describing a Product or Mechanism. In the solution section of your proposal, you may need to describe how equipment or mechanisms work. Here's a simple outline that will keep your discussion organized and make it easy for your reader to understand:

I. Introduction: *Be sure to mention your controlling strategy or one of your win themes in the introduction*
    A. Define/identify the mechanism or equipment

1. Indicate its function or purpose, linking it to customer needs or issues
2. Describe its general physical characteristics (including a comparison or analogy to a more familiar object)
3. Divide it into its principal parts

   B. Indicate why the mechanism is important to the reader: this is another good spot to introduce or reinforce your value proposition

II.   Provide a part-by-part description

   A. Part number one

1. What the part is (definition)
2. Function or purpose of the part
3. Physical characteristics (including comparison)
4. Division into subparts

      a. Subpart number one

        (1) What the subpart is
        (2) Its function or purpose
        (3) Appearance
        (4) Detailed description

           (a) Relationship to other parts
           (b) Size
           (c) Shape
           (d) Methods of attachment
           (e) Material
           (f) Finish

      b. Same as "a" above for subpart number two

   B. Same as "A" above for part number two

III.   Closing*: Return here to the win theme*

   A. To bring the description to a close with an emphasis on function:

1. Briefly describe the mechanism in a complete cycle of operation
2. Mention variations and options of the mechanism
3. Indicate the importance of the mechanism to the customer's operating environment

   B. To bring the description to a close with a more persuasive slant:

1. Compare the mechanism to other makes and models, in terms of features and advantages—this is a chance to "ghost" the competition by pointing out important differentiators or design features without disparaging your competitor
2. Recommend the use of the mechanism in the client's environment, or reference successful uses in similar environments

Describing Processes. Your proposals may also need to describe processes and operations, particularly when the solution is primarily a service:

I.   Introduction: *Announce your value proposition or a supporting win theme here*

   A. Define or identify the process

1. Formal definition: what is the process
2. Statement of significance: why is it done, why does it happen
3. Underlying principle which governs this process

    B. Indicate the time, setting, operators, equipment, and preparations necessary
        1. Time and setting: when and where it is done or how it happens in a natural setting
        2. Personnel: who (or *what* for automated processes) performs it
        3. Equipment: what is needed
        4. Necessary conditions: the requisite circumstances
    C. Indicate the point of view from which the process will be considered
    D. List the main steps

II. The main steps
    A. Step number one
      Note: each step is itself a process. Organize it by following the format outlined in the Introduction above.
    B. Step number two, etc.
      Note: the simplest and most logical way to organize a process description is chronologically. For a cyclical process, simply choose a reasonable starting point and follow the complete cycle.

III. Closing: *Return here to your strategy or to one of your win themes*
    A. Techniques for closing the description:
        1. Simply stop after the final step—this is effective for a short description
        2. Summarize the key steps again—this is effective for a lengthy, multipage description. *However, if you use this approach, emphasize the value of following these steps or the importance of expert knowledge in executing the steps correctly.*
        3. Comment on the process's significance, particularly in the context of achieving the customer's objectives
        4. Indicate the process's place in a larger scheme of operation
        5. Mention other methods by which the process can be performed and why you are recommending this method (an opportunity to ghost the competition.)
        6. Discuss the consequences of modifying time, setting, operators, equipment, or other conditions (another ghosting opportunity)
        7. Predict or forecast improvements in productivity, cost efficiency, etc.
        8. Recommend implementing or using the process

Link the Customer's Needs and Goals to Your Solution

Customers do not automatically recognize that the solution you are proposing will give them the results they want. You must clearly, explicitly link the elements of your solution to their needs and to the outcomes they seek. This is particularly important for a highly complex or technical recommendation. Imagine the client asking after each mention of a feature, "So what? Why should I care?" If your proposal answers those questions, it's on the right path.

Many presentations of the solution are descriptive, often consisting of long lists of bullet points that enumerate so-called "features" *ad nauseam.*

Unfortunately, readers tend to skip over long lists of bullet points, because they assume that a list of ten or twenty bullet points probably contains a lot of irrelevant detail. By breaking up your description into thematic units, you can limit the number of features you bullet point to a manageable amount—somewhere between five and ten per category at the most.

When presenting your recommendations, don't mention a feature without linking it to the customer's issues and to the benefits that feature will provide. (Those benefits should be the goals or outcomes the customer seeks, of course.) Remember: a feature is a component of the solution, but a benefit is an impact on the client's operations that the client will find desirable.

To create solution presentations that are more persuasive and client focused, use the structure in Figure 12-12 as a basic guideline for organizing descriptions of products and services. Figure 12-13 provides an example of an effective solution description.

Figure 12-12. Guide for Organizing Solutions.

Introduction/positioning statement

Brief overview of the product or service to provide general understanding

Customer's issues, problems, or needs	Solution component: feature 1	Benefit of the feature	Brief mention of proof statements/ evidence that the benefits are real
Customer's issues, problems, or needs	Solution component: feature 2	Benefit of the feature	Brief mention of proof statements/ evidence that the benefits are real
Customer's issues, problems, or needs	Solution component: feature 3	Benefit of the feature	Brief mention of proof statements/ evidence that the benefits are real

Transition to more detailed content or discussion of project steps, pricing, and so forth

Figure 12-13. Sample Solution Description.

The DataMaster System from ComStar

We at ComStar recommend using the DataMaster System as a platform for developing American Cellular's EtherSwitch system. The DataMaster system is a new generation of data management tools, designed specifically for the cellular marketplace. Its design incorporates all of the elements of traditional call management and billing systems, but is based on a new, modular platform that allows for easy customization to meet unique needs.

You indicated to us that you are looking for a vendor who can address four specific needs in your business:

1. Capacity to handle current and projected volume of transactions without requiring system add-ons or expansion
2. Enhanced customer support and service
3. A customizable solution
4. A complete solution, including service bureau options

The DataMaster system, in conjunction with our services, provides you with exactly what you want. We are confident that meeting your business needs, as listed above, is your most important objective.

Capacity to handle the volume of billing transactions your business needs	ComStar is the only provider of cellular billing systems with existing capacity to handle the volume you specify in your RFP. With our combination of software designed specifically for the cellular market and our extensive service bureau capabilities, we can provide American Cellular with the right mix of products and services regardless of the volume your business demands today or in the future.
Enhanced customer support and service	Your billing systems are a fundamental part of your total customer support and service system. By outsourcing the management of billing to a third party, you must feel confident that your customers will receive the highest-quality service and that the relationship will be transparent. ComStar has received awards from industry groups for the quality of our customer support. In addition, because the DataMaster system is customizable, it can provide your

(continues)

Figure 12-13. (Continued).

	customers with exactly the kind of billing information they want. Finally, as your first line of customer support, we handle all customer inquiries in a timely fashion with a documented 97.9 percent closure rate on the first call.
A customizable solution	Everyone wants choices. Unless your business partner can offer you a wide range of options, you may feel that you are forced to take less than or something other than what you really need. ComStar offers a broader range of product and service offerings than any other provider in the wireless market. The DataMaster system was specifically designed as a modular, N-tiered application with a mathematically infinite number of potential configurations.
A complete solution	ComStar is a pioneer in creating and providing cellular billing systems, and we continue to be the industry leader. But we are also the largest provider of service bureau operations with the ability to handle the complete range of customer billing, service and support functions, including problem resolution, collections, marketing, and more. As a result, we can tailor a solution specifically to your needs.

As you can see, the use of the DataMaster platform addresses your four primary objectives. In addition, it delivers all of the technical functionality you have specified in your RFP. In some cases, we provide the functionality that you specify, but because that functionality will be delivered from an innovative platform, the system architecture may not conform exactly to the design specifications you have included in the proposal. These differences will be invisible to the user. However, we do want to be clear that in some instances we deliver the functional requirement but do it in a different part of the system or with a different logical flow of processing steps.

We believe it makes good business and technical sense for American Cellular to use DataMaster as the platform for your EtherSwitch. It will provide you with a comprehensive, flexible, high-quality product at a much lower cost than would be possible if the entire system were created as a custom product.

Writing Effective Case Studies

Case studies can be effective tools for building credibility, minimizing risk, and helping the decision maker develop a "vision" of the results you can produce.

Keep your case studies short, one or two pages at most. Focus them on the success your previous client achieved, not on the details of the project you managed or the product you delivered. (See Figure 12-14 for a sample case study.)

Figure 12-14. Sample Case Study.

What our client needed: In the highly competitive executive recruiting business, success is based on who you know and what you know about them. REX Recruiting found that they were not able to keep track of their contacts and leads in a systematic way. As a result, opportunities to place executives were sometimes lost.

What we created: After investigating costly, high-end products designed for sales forces or customer service organizations, REX Recruiting contracted with Mustang Software to create a data storage and tracking tool that was right for them. REX Recruiting defined exactly what kind of information they wanted to store, how they wanted to use it, and how they needed to access it.

Mustang took it from there. Creating simple data screens that required no knowledge of databases, we created a user-friendly system that was compatible with REX Recruiting's Microsoft-centric environment. Each executive, each job opening, and each company for which REX has previously provided an executive is available in the system. For each of these categories the company defined significant attributes and details that needed to be tracked. The user can search on any of those categories or attributes or can combine any number of them to create a custom report format simply by clicking on the screen. When one of REX's recruiters receives an inquiry from a client, he or she can generate a report that lists all available candidates with the right qualifications. Recruiters can also generate candidate profiles and status reports to keep clients informed about the status of the search and document effort.

How it worked: REX Recruiting has seen 17 percent growth since the system was implemented, which is all the more remarkable since it coincided with a general downturn in the economy. With seven new offices on the west coast, REX has grown to be the largest firm specializing exclusively in executive placements.

Try to use case studies about customers that are similar to the company or agency to which you are proposing. Match a municipality with a municipal or county government client. Use a bank with another bank or financial institution. And so on. Although using a case study about a company from the same industry is ideal, it's also helpful to at least use a client that is similar in size and that had a similar problem as your prospect.

To get the right emphasis in your case studies, structure them using the P-A-R format. P-A-R stands for Problem/Action/Results.

Problem or objective

Briefly describe the previous customer's situation, the problems they were facing, and/or the objectives they had in mind. The first part of the case study should provide your prospective customers with enough information that they can identify with the one being described.

It's most effective to name the previous customer, but you don't have to. You can use a general description: "A large, international biotechnology firm with complex requirements for warehousing and transporting volatile compounds and controlled substances."

Actions taken

What did you do to help them solve their problem? Be specific about the solution you provided, highlighting your differentiators.

Obviously, the actions you took should be very similar to the actions you are recommending. Otherwise, your case study will demonstrate that you are competent in ways that aren't fully relevant to the current situation.

Results obtained

Outline the results the customer obtained. Whenever possible, quantify the impact: 15 percent reduction in total project length, 20 percent lower operating costs in the outbound telemarketing function, 17 percent higher productivity among hourly employees.

If quantifiable results are not available, use a quote from a key executive within the customer organization.

Creating Persuasive Resumes

Research conducted among evaluators for the U.S. Department of Defense and the National Aeronautics and Space Agency found that they thought the following content was most important in a resume (listed in order of priority):

■ Recent, relevant experience

■ Education, particularly in specific skills or technologies applicable to this project

■ Professional licensing or accreditations

■ Professional affiliations

■ Publications

■ Patents

Experience is more important to most people than any other factor. When you write a resume for use in a proposal, emphasize the skills of the team members and how they apply to the project.

Keep the resumes short. Two or three paragraphs will usually be enough. But edit them or rewrite them so that they really match up to the opportunity being proposed. Using the same resume every time you include someone in a project is a bad idea.

Writing Persuasive Answers to RFP Questions

Customers and consultants issue formal RFPs to obtain a consistent body of information by which they can compare offers.

RFPs almost never identify the business issues that underlie the proposal as a whole, nor do they indicate why a particular question is being asked. But those factors matter. You'll improve your chances if you address the business issues that underlie the RFP as a whole and the critical questions in particular.

Product and service descriptions written in-house or by vendors are almost always factual, not persuasive. Often they are not customer centered in that they don't discuss functional value. Critique them carefully before using them. Eliminate jargon, or find ways to define it before it's used. Remember that your company's product and process names are jargon outside the company. Also, be wary of using undefined acronyms.

Writing an effective answer in your RFP response is more than a matter of "answering the mail." Use the following format to respond to questions or requirements that seem to be particularly significant. Obviously, it's not an appropriate format for answers that are extremely short or that require a simple, factual answer. If the customer asks, "When was your company founded?" you can feel confident in just writing "1976." For the few questions that are particularly significant, however, use this approach:

■ **Acknowledge:** Restate the customer's question or requirement in general terms, empathizing with the concern that probably lies behind this question. In the case of a requirement, position your response in terms of a broader principle, such as efficiency, customer satisfaction, and so on.

■ **Persuade:** Incorporate a *value* or *benefit statement* into the description as quickly as possible—something that the decision maker cares about. Do this even in RFP sections where the original question only asked, "How do you do something?"

■ **Substantiate:** Provide the factual answer next: describe the product or service, outline the steps of the process, provide the details necessary. Do not include every feature—focus on including only those features that matter to the given customer.

Here are two samples, showing different approaches to answering the same question. The sample in Figure 12-15 shows how a provider of medical insurance answered a question that was asked in nearly every RFP they received. The first answer was their original version; the second incorpo-

Figure 12-15. RFP Responses Sample Answer 1.

Question:
What information appears on the Explanation of Benefits? Can EOB information be customized by the client? Please provide a sample EOB.

Original Answer:
See the enclosed EOB.

Generally all EOB messages are predefined for all clients to meet readability, accuracy, and legal requirements. Limited customization is available, including the addition of logos and personalized remarks in the remarks area.

Revised Answer:
It's important for plan members to understand how their benefits were determined. The Explanation of Benefits is a vital tool in our overall effort to provide good communications and to avoid confusion or misunderstanding when plan members file a claim.

At American Health we have spent considerable effort to design and write our EOB forms for maximum readability and accuracy. In addition, our forms' layout and content has been developed to address certain legal requirements. Within that framework, we can provide some customization to the EOB form, such as adding your logo or providing personalized information in the remarks area of the form.

The enclosed EOB is a sample of what we will provide to your members.

rates the three-part structure. Which of the two sounds more persuasive to you?

The first answer sounds perfunctory, doesn't it? And do you detect a tone of negativity? The provider doesn't seem interested in customizing the EOB if it doesn't have to. The second answer says the same thing exactly, yet it manages to sound positive and cooperative. It's basically a matter of the structure of the answer.

The sample in Figure 12-16 comes from a proposal written by an I.T. services provider. You couldn't even call the original answer factual.

The Compliance Matrix: Simplifying the Evaluator's Job

What's a compliance matrix? It's a chart that makes it easy for the evaluator to determine which proposals are worth looking at and which can be discarded. Remember that the evaluator's first job is to reduce the number of proposals down to a manageable few. An easy way for a gatekeeper to do that is to glance through your proposal to see if it complies with the basic requirements. A compliance matrix shows the evaluator that your response is worth keeping and looking at in detail. The absence of one may suggest that it's not.

As in Figure 12-17, a compliance matrix should show the evaluator how well you meet the requirements of the RFP and should make it easy to locate more detailed information. In this case, the page numbers are hot links that jump directly to the relevant answers.

Creating Graphics for Your Proposal

There are lots of reasons to incorporate graphics in your proposal. Graphics—diagrams, flow charts, photos, organizational charts, bar charts, line

Figure 12-16. RFP Responses Sample Answer 2.

Question:
We need an integrator that can be responsive and available 24x7. Please provide the pricing and options for this type of coverage in Appendix G.

Original Answer:
Please see pricing in Appendix G.

Revised Answer:
With a business critical system, such as the one being proposed here, you need to know that you have support available around the clock. That's why SysTemPro has created a support program that gives you 24x7 coverage at an extremely affordable price.

In Appendix G, we detail the levels of support available to you within the framework of 24x7 and the pricing for each.

Figure 12-17. Compliance Matrix.

HOW OUR PROPOSAL COMPLIES WITH YOUR REQUIREMENTS

The compliance matrix below illustrates graphically the extent to which our solutions match up with Urban Bank's key requirements. Detailed answers and explanations for each question or requirement can be found in the following pages, as indicated by the page numbers.

Compliance Key:

EX = Exceeds the requirement
F = Fully complies
P = Partially complies
N = Noncompliant

QUESTION	EXTENT OF COMPLIANCE				PAGE	COMMENTS
	EX	F	P	N		
Urban Bank Corporation needs to streamline the proposal generation process.		√			21	Our recommendations will eliminate eleven steps from the current proposal process at Urban Bank.
Internet accessible and mobile proposal and presentation generation capability integrated with a product and price configuration system.		√			22	We offer a Web-based (not merely Web-enabled) system that includes presentation capabilities. We provide built-in integration with the pricing tools Urban is considering.
Produce consistently high-quality customized proposals, request for proposal responses, and customer presentations.		√			24	Our system produces the full range of documents in an easy-to-use format.
Automated interface to configuration systems.		√			25	Our system accepts output from configuration systems if formatted as an Excel or Word file.

QUESTION	EXTENT OF COMPLIANCE				PAGE	COMMENTS
	EX	F	P	N		
Knowledge transfer.		√			26	
Guidance leading to a prospect/customer needs analysis and solution.		√			27	Our system coaches the user to define the opportunity, including needs and solution.
Supplemental product support.		√			29	We provide exceptional technical and customer support.
Catalog product and service proposal language, promotional text, graphics, and promote the Urban Bank brand ID.		√			31	Our system serves as a library for all types of content and automatically formats documents to match Urban's identity requirements.

drawings, or creative visualizations of key concepts can be tremendous aids to communicating effectively. Many people understand complex ideas better if they are presented visually. For readers who tend to skim text, graphics often focus their attention and help stimulate their interest. Evaluators typically like graphics that help them see the points you are making quickly.

Here are some ideas for using graphics to enhance your document:

- **Think about graphics while you're outlining** or organizing your document, before you have written any text. Graphics that are thrown in as an afterthought typically look like afterthoughts.

- **Avoid using clip art.** Clip art is the frozen burrito of graphic design: a choice of last resort and one you usually end up regretting. It usually doesn't enhance your document.

- **Incorporate your customer's logo into your design.** For example, use the customer's logo on the title page or in the header or footer of your proposal. Ask the client's permission first, and then ask them to provide you with a clean, digital image of the logo. Copying the logo from the Web site or scanning it from the letterhead can produce a jagged, poor-quality version.

- **If the customer has a "company color," incorporate it into your design.** For example, use a line at the top of the page in their color to separate the header from body text, or print your major headings in their color.

■ **Avoid highly technical graphics, complex diagrams, and charts.** Simple graphics are better. They will attract more attention and will be easier to understand.

■ **Graphics should be oriented horizontally** on the page, just like the text. The reader should never have to turn your document sideways to look at your graphic.

■ **Write an active caption** that not only explains what the graphic is showing but also emphasizes a customer benefit. For example, rather than calling a product illustration "Figure 3: The Turboencabulator Model 2000," you could caption it "Figure 3: The Low-Maintenance Design of the Turboencabulator Model 2000."

■ **In long proposals, it's a good idea to number the graphics sequentially.** In formal proposals, you should also list them in a Table of Illustrations, right after the Table of Contents.

■ **Discuss an idea in the text and then illustrate it graphically.** That is usually more effective than showing the graphic first and then discussing it.

■ **Never put all the graphics at the end of the document.** If people have to flip back and forth between the text and the graphics, they won't get the full value of either.

To gain the maximum benefit from your graphics, use the kind of graphic that best suits a certain kind of message. Here are some ideas:

The Point You Are Making	*A Type of Graphic You Could Use*
We fully comply with all of your requirements	• *Compliance matrix*
Our system or approach offers better performance	• *Comparison table* • *Bar chart* • *Stacked bar chart* • *Pie chart* • *Trend curve*
Our system will meet your performance expectations	• *Schematics* • *Flow chart* • *Table* • *Matrix*

We will assign the right people to this project	• *Table of tasks with associated personnel assigned to the tasks* • *Table of personnel with associated experience, past projects, publications, etc.*
We can meet the deadline	• *Critical path chart* • *Gantt chart* • *Schedule*
We have the right experience to do this job	• *Tables of past projects, objectives, outcomes, dates, clients* • *Maps showing locations of similar projects*
We have a history of successful projects	• *Testimonial letters scanned into the text (make sure they stay readable!)*
We are committed to quality	• *Diagram of project activities, showing regular reviews and QC*
We offer unique features, strengths, and/or benefits	• *Bullet points* • *Side bars (boxed text, possibly with shading)*

Presenting Your Price and Value

You need to talk convincingly about price. If your pricing seems too low, your proposal may be rejected for lack of "cost realism." If it seems too high, the consequences are obvious. To address price convincingly, link your fees to the deliverables clearly and plausibly. Some RFPs include explicit instructions about presenting cost information. Some require cost details in a separate volume. Some give you no direction at all. If your proposal is unsolicited, of course, you can probably handle pricing issues as you wish. Regardless of how you handle them, you should always strive to put cost in the larger context of your solution's return on investment.

Use the following techniques to handle cost and price issues effectively:

1. Introduce price only after presenting the solution and its potential for positive impact in detail.

2. Don't talk about price in the first or last paragraphs of the cover letter.

3. Whenever possible, introduce pricing in a sentence that also talks about benefits and results. For example: "The cost for a system that can handle all of your payroll, budgeting, forecasting, and analysis needs is surprisingly low, probably less than $3,000 per month for a company the size of yours."

4. As in the preceding example, try to state the price in a complex or compound sentence, putting the actual price in a dependent clause.

5. Also as shown in (3), state the price in the smallest logical unit—$3,000 per month instead of $36,000 per year.

6. If you have the facts, quantify the impact of your solution. Tell the customer how much time or money they will save, exactly how much lower the total cost of ownership will be for your system compared to the competition, or how cost-effective it will be in comparison to the system currently in use.

7. Avoid providing detailed pricing on an item-by-item basis. Line item pricing encourages the detail-oriented to nitpick and makes it easier for unscrupulous customers to shop your proposal to your competitors.

Appendix

The appendix contains supplementary information and attachments, material that may help your client understand your solution better, understand your differentiators, or see that you are competent to deliver. It's not a garbage can into which you should throw anything and everything that might conceivably be of interest. Instead, think of it as the section of the proposal to which the true specialist will turn to get highly specific, detailed information.

Appropriate content for the appendix might include technical specifications, additional case histories, or research studies. You can also include product brochures, annual reports, and capabilities statements for your company and/or any partners. Often the appendix is the appropriate place to put a detailed statement of work and your company's terms and conditions.

Some Final Thoughts

Here are some additional tips that will help you organize your formal proposal effectively:

1. **When responding to an RFP, respond completely.** Answer every question, no matter how irrelevant, annoying, or stupid it may seem. Even if a question has already been asked in a previous part of the RFP, answer it completely all over again. Do not make perfunctory comments, such as "See above" or "See attached brochure" or "Comply." Failing to answer or giving perfunctory answers may be seen as nonresponsive.

2. **Figure out ways to make your business case.** Some RFPs limit the content or length of your proposal. For example, an RFP may state that you must answer the questions only on the form provided, that you may not include any "marketing" or "sales" material. Sometimes the RFP is issued in the form of a spreadsheet into which you must insert your answers. You can still make your case, though. Here are some suggestions:

   - Turn the cover letter into an executive summary.

   - Write each answer as completely and persuasively as possible.

   - Use language that suggests the reliability, efficiency, and scope of your solution.

3. **Avoid using boilerplate sections that have been written for other proposals or for generic applications.** They may not work, and they may not emphasize the right points. Rewrite them as necessary so they sound like they belong.

4. **Write technical sections with an eye to organizational impact.** Do not include technical data for its own sake, and do not include any internal technical documentation without thoroughly rewriting it. Technology for its own sake does not persuade.

5. **Avoid banal headings and titles.** Rather than "Technical Section," write "Five High-Productivity Features of Amalgamated's Controllers." Try to use strong verbs in your titles and headings, especially verbs that imply a benefit to the client.

13 *Writing Research Proposals and Proposals for Grants*

Proposals are not exclusively written in business-to-business or business-to-government settings, of course. Researchers, nonprofit organizations, charities, and others with a social service, educational, or artistic mission must seek financial support from sponsors by writing proposals. Writing an effective proposal to win research funds or grant money can be just as challenging as writing a sales proposal for millions of dollars' worth of equipment and services. And the challenge can be met only by writing the proposal as persuasively as possible.

Most of what we have already said about persuasive structure and audience analysis applies to research proposals and grant requests. The primary difference is that instead of focusing on solving business problems that are having a negative impact on profitability, productivity, quality, or some other metric of business performance, you need to position your proposal to show that it will help the target agency or foundation achieve its mission. For your funding source, the primary "problem" is distributing scarce resources in the most effective way to promote the purpose for which the agency or foundation was created. Your proposal must make it clear that your proposed project is fully compatible with the proposed sponsor's interests, policies, and values.

As you look for sponsorship, go through the same steps that a salesperson goes through when qualifying a lead. Ask yourself:

- What is this organization's purpose? Why was it created? What broad objectives does this foundation or agency seek to achieve through its funding activities?

- What size of grants does it award?

- Where does its money come from? What type of support does it provide (for example, capital funds, endowment funds, matching funds, research grants, educational project support)?

- What are some of its past and current funding activities? What are its program interests for the future?

- Who makes the decisions regarding allocation of funds?

- What criteria are used?

- Does the organization or agency impose any geographic limitations on its grant activity?

Accurate answers to these and similar questions should save you from wasting time and effort in pursuing funds for which your initiative is not qualified.

Usually funding is awarded because of the specific research plan and special competence of the individual researcher or the small group of researchers who will execute the work outlined in the proposal. However, the actual award is usually made to a university, hospital, or other institution within which the research will be conducted, rather than to the individuals. If you work within such an institution, you will probably have to submit any formal proposals seeking external support to the appropriate sponsored programs office for review before you can submit them to the potential sponsoring agency. Check with the administration of your institution for specific guidelines. Keep in mind that such a review can be time consuming. You should allow for it as you schedule your activities to ensure that you get your proposal submitted before the funding agency's deadline.

There are three main types of external funding:

▪ **Grants and contracts.** Grants and contracts arise directly from proposals and/or applications prepared by individual researchers. Grants are awarded by government agencies, corporations, or private foundations as a result of an unsolicited proposal sent by an investigator who is interested in a basic research project. Contracts are normally awarded as a result of a proposal submitted in response to a bid solicitation or an RFP issued by a federal or state government agency or, in some instances, by a private company. Contracts often have stricter reporting requirements than grants. If you seek a contract, you may find yourself in competition with private enterprise. You may also find that contracts are very explicit about the ownership of intellectual property, patents, and work products arising from the contract.

Some government agencies award "cooperative agreements," which are similar to grants except that substantial agency involvement is anticipated during the performance of the project.

▪ **Fellowships (faculty, predoctoral, postdoctoral).** These awards are normally given directly to the individual researcher, bypassing the institutional hierarchy. The fellowship usually pays a specific dollar amount in the form of a stipend. Many private foundations and government agencies offer this type of support, particularly to new or inexperienced investigators.

▪ **Unrestricted gifts.** Awards of this type, unlike sponsored programs, usually have no reporting requirements of any kind.

Preparing Your Research Proposal

When you seek external funding, you need to write a clear, convincing, persuasive proposal because you are almost certainly competing for limited funds. Here are some basic steps to help you produce a winner.

Initial Contact

Usually an agency or foundation publishes guidelines, an annual report, or some other kind of document outlining the procedures you should follow in submitting an application for funding. However, you may find it helpful to contact the agency directly to obtain current application forms, to clarify a policy, or to present a project in outline form to see if it's suitable. Some agencies or sponsors prefer this kind of preliminary contact to help reduce the volume of inappropriate proposals they receive. For projects that arouse their interest, agencies may provide suggestions to strengthen the proposal and make it more competitive. Be careful not to make commitments during this stage, particularly budgetary or scheduling commitments.

Pre-Proposals

As the term implies, pre-proposals are informal, preliminary documents, intended to "test the waters" in an agency or foundation without requiring the extensive time and effort a formal proposal will take. Another advantage of the pre-proposal is that you can submit one to several different sources of support simultaneously.

The pre-proposal usually contains the following five sections, depending on the project:

1. **Cover letter.** This should contain:
    a. An introductory paragraph containing the title of the project
    b. A persuasive statement of objectives and intended outcomes, explicitly linked to the agency or foundation's mission
    c. An offer to develop a formal proposal
    d. A description of the unique qualifications of the research team, institution, or facilities, or a summary of relevant prior projects that will contribute to a successful outcome
    e. A final paragraph indicating your willingness to negotiate or discuss further the project's objectives or budget

2. **Statement of proposed research.** Include a brief, clearly written description that provides a general understanding of your project. Remember that some of the people who read this description may lack expertise in your field. Keep it simple, focus on basics, and emphasize the probable benefits, potential breakthroughs, or positive outcomes of the project.

3. **Resumes.** Provide a brief curriculum vitae or summarize your relevant biographical data, emphasizing any special experience that qualifies you for the proposed study. Remember that recent, specifically relevant, and successful work is more convincing than general academic achievements.

4. **Facilities**. Briefly describe any special equipment, laboratories, or other capabilities available at your institution that justify conducting the project there. Also indicate the major equipment needed, if any, carefully explaining any unusual needs.

5. **Budget**. Provide a rough estimate of the project's budget. At this stage an itemized budget is not necessary. All the agency or foundation needs to know is what range the project falls into: $5,000 or $50,000 or $500,000.

In summary, your preliminary proposal should be brief (four to ten pages) and easy to understand. It should leave room for negotiation and contain defined next steps for follow-up telephone calls or visits.

Formal Proposals

Most federal and state agencies provide very specific guidelines and application forms that you must follow in submitting your final proposal. Use them and be careful to follow directions exactly.

However, some agencies, and private foundations in particular, may not provide an application form or guidelines regarding format. Although your formal proposal is obviously a much more structured document than a pre-proposal, there really isn't just one "right" way to do it. In fact, it's important to be flexible. Allow the nature and scope of your proposed sponsored project and the values and interests of the decision maker to determine the proper order of the sections and the appropriate length of your discussions.

Here's a general outline you can use in preparing a formal proposal if the agency doesn't provide any specific guidelines:

1. Letter of transmittal

2. Cover or title page

3. Table of contents

4. Abstract

5. Overview/statement of problem

6. Body of proposal
   a. The need for this project
   b. Objectives and positive outcomes (benefits) of the project and their significance
   c. The proposed project designs and/or procedures

7. Facilities/location of the project

8. Project personnel

9. References/bibliography/literature review

10. Budget/budget justification

11. Certifications and representations

12. Appendices

Letter of Transmittal. The letter of transmittal officially introduces your formal proposal to the sponsoring organization. Although you might write it, it is typically signed by a high-ranking official of your institution, giving the proposal the stamp of authority.

Cover or Title Page. Federal and state agencies usually provide their own form for this page. If you haven't worked through one before, they can seem hopelessly confusing and cluttered. Have patience, and take your time. After all, they're probably no worse than filling out your taxes—which may or may not be an encouraging thought!

Most private foundations and industrial sponsors do not provide a title page. In such cases, create your own title page, containing the following data:

1. Title of the proposal. Choose the proposal's title carefully. The same principles apply to a research proposal as apply to any other kind of proposal. Try to stress a benefit or tie your proposal to the funding agency's mission or goals. Vague, flat, or highly technical titles are seldom persuasive.

2. Request for Proposal or Solicitation number, if any.

3. Name of the institution to which the award will be made.

4. Name of the funding agency to which the proposal is submitted (for example, the National Science Foundation, the National Institute of Health, the Ford Foundation).

5. Endorsement. The sponsoring agency may require various endorsements on the cover page. The two most commonly requested are the principal investigator(s) and the authorizing official. For both, include the person's name, title, departmental or official affiliation, and phone number.

6. Other items. Additional information on the cover page might include the start date of the project, the amount of funding requested, or the program from which the funds will come.

Table of Contents. The table of contents usually follows the title page, although sometimes it is preceded by the abstract. The table of contents should serve as a convenient navigation tool through the proposal, and should also provide a general outline of the project. Don't break the contents down beyond one or two levels of subheadings, but make your headings and subheadings substantive so that the reader can get a sense of your project and its value from them. Do include page numbers in the table of contents. Number the pages consecutively throughout your proposal, rather than starting over with each section.

Abstract. The abstract is roughly the equivalent of the executive summary in a sales proposal. It is one of the most important parts, because like the executive summary written to win commercial business, its job is to persuasively explain the nature of what is being offered, why it matters to the audience, and how their constituency will benefit. Write the abstract in general terms geared to individuals who may lack expertise in your field.

Keep it brief—about 250 to 1,000 words will usually be sufficient—and use plain English. A good abstract states in simple sentences what the problem or opportunity is, how the challenge posed by that problem or opportunity will be met, and what benefits or positive outcomes will result from the research. Although you don't have to summarize every part of your proposal in the abstract, you should include a basic summary of budgetary requirements. This is a key difference between a research proposal or proposal for grant money and a sales proposal's executive summary.

Overview/Statement of Problem. The overview orients the decision maker to the background of the study, discusses the reasons for the study, and presents the conditions leading to the need for the project. It includes an explanation of the specific problem and how it relates to the need. Pertinent references to related research should be included to demonstrate that the researcher has knowledge of all relevant previous work in the field. Make clear how the new research you perform will build on that previous work.

If your request is for funding of a social service or arts initiative, the overview serves the same basic purpose: define the problem or gap being addressed, why that problem is serious enough to merit attention, and how the community will benefit once your project has been executed.

Body of the Proposal. The body of your proposal contains the detailed information regarding your proposed research or activities. Evaluators who look at this part of your proposal are more likely to be specialists, so you can write in a more technical style. However, clarity is always a positive quality, and technical information for its own sake is never persuasive. For each point you cover, ask yourself the same question your evaluators will ask: So what? If your proposal doesn't answer this question, rewrite it. Linking the details of your research or project to the desired outcomes or the general objectives supported by your funding agency is still important.

Evaluators will be interested in finding answers to questions such as the following:

■ What are you requesting?

■ Why is this project needed?

■ What is the significance of the project?

■ What are the major objectives, and how do they relate to the problem?

■ Can these objectives be evaluated? Can they be measured?

■ What are the procedures you will use in the project?

■ How will you do the work?

■ How will you manage the work?

■ What data will be gathered?

■ What is your research design?

■ What are the technical details?

■ How large is the scope of the project?

■ What is the time schedule for various phases?

■ Is this project a continuation of earlier work?

■ Will future projects grow out of this work?

■ What specifically will be accomplished by this project?

■ What are the expected end results?

■ How will you evaluate and disseminate the results?

■ Will there be any form of peer review process for the results?

■ What plans for publishing or patenting the results do you have?

Facilities/Location of the Project/Special Equipment. In this section, discuss any unique aspects of the available facilities. Is special equipment available? Will you be using a nationally recognized laboratory? Does the location have unique computing capabilities? Is there an advantage to your geographic location? Will you subcontract any part of the study to take advantage of someone else's unique facilities, equipment, or location?

Project Personnel. This section should contain the information needed for evaluators to assess the qualifications and competence of the personnel proposed for the project. A brief description of key personnel and their proposed roles in the project should precede their resumes or curriculum vitae.

Resumes and curriculum vitae for research projects, particularly those involving faculty and research staff at a college or university, will typically be more detailed than the personnel data provided in sales proposals.

References/Bibliography. For a research proposal, you should include a numbered listing of the relevant literature in your research area. This shows that you have done the necessary preliminary work to avoid duplicating work that has already been completed and to keep your project focused on the main lines of inquiry.

Budget/Budget Justification. List the anticipated costs of the project in this section. The RFP or application form will usually call for a statement of the total cost of the project, with a breakdown of costs per year and by category of expense. The following checklist covers most of the items that typically occur in a research budget. However, it may not include every cost a particular research project might incur, so use it as a starting point.

A. Direct costs
   1. Salaries and wages
      a. Professional personnel (faculty, for example)
      b. Senior assistants (exempt staff or postdoctoral students, for example)
      c. Administrative personnel (nonfaculty exempt employees)
      d. Technicians (exempt or nonexempt)
      e. Graduate research assistants
      f. Students
      g. Support personnel, office management staff, secretarial support (nonexempt staff)
      h. Hourly help (nonexempt staff or students)
      i. Salary increases (for proposals lasting more than one year)
   2. Fringe benefits on all salaries and wages, including hourly help
   3. Equipment
      a. Equipment purchase costs (list items individually)
      b. Equipment installation, if included on bid
      c. Freight, if included on bid
   4. Travel
      a. Domestic
      b. Foreign
      c. Subsistence costs or per diems
   5. Computer services, computer equipment, and software
      a. Central computer system costs
      b. Department usage fees
      c. Personal computers, printers, networking equipment, and related hardware
      d. Software
      e. Maintenance costs
   6. Materials and supplies
      a. Laboratory supplies
      b. Books, reprints, journals
      c. Chemicals and glassware
      d. Expendable items of equipment (less than two years' useful life)
      e. Office supplies
      f. Photo duplication, illustrations, film

      g. Printing services not considered part of standard publication costs

  7. Publication costs for page charges in professional journals

  8. Consultant costs

      a. Professional fees

      b. Travel, food, and lodging expenses

  9. Subcontracts

      a. Third-party costs for portions of the research done outside the institution

      b. Overhead costs associated with managing subcontracting relationships

 10. Other costs

      a. Alterations, construction, renovation costs

      b. Communications, particularly telecommunication expenses, delivery fees, and postage

      c. Conference and meeting expenses

      d. Equipment leasing or rental costs

      e. Insurance premiums

      f. Off-site rental of space

      g. Participant support costs

      h. Patient care costs (if appropriate)

      i. Purchase and care of lab animals (if appropriate)

      j. Recruitment costs

      k. Royalty and patent costs

      l. Specialized service facilities

B. Indirect costs (these are determined by the type of project and whether it will be conducted on or off site)

C. Cost sharing (if required)

Certifications. Sometimes you need to document that you comply with various policies and regulations. For example, a proposal for funding for medical research will require evidence that you have obtained informed consent from the patient participants. If your research involves laboratory animals, you may be required to provide evidence of humane treatment. If you are using radioactive materials, you must certify that proper safeguards and handling procedures are being observed.

    Other information you may need to provide includes:

- Your institution's congressional district

- IRS employer ID number

- Tax-exempt status letter

- Institutional financial statement

- Representations and certifications regarding civil rights, affirmative action, drug-free workplace, contingent fees, and so forth

Appendices. Any supplementary materials, such as papers, reprints, charts, letters of support, course descriptions, or special brochures, should be included here. Remember, however, that reviewers do not usually read appendices. They may skim through them in reference to particular sections of the proposals. Never put anything in the appendices that must be read thoroughly. And don't throw material in just to beef up your proposal.

Figure 13-1. Sample Research Proposal

Part I

This section introduces the proposal, describes the project, lays out the work plan and time schedule, and identifies the project principals and their qualifications.

Introduction

The proposed project is the development of a second-generation portable glass pulverizing plant that recycles glass by completely separating on site the glass particles from all wrappers, metal attachments, and nonglass components. The plant and all related apparatus are mounted on a flatbed trailer and towed by truck wherever glass recycling is required. The processed glass may then be used in fabrication of new products.

The project is based on a patented invention that pulverizes materials such as glass bottles, plate glass, and laminated glass, producing a desired particle of clean glass. The recycled product's relative freedom from contamination is important to manufacturers. Current methods and equipment do not remove enough of the metal caps, neckbands, wrappers, and the like to produce a clean product.

The plant's portability offers several significant benefits:

1. Portability means that the plant can be taken wherever glass is most conveniently recycled, reducing transportation costs by eliminating the cost of moving the glass to be recycled.

2. Portability also means that each site can arrange for recycling as needed, rather than maintaining a permanent and separate facility.

3. Even the smallest local communities can get rid of waste glass safely and efficiently.

The portable facility processes all three types of glass—clear, brown, and green—for market.

DAG, Inc. believes that the process technology may be transferable to other kinds of recycling, such as ceramics, in addition to glass.

(continues)

Figure 13-1. (Continued).

Project Description

The greatest challenge in producing small glass particles for use as raw material is achieving a clean product. Conventional hammermills are unsuitable for this purpose because they crush the metal parts as well as the glass. The hammermills also overheat and require frequent maintenance.

The portable plant based on this invention separates attachments to the source glass—aluminum caps, neckbands, Styrofoam, etc. Bulk glass is loaded into the feed hopper, transported by a feeder belt to a mill, pulverized, screened of nonglass contaminants, and discharged directly into a truck, trailer, or roll-off container for market.

The invention on which this project is based provides [*proprietary description, deleted from this sample but included in the actual proposal*].

Mill Components and Functions. Following are the main components of the pulverizing mill:

[*Components are itemized in bullet points.*]

Plant Operation. The pulverizing mill mounts on a flatbed trailer. The hopper (Figure 1) controls the flow of raw material to a conveyor belt, which transports the material to the pulverizing apparatus of a motor-driven mill. The mill deposits the crushed glass on a second conveyor for delivery to the separation unit. Waste is ejected to a bin or caught on the screen for disposal. This unit extracts the pulverized glass and deposits it onto a third conveyor, which transports it to a removable receptacle of the user's choice.

All components are mounted on a standard-size flatbed trailer, which may be towed by a tractor, dump truck, or similar hauling vehicle.

Three capacities are available:

1. A miniplant capable of six to eight tons per hour

2. A medium-size plant capable of fourteen to sixteen tons per hour

3. A maximum-capacity plant processing twenty-four to thirty-two tons per hour

Variables. Changes in the arrangement of the mill components allow for different raw materials and varying particle outputs. Variables include the size of the component elements, their number of sets, the number of elements per set, their rate of rotation, and the size and location of [*proprietary*]. Also the composition of the crushing apparatus can vary to accommodate the products being rendered.

Work Plan and Time Schedule

Glass recycling is widely practiced in the United States, virtually all of it accomplished by hauling the material from collection points to a processing facility. No other portable plant is now in operation, and the authors of this proposal hold a patent-pending certificate (61, 221-378) and a foreign patent number on the process.

The bulk of the grant funds will be used for research and development of a second-generation machine that is more efficient and cheaper to operate, leading to a demonstration model suitable for EPA evaluation.

The work will be supervised by Project Manager Albert P. Gurney and will begin upon receipt of grant funds.

[*Schedule of tasks and target dates for overall completion by February 2004.*]

Experience and Personnel

[*Resumes of the key members of the team.*]

Part Ii

This section provides the cost estimates for performing the project. Following the budget sheet is an explanation of each line item.

Budget Proposal

COST CATEGORY	TOTAL	EPA SHARE	PROPOSER'S SHARE
Personnel	$30,000	$21,000	$9,000
Travel	1,200	900	300
Equipment	12,000	12,000	
Supplies	3,000	1,500	1,500
Subcontractor	6,000	5,000	1,000
Other	900		900
Overhead	15,000	12,000	3,000
Totals	$68,100	$52,400	$15,700

Explanation

Personnel

- Albert P. Gurney, Project Manager: $15,000 (200 hours @ $75/hr.)
- Tom Richardson: $15,000 (200 hours @ $75/hr.)

(continues)

Figure 13-1. (Continued).

Travel
   • Pennsylvania to Washington, D.C., to present project results to
     the Environmental Protection Agency: two people, $1,200

Equipment
   • Upgrade motors on the plant to process a higher rate of glass:
     $7,500
   • Upgrade controller hardware: $4,500

Consumable Supplies
   • Maintenance supplies: $600
   • Paper and office supplies: $1,500
   • Oils and grease: $900

Subcontractor
   • Engineering Associates: $6,000

Other
   • Telephone and Internet access: $300
   • Photocopying: $60
   • Videotaping: $540

Overhead
   • Estimated overhead: $15,000

14 *What to Do After You Submit*

There are a number of activities you can engage in after you have submitted the proposal. Some of these are ongoing steps in the sales process. Others are intended to help you improve your next proposal. Both kinds of activities should be a regular part of your postsubmission regimen.

> *Sometimes government bids prohibit you from communicating with the contracting officer after a certain date. Attempting to do so could disqualify you from competition.*

Following Up with the Prospect

In the private sector, and even in some government bids, contacting the decision maker after your have submitted your proposal is not a problem. In fact, it's a good idea. Maintaining open communication after submission may help win the deal, since it can be an opportunity to begin closing the deal and negotiating terms. The kinds of communications to use in following up with your client include:

- Confirmation and clarification
- "Best and final offer" (BAFO) and other negotiations
- Presentations

Confirmation and Clarification

Immediately after your proposal has been submitted (allowing time for it to arrive and for the client to read it, of course), call the client's office and confirm that the proposal arrived on time. If you can reach the decision maker, this is a good opportunity to "confirm and clarify" basic facts about the decision process:

- Ask if the evaluation team has any questions.
- Ask the name of the person to contact for information about the final decision.

■ Ask about the evaluation process, the people involved, and the decision timeframe.

■ Ask if there will be any intermediate steps—a "finalists" list, for example, or an opportunity to present in person.

If you do receive requests for clarification of your proposal, questions about your terms and conditions, or other factors that suggest buying interest, respond quickly.

Best and Final Offer (BAFO) and Other Negotiations

Sometimes you will be notified that you have made the short list. At that point, the customer may want you to submit your "best and final offer." In such a situation, you should prepare a supplemental proposal and/or presentation that summarizes your offer. Stress the value proposition at this stage. The temptation is to cut your price in an effort to sweeten the deal, but in reality you may do just as well to look for opportunities to supplement your offer with additional value-added services—free training, or an extended warranty, or customized documentation. Cutting your price too quickly and too much suggests that your original price wasn't realistic to begin with and may encourage the decision maker to put even more pressure on you for concessions.

Presentations

Seek and welcome the opportunity to present your solution in person. Getting in front of the decision team or selection committee is always desirable.

After the Decision Has Been Made

The decision has been made. You won. You lost. The award was split between you and a competitor. Regardless of the outcome, there are still things you can do to learn and possibly to influence the future. Some of these activities include:

■ Debriefings

■ Win/loss analyses

■ Research to prepare you for the next opportunity

■ An internal review of the proposal creation process, identifying any lessons learned

Debriefing

If you were competing to win business from the federal government and have been notified that you did not win, you have the right to receive a debriefing after the decision has been announced. This is a legal right which you can exercise under Federal Acquisition Regulation Part 15.506. Among state and local governments the rules vary, but often you can request a debriefing in those situations, too. And if you have been competing in the private sector, there's nothing to prohibit you from asking the prospective client to provide you with some insight into its process and how well your proposal stacked up.

If you do arrange for a debriefing, use it as an opportunity to learn as much as you can about how the agency handles acquisitions, what their key decision criteria are, whether or not they followed their own guidelines, and anything else that may help you in the next opportunity.

You should also focus on specific content about your proposal and how it was reviewed:

- Where was it weak, particularly in comparison to the winning submission?

- Were there any critical areas where your proposal was deemed to be noncompliant or nonresponsive?

- How did you do in terms of pricing and in terms of your value proposition?

- Did existing relationships, prior experience, references, case studies, or expertise in a specific area make a difference for your competitor?

- How did your proposal rank compared to all the proposals submitted?

- What were the key criteria that the evaluators used in determining who won? How were these criteria weighted?

- Were the procedures outlined in the RFP (if any) actually followed? Were other processes used?

- Besides the evaluators, did anyone else participate in making the decision? What role did senior management play, if any?

Win/Loss Analysis

Conduct a win/loss analysis the same way that businesses conduct customer satisfaction surveys. That is, select a specific percentage of all the opportunities you propose and seek feedback. Conduct the analysis whether you win or lose. You can do it in the form of a questionnaire, a telephone interview, even a site visit if that's convenient. Be sure to make it clear that you are not trying to reopen the decision process, but are interested in getting feedback to improve future proposals.

Many of the questions listed above for a debriefing are appropriate for a win/loss analysis. Some other questions you might ask focus on specific areas of your proposal:

Format and Content

1. Did our proposal correctly respond to your needs and requirements?

   ■ If no, where did we fail?

   ■ Did we exceed your expectations in any areas?

2. Did we correctly understand and address your needs, objectives, and goals?

3. Did you think our proposal was well organized?

   ■ If yes, what features did you find helpful in understanding its organization and using the proposal efficiently?

   ■ If no, how could we improve its organization?

4. Was our proposal easy to understand?

   ■ What specific areas were unclear or difficult to follow?

   ■ If no, how could we make it clearer?

5. Did we provide enough detail on our products and services?

   ■ Did we spend too much time on our products/services?

   ■ Did we clearly demonstrate how specific features would provide solutions to your problems or meet your particular needs?

6. After receiving the proposal, did you have to ask us for more information?

7. Was the proposal:

   ■ Too long/detailed

   ■ Too short/cursory

   ■ About right

8. Do you feel we responded to your request in a timely manner?

Pricing

1. Did we provide sufficient pricing detail?

2. Was our pricing too detailed?

3. Did we fail to include any of the pricing you needed to see?

   ■ If yes, what did we leave out?

4. Did we adequately explain our pricing?

5. Did we provide a satisfactory analysis of ROI/payback?

   ■ If no, what made it unsatisfactory?

6. How did our pricing compare to other companies responding to this RFP?
   a. Higher
   b. Lower
   c. About the same

Proposal Effectiveness

1. What were your key reasons for selecting/not selecting us?

2. What were your key reasons for selecting our competitor?

3. We attempted to develop a specific message or theme in our proposal. Can you summarize to the best of your memory what that theme was?

4. In recalling our proposal, are there any graphics or sections that you remember as standing out? Do you have a clear picture of any part of our proposal?

Research Into the Next Phase of Business Development

Win or lose, maintain contact with the client organization and listen for opportunities that may lie ahead. Sometimes a client will realize that they misjudged your proposal and will want to rectify that on the next opportunity. Sometimes your persistence and professionalism will create a level of trust that opens up new opportunities.

The In-House Assessment

To engage in continuous improvement, you need to make a conscious, consistent effort to gather information about how effectively each proposal succeeds in achieving its purpose. Keeping track of the "lessons learned" from each project will help all team members deliver more value, communicate more persuasively, and enhance your contributions to your company. Unfortunately, the "lessons learned" are often ignored, meaning we continue to repeat the same mistakes over and over.

At the conclusion of each proposal project, after a suitable period of rest and healing for the proposal team, conduct an internal review for about an hour. The main goal is to review the process and the deliverable to find out how you can do a better job next time.

Here's a checklist for conducting a lessons learned session:

The Proposal Document

1. Does the proposal (or other persuasive message) look attractive and professional?

2. Does it reflect the image we want our company to convey to clients?

3. Does the proposal present a clear, consistent, and integrated message? Does that message appear throughout the document?

4. Is the total proposal organized persuasively? Is the executive summary focused on the client's key issues and outcomes?

5. Does this proposal clearly differentiate us from the competition? Have we made the value of that differentiation obvious?

6. Are our win themes presented clearly and emphatically? Are they substantiated with specific details and proof?

7. Is it easy to read? Is the writing style consistent throughout? Does it use graphics effectively?

8. Does it conform to the RFP requirements for format?

The Proposal Process

1. How well positioned was our company before the RFP was released? What kind of relationship was already established with the customer? Who owned that relationship?

2. Were we able to influence the RFP in any way before its release?

3. Was the proposal team brought in at the outset or did the opportunity lie on someone's desk for a while? Was the development schedule realistic?

4. Did we have an accurate idea of who the competitors would be? Did we analyze the competitors to develop the most effective win themes? If not, why not?

5. Did we spend time to define our strategy for winning at the outset? If not, why not?

6. Were key win themes identified before writing began? Were all contributors made aware of them? If not, why not?

7. Was a red team review conducted? If not, why not?

8. Did the red team cite any major deficiencies? Were they resolved before the proposal was submitted?

9. Were there any bottlenecks in the proposal development process? If so, who or what were they? How could they be resolved or avoided in the future?

10. Did the team work well together? If not, why not? How can it be improved in the future?

11. How effective was the communication between the proposal team and senior management? Was senior management involved at the outset or only at the end?

12. Did any unexpected problems arise during the proposal development process? If so, what were they and how did we resolve them?

13. Was any new content developed for this proposal? If so, has it been stored for future use?

14. What worked well? What didn't work so well in the overall process? What can be done to improve our proposal process in the future?

15 *Writing in the Midst of a Storm*
How to Deal with Bad News and Negative Publicity

We said earlier that people like to buy from people they trust. We further defined trust as a combination of rapport (how well they like you and your colleagues) and credibility (how well you seem to understand your own field), divided by the perception of the risk of doing business with you. Trust is generally earned over time, built up from repeated positive experiences.

Trust can be damaged very quickly, however, from just a single negative experience or from bad publicity or news reports. We have seen examples in recent history of once mighty and prestigious companies that were brought down by the loss of trust.

Every business relationship will hit a rough spot from time to time. The customer may be disappointed in our execution on a given contract. Negative press coverage may raise some concerns. As long as the experiences and the reportage aren't so bad that they become toxic to the relationship, we can usually recover. We regain trust through honesty, accuracy, and effective communication.

But what do you do if you're trying to write a proposal in the middle of churning seas of bad publicity? The kinds of negative publicity are legion—product defects, product recalls, lawsuits, accidents, regulatory violations, malicious tampering with your products in the marketplace, defections of key personnel, loss of a major client. All of these may cause eyebrows to go up and frowns to turn down.

Or what if you are trying to win business from a client who is currently unhappy with your firm? They have refused to sign off on the most recent phase of a project. They are invoking service-level agreements and demanding refunds. They are claiming that your product does not perform in full compliance with the specifications contained in their original RFP. They are unhappy because of personnel changes your company has made that affect their project.

Figure 15-1 shows the range of options available to you in dealing with these situations, assuming that the accusations or bad news is basically correct. Lying, denying, and ignoring are negative approaches that are predicated on the notion that your customers (or the public in general) are stupid, that they have short memories, and that they have even shorter attention spans. History is full of examples of businesses that decided to use one of these approaches, only to have it blow up in their faces like a land mine.

Figure 15-1. Ways to Handle Bad News.

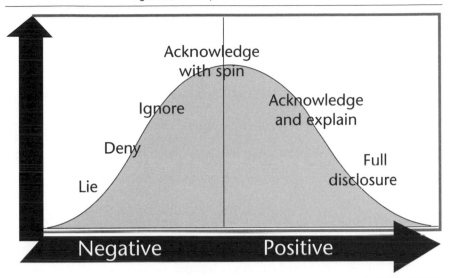

That means you're better off confronting the situation directly. Your options there are to acknowledge that the situation is essentially true, but to put a spin on the way the facts are interpreted to minimize the damage. Thus, if your CEO was indicted on charges of embezzlement and tax fraud, you may want to indicate that although charges have been filed, not all the facts are yet known in the case. It would be unfair and contrary to the justice system to pronounce someone guilty before that person has had a full and fair trial. In the meantime, the company is moving ahead with an acting CEO.

It's not great, but it may relieve some of the heat. A slightly more courageous approach is to acknowledge the facts as they are known and explain how this sad situation came to pass. In the case of the felonious CEO, your response might be that the indictment has been handed down and that although there is still much evidence and information which must be disclosed, at this time the company is changing the way sales are recorded and the way cash accounts are handled. The situation has brought to light weaknesses in the internal controls that are being fixed.

Finally, full disclosure is a rare and somewhat risky approach. Basically, you grab the advantage by telling the public everything and taking fast action to rectify the situation. The most famous example of this approach is the way Johnson & Johnson responded to the deadly product tampering with their pain reliever, Tylenol. Rapid action, full disclosure, and aggressive change managed to preserve an extremely valuable brand name.

If you are writing a proposal, the "acknowledge and explain" approach is usually your best choice. It gives you the opportunity to be forthright without necessarily conceding that the situation is completely bad. Warren

Buffett's advice on communicating during a crisis applies to the proposal writer or salesperson who is trying to close a deal during one, too:

■ Admit that not all of the facts are known.

■ State the facts that you do know.

■ Make sure you get them right. At this point, you start reestablishing trust by communicating accurately.

■ Quickly shift to a discussion of what you are doing to solve the problem, to minimize its impact, to correct any damage done, and to prevent similar problems from occurring in the future.

When the negative situation is based on the customer's unhappiness or dissatisfaction with your firm's performance, avoid blaming the customer for the problem. That's just not going to get you anywhere. It is reasonable to point out that situations are never black and white and that a number of variables contributed to the current situation.

In your proposal and presentations, stick to your core message. This message is based on the assumption that the client has a need, that you can meet this need, and that you can deliver superior value in the process. The negative news or unpleasant experience is undercutting the issues of credibility, but if you have the problem right and if you have a compelling value proposition, all is not lost.

If the customer's unhappiness is based on your team's poor execution of the contract terms, maintain an attitude of candor. You need to say: "Yes, there have been problems, but this is an extremely complex environment and a challenging project. We may have underestimated the challenge at the outset, but we fully understand it now and remain the best choice for managing the project to a successful conclusion."

In the case of bad news, you may want to reframe the issue. This can work well both in a proposal and in an oral presentation. By reframing, I mean changing the nature of the questions being directed at you in the RFP or during the question and answer period following your presentation. Here are typical reframing statements:

■ This is an important issue, of course, but we believe the most important issue is . . .

■ You're right to be concerned, and what we have done is . . .

■ In the past that was a problem, but let's focus on what we have done about it because these changes will help guarantee a successful project for you . . .

■ It's important to look at what the facts are, all of the facts, and to separate the facts from rumors . . .

■ This is a complex issue. We are continuing to gather information and opinions from experts and a variety of sources, both within our company and from outside, including . . .

What if the bad news that has been reported about your company is actually false? In a way your task is more difficult. Refuting a negative report is much harder. Your best options are to draw upon third-party evidence to establish a strong record of performance. Also, focus on the policies and procedures in place that were designed to prevent exactly the kind of problem your firm is accused of. You might be able to use traditional forms of credibility-building content, such as references and case studies, to counterbalance false accusations. Finally, if you know what is being claimed is not true, you might consider offering guarantees, service-level commitments, or other tactics designed to minimize the customer's perception of risk.

When you're faced with the challenge of writing a proposal or presenting a solution during a period of negative coverage or during a crisis, ask yourself what part of the trust relationship is broken. Is it your firm's credibility? Is it the sense of rapport and shared values? Is it the client's perception that working with you does not pose significant risk for them and their company? Keep your content as accurate as possible and strive to overcome negative news with superior value.

Above all, don't bluff and don't lie. Just like your momma told you, honesty is the best policy. Even if you lose this particular battle and don't win the business, your candor and directness may go a long way to healing the wounds and helping the client start to trust your firm again.

16 *Creating a Proposal Center of Excellence*

I'm often asked whether it's better to have salespeople write proposals themselves or to create a separate unit that writes the proposals in support of a sales organization. Well, unfortunately there isn't a single correct answer. Either approach can work. Which one you follow will depend in part on the caliber and training of your salespeople, the complexity of the proposals you must create, budgetary considerations, and what your competitors are doing, among other factors.

If you do decide to create a unit focused solely on proposal preparation, you'll certainly be in good company. All kinds of companies have centralized their proposal function—large corporations and consulting organizations; firms that specialize in government contracting; organizations that depend for their funding on grants; companies that compete in specific, proposal-dependent industries, such as insurance, financial services, and information technology; and even small firms that handle a lot of RFPs. In all of these environments, the proposal is such a vital part of the sales process that creating a specialized team of experts to handle proposals seems like the obvious, intelligent course of action.

In this chapter we will look at the various elements involved in creating a proposal center of excellence.

The Proposal Unit: Defining Its Mission

A proposal center can define and implement best practices for proposal development, standardize the company's output, and raise the overall level of quality. It can create and maintain a pool of information and reusable content. It can become a repository of expertise in the intricacies of procurement rules and contracting policies. It can supply expert help to get major proposals done on time. And most important of all, a dedicated proposal team can be a valuable asset that helps the company win more business.

Typically, a proposal function that is well integrated into marketing and customer relationship activities will play a broader role in business development than simply writing proposals. Other roles and contributions for the proposal team may include:

■ Developing standard tools for customer assessments, such as an Opportunity Assessment Worksheet, that focus on customer needs, issues, goals, and so on.

■ Participating in account planning and competitive assessments prior to or at the outset of a bid opportunity

■ Participating in bid/no bid analysis

■ Assuring that proposal development resources are applied to those opportunities with the most strategic value to the organization

■ Maintaining a repository of current, persuasive, reusable content

■ Developing and maintaining win themes related to specific product and service offerings

■ Researching trends, issues, and themes, both on a customer-specific basis and in terms of the market in general

■ Acquiring expertise on the procurement rules that govern how contracts are awarded, particularly for government clients, so the account manager will know how much he or she can do before the release of the RFP to influence its content or even to circumvent it by moving the opportunity to sole source status

■ Implementing formal methods to assess the competition, both for specific opportunities and in general, and publishing competitive information to benefit the organization as a whole

■ Writing or assembling a large percentage of each proposal

■ Attending bidders' conferences

■ Attending customer debriefings, regardless of a win or loss

As the preceding list suggests, in defining the mission of your proposal center, you should probably think a little beyond proposals.

If your proposal operation is a support organization, you may find it necessary to establish a formal process by which you take on projects. By requiring your internal clients to enter into a "contract" with your operation, you can clearly establish roles, responsibilities, and expectations on both sides. The contract should define the proposal project, timeline, charge rate (if any), scope of effort, and deliverables. Using a contract will prevent conflicts and missed expectations and may even enhance your role as a strategic resource within the firm.

Integrating the Proposal Center Into the Overall Organization

I have seen large companies spend a ton of money recruiting quality people, setting up facilities, and otherwise creating a proposal center, only to find a year or two later that the center had become little more than a copy and production shop. What happened to the strategic vision? Where is the contribution to big wins and dramatic improvements in quality?

Usually what happened is that they were never feasible in the first place, because the proposal center was slotted into the wrong part of the organization and was not able to count on top management support.

So what is the right place to fit the proposal operation into the organization? The best choice is to make it part of the sales or marketing organization. The worst choice is to put it in engineering or operations. After all, the proposal team is creating sales documents, not technical manuals. When the proposal function originates within the sales/marketing organization or in the business development function, it is typically viewed as a critical element in the overall business capture process. If it's part of engineering or operations, it's likely to be seen as part of order entry, pricing, configuration, or contracts.

People: Putting the Right Staff in Place

The cornerstone of a successful proposal center is a staff that can focus on delivering strategic, client-centered, winning proposals.

In top-notch proposal operations, everyone's roles and responsibilities are clearly defined in detail and everybody is focused by management directive on improving the organization's overall capabilities to bid successfully. To attract quality people, the company creates an environment that is creative and challenging. In addition, the company develops a career path for people who work in the center so they can see a future for themselves.

At the minimum, an effective proposal team will have three key members: the proposal manager, the writer, and the graphics expert. From time to time, you will also need to draw upon subject matter or technical experts.

Proposal Manager. The proposal manager is responsible for bringing the proposal project to an on-time, successful completion. Just as important, the proposal manager develops or facilitates development of the overall proposal strategy and makes sure that the strategy is executed throughout the proposal. The proposal manager will typically make assignments to other contributors, monitor their progress, and either edit their submissions or assign them for editing. In addition, the proposal manager will assure the technical accuracy of the proposal, will gather and monitor cost data, will make sure the costing is reviewed and approved, and will monitor the overall effort to keep the cost of proposal development within budget.

The manager should have in-depth knowledge of the customer and the opportunity, and should share that insight with the rest of the proposal team during a kick-off meeting and throughout the project. Ideally, the proposal manager should be someone who can assimilate knowledge quickly, sort the useful and relevant from the superfluous or irrelevant, stay organized, think strategically, stay focused on deadlines, and maintain a high level of energy and stamina, even during difficult periods when the hours are long. The proposal manager will also need leadership skills, because he or she will be organizing a team and moving a complex project to conclusion.

Other qualifications and experience that will lead to success as a proposal manager include:

- Self-starter

- Savvy about marketing and sales

- Excellent writing skills

- Good communication and negotiation skills

- Solid, applications-oriented knowledge of products and services being offered

- Field/product experience, either in sales, installation, or customer support

Writer. Proposals are communication vehicles. It goes without saying that you'll need people with strong communication skills, especially the ability to write clearly and quickly. In my opinion the best kind of background for proposal writing is journalism. Someone who has made his or her living as a reporter, particularly if that person has a business background, can crank out the text you need in a fast and dependable way.

Besides having good writing skills, this person must be computer literate. Advanced knowledge of word processing techniques will make the writer more productive. (It's extremely frustrating to discover that someone's contribution has lost all formatting because the person didn't use the style sheet.) But computer literacy goes far beyond just word processing or desktop publishing programs. Your writer will need to be able to navigate around the Web, both within the company's private sites and externally, to locate information. He or she will need to be comfortable using e-mail, working on a network, using backup software, and possibly creating materials in a presentation system, such as Microsoft PowerPoint.

Graphics Expert. The graphics expert is the person most likely to be missing from a fully staffed proposal team. Often, proposal units draw on the marketing department for graphic support, or they turn to outside vendors on a contract basis to create graphics. From a budgetary standpoint that might make sense, but ideally you should have someone on the team who thinks visually and who can translate proposal-specific messages into crisp, interesting images.

A good graphics person should also be skilled in page design and layout issues. If you can find a contributor who can create a simple, clean, but distinctive format for your proposals, grab that individual around the knees and hang on. That's one extremely valuable person.

Subject Matter or Technical Experts. In addition to the three core functions found in a proposal team—the manager, the writer, and the graphic designer—you may need special expertise from time to time. Although not likely to be an employee of the proposal center, the subject matter expert is often indispensable. When you really need somebody with a deep knowledge of the technology underlying your recommended solutions, you realize that's the kind of content that just can't be faked. You need an expert. The problem comes from the fact that your technical experts (1) don't think proposal writing is part of their job and (2) don't know how to communicate their in-depth knowledge in language that's appropriate to a customer. Store whatever contributions your technical experts make so that you don't have to go back to them and ask them to do it again. They hate that.

Skills: Assessing and Training for Outstanding Performance

Putting the right people in the right jobs is a critical factor in developing a center of excellence. Training them to do those jobs to the best of their ability is another. Based on having clear definitions of roles and responsibilities, you should be able to develop a training map for each job in the proposal unit. The three components of effective training include *formal training, mentoring activities,* and *on-the-job experiences.* Thus, your training maps should integrate all three of these activities—in conjunction with proper goal setting—to give your staff the highest opportunity for success.

In terms of the necessary formal training, your proposal specialists should receive some of the typical training already offered within your company. But much of the curriculum will be specific to the skills required of a proposal center employee:

The Basics of Writing a Winning Proposal: Curriculum

Principles of Persuasion
■ Structural patterns for effective proposal writing—the persuasive paradigm, the structure of the executive summary, the pattern for effective case studies, resumes, answers, and so on.
■ Value propositions and win themes
■ ROI models and company differentiators

Proposal Project Management
- Managing the project
- Collaboration skills
- Analyzing the RFP
- Bid/no bid issues
- Developing a writing plan, distributing effort
- Handling production issues
- Time/organization management

Writing Skills
- Sentence structure for clarity
- Modifying text for different audience types
- Techniques for writing component parts of proposals

Use of Office Tools:
- Word processing, spreadsheet, and presentation software
- E-mail system
- Proposal automation tools
- Web-based search tools, particularly internal sites

Methods: Incorporating Best Practices

If your proposal center has clearly defined processes that enable the entire team to understand a customer's needs and requirements fully, your center will be seen as a professional unit focused on business development. If it has processes that it consistently follows that control how a proposal gets printed and bound, it will be seen primarily as a production shop. Obviously, both kinds of processes are important, but in my experience proposal teams usually ignore the importance of the first kind, those that are directed outward toward the deal.

To operate efficiently and effectively, a proposal center must be based on a solid process model for handling opportunities and collaborating with the rest of the firm, particularly the sales organization. That process model must be:

- Rigorous enough to capture the complexity of creating proposals

- Flexible enough to work in the company's dynamic business environment

- Simple enough to be communicated to internal customers and learned quickly by new employees

- Metrics-based so proficiency and progress can be tracked

You need a clearly defined and documented methodology for handling each proposal, supported by checklists, guidelines, and other job aids.

When you develop and implement your process for managing proposals, be sure to publicize the linkage between that process and your company's overall sales or business development life cycle, so that others in the company will see that you are supporting their interests, too. Establish a formal process for waiving or deviating from standard procedures.

The actual production of a proposal is generally a low-level activity, primarily involving final editing, formatting, binding, and delivery of the document. However, one aspect of proposal production that should be owned by the proposal organization is the development and use of electronic processes and systems to store, manage, retrieve, and distribute information and reusable content. Developing electronic stores of reusable information will provide more time for strategic thinking.

A proposal operation can provide leadership in two other areas of production without diminishing its role as a strategic resource. First, you can take the lead in identifying requirements for your company's visual identity and in assuring consistent implementation of the identity guidelines. This responsibility is usually owned by the marketing department, but if they aren't doing it, the proposal team should.

Second, the center should create formal review processes and integrate them into the production process to assure high-quality output. The focus should be on both document quality (spelling, grammar, formatting, and so forth) and content quality (customization to the client, effective presentation of a win theme, accuracy of information, relevance of credentials and other supporting materials included).

Tools: The Right Resources and Facilities for Optimum Performance

The proposal operation must be designed for efficiency. This includes having the equipment necessary to do the job and the specialized tools to operate at peak effectiveness:

- Proposal generation software

- Individual workstations, fully networked and equipped with up-to-date office productivity software (given the realities of the marketplace, I recommend Microsoft Office for consistency across the enterprise and with the vast majority of clients)

- Printers, phones, faxes, and high-bandwidth access to the Internet to facilitate collaboration within the center and with internal clients

- Whiteboards, flip charts, libraries of resource material, and other materials for planning and managing proposal projects

■ Easy access to electronic stores of reusable content and other information

A few years ago I would have added that the proposal unit needs a dedicated workspace where team members can collaborate. That seems less important now. Working remotely has become such a standard part of doing business that the only concern is whether or not employees have sufficient bandwidth to participate in a Web-hosted meeting and whether they can sort out the time zones.

Surviving and Prospering

In tough economic times, support organizations often feel the sharp edge of the budgetary paring knife. To keep your proposal operation from falling victim to cost-cutting measures, there are a couple of things you should do.

First, publicize the proposal unit's contributions and successes regularly. Make sure senior management is aware of the group's contributions. Self-promotion is a necessary element of survival.

Second, expand the value you provide. One area you should think about seriously is providing generalized information management for the company, or at least for the sales and marketing organization. Chances are your proposal operation is probably the best-organized repository of facts and insights in the company. Look for opportunities to open access to your knowledge stores, publicize the importance of maintaining the information so that it is current and accurate, and make yourself indispensable to other areas of the company.

17 *Proposal Metrics:*

How to Measure Your Success

You should regularly take the pulse of your proposal operation by measuring both performance and proficiency. In measuring performance, you want to make sure the work you are doing and the results that work is producing are in alignment with the company's goals. In measuring proficiency, you need to define what tasks proposal writers perform and which of those tasks have the greatest impact on producing successful projects. Then you can measure whether or not the people involved have the right skills at the right level of proficiency.

Why bother measuring all of this stuff? Well, if you want to improve your proposal process, if you want it to produce more wins and require less time and money, you have to be able to track what you're doing and measure the results.

Measuring Success—the First Steps

To improve your proposal process in a systematic way, you must first decide what it is you want to measure. Which measurements are truly meaningful?

The second step is to develop a baseline of data based on the "old" way of handling the task. If you don't know where you are, it's pretty hard to figure out if you're moving in the right direction.

The third element in measuring results is to implement a system that will collect the appropriate measures from the "new" process. This may be a matter of self-reporting on the outcome of each sales opportunity, but it could require a more structured effort, such as conducting a win/loss analysis or tracking hours of effort.

Take a Three-Dimensional View

To get a complete view of the impact of any changes you make, measure results in terms of three goal areas—business performance, process improvements, and customer satisfaction. This will give you a three-dimensional view of your success, which is much more likely to be accurate and meaningful for you.

Business results are typically measured in financial terms or in terms of productivity. In looking at your proposal processes, you might measure the gross revenues you win, or the total number of proposals prepared per center employee, or the total dollar volume won by your proposal center on a per employee basis.

Second, look at the impact of technical improvements to your proposal process. Technical improvements usually produce process efficiencies that can be measured in terms of reduced time or effort. They might overlap with business results, but not always.

The third area where you should measure results is customer satisfaction. You obviously have one all-important customer—the one who signs the contract and sends you the check. But it's possible you have other customers, too. For example, if you're a proposal writer who supports salespeople, those folks out in the field are your customers, too. Are they satisfied with the work you do?

Five Ways to Measure Business Results

1. Win Ratio

The point of this sort of metric is pretty obvious. It's like glancing at the baseball standings—the team with the highest winning percentage is on top. For most sales executives, increasing the win ratio may be exactly the kind of success they want to see. It's simple and straightforward.

2002: 500 proposals submitted, 200 deals won = 40 percent win ratio
2003: 400 proposals submitted, 185 deals won = 46.25 percent win ratio

The interesting thing about these numbers is that even though fewer deals were won, the win ratio was higher. This could stem from putting in place a better bid/no bid analysis process, or from fewer opportunities in your industry due to economic conditions. But it could also mean the sales team was not doing as good a job of uncovering opportunities, even though you managed to win more of the deals they did find. You can see why measuring win ratio alone may not be adequate. But it is a starting point. And it's one measure that's obviously relevant.

2. Ratio of Opportunities Won/Total Opportunities

To address some of the inaccuracies inherent in measuring nothing but win ratios, you might consider tracking how you are doing compared to the total number of opportunities that were available for you to compete on. If you are working in a focused market, such as local government, where all opportunities require an RFP as part of the formal procurement process, you may know exactly how many deals were on the table. For example, suppose the numbers look like this:

2002: 750 RFPs released, 200 deals won = 27 percent hit ratio
2003: 600 RFPs released, 185 deals won = 31 percent hit ratio

Again, although there were 20 percent fewer opportunities available to bid on, the number of total deals you won declined only 7.5 percent. Your "hit ratio" went up.

3. Win Ratio in Target Markets

A useful measurement is to segment your success by markets, particularly if you're trying to grow your business in a specific area. Suppose you have traditionally been a government supplier, but your firm has decided that it must expand into the commercial market. Tracking revenue by market will show whether or not you're making progress toward that goal, as these number indicate:

2002: 85 percent revenue won in government contracts
       15 percent revenue won in commercial
2003: 78 percent revenue won in government contracts
       22 percent revenue won in commercial

4. Ratio of the $ Won/Total $ in All Potential Bids

If you are winning a lot of deals, but those deals are all the small ones, and you're not winning any of the large opportunities, you may have a high win ratio and yet unexpectedly low revenues. By tracking the total value of all the contracts for which you compete and comparing that to the total amount you win, you can track your capture rate, like this:

2002: won $4 million revenue/$24 million potential revenue = 17
       percent capture rate
2003: won $3.8 million revenue/$21 million potential revenue = 19
       percent capture rate

On a year over year basis, your revenues went down, but you captured a larger share of what was available, which means you actually did a better job in a declining market.

5. Ratio of the Cost to Win/Value of Wins

Finally, a measure of business performance that is relevant to a dedicated proposal operation is how much it costs to run that operation compared to how much the proposal team has helped win. A well-managed proposal operation should learn to operate more efficiently and effectively over time.

If this measurement is trending in the right direction, the ratio between the cost of running the proposal operation and the revenue won from proposals produced by that operation will grow larger:

> 2002: *Proposal Center budget = $850,000*
> *Revenue won = $38 million*
> *Ratio of revenue to cost = 44.7:1*
> 2003: *Proposal Center budget = $850,000*
> *Revenue won = $64 million*
> *Ratio of revenue to cost = 75.3:1*

Measuring Technical Results

As we defined them, technical results are the direct consequence of improvements to the infrastructure. These improvements result in greater productivity, better utilization of resources, lower costs of operation, or similar measures related to time and effort. Here are some ways of measuring technical results:

1. Decreasing the Cost per Page

How much does it cost to produce a proposal? One way to measure the costs is to calculate how much you spend per page. For example, let's look at two years' operation in a large proposal operation:

> 2002: *Proposal Center budget = $850,000*
> *Total proposal pages produced = 50,000*
> *Cost per page = $17*
> 2003: *Proposal Center budget = $850,000*
> *Total proposal pages produced = 60,000*
> *Cost per page = $14.17*

The cost per page has gone down considerably, an interesting measurement, but it ignores issues of quality and effectiveness. Producing 20 percent more garbage isn't necessarily an improvement. But if you couple this kind of metric with careful tracking of business results, you will have a useful insight.

2. Decreasing the Cost per Outgoing Page/Incoming RFP Pages

This is an attempt to account for the complexity of the proposals being handled. The assumption behind this is that responding to a twenty-page RFP is probably less demanding than responding to one that's 200 pages.

3. Reducing Access Time to Existing Information

Good proposals require good information. A proposal operation that can find the right information quickly will be more efficient than one that struggles to locate the information needed for a proposal.

> *2002: Finding an RFP answer among existing proposals: 42 minutes average*
>
> *2003: Finding an RFP answer from redesigned database: 3 minutes average*

Measuring Customer Satisfaction: The Process

The final area of measurement is customer satisfaction. Are you producing proposals that your customer thinks are high quality? Easy to use? Clear? Persuasive?

To use customer satisfaction as a metric, you first must define who is the "customer." The obvious choice, the final decision maker or the client evaluation team, may be only part of the answer. There may be consultants involved in the selection process. In addition, you may have internal customers whose satisfaction matters.

After you've defined who is the customer, your next task is to gather quantifiable, objective measures of customer satisfaction. Win/loss analyses, focus groups, interviews, surveys, and other research tools will help you get the data you need. One useful measure of internal satisfaction is to track red team scores. Are they going up? (Another interesting question is whether good red team scores correlate to winning proposals. If not, it's time to shake up the red team process!)

Implementing Metrics to Improve Your Proposal Processes

In summary, remember to look for three-dimensional measures of impact: business performance, technical or process improvements, and customer satisfaction. Establish solid baseline data before you start measuring the impact of changes. Without a baseline, there's no way to know if your changes have helped or hindered the process.

Also, remember that external economic and business factors can make good numbers look bad and vice versa. Process improvements need to be measured over a long enough period to account for cyclical variations in business performance.

4

Writing to Win

18 *Give the Reader a KISS!*

If you ask people what they like to see in the business writing they receive, most of them will say something like, "Gimme a KISS!" In other words, Keep It Short and Simple.

As readers, we all know what we like: Conciseness. Clarity. Simplicity. Unfortunately, when we sit down to write, we too often fail to deliver anything like that. We produce lengthy, verbose, and complicated documents. Especially when writing proposals, many people subscribe to the "bulk" theory.

That's ridiculous, of course. To my knowledge, nobody has ever made a buying decision based on the thud factor—which proposal makes the loudest noise when dropped on the desk. It's true, of course, that an analytical decision maker will want quite a bit of detail, but details in and of themselves have no value.

One of our clients asked for advice that would help them improve their win ratio. When we reviewed their proposals, we were very impressed with their quality. In fact, we identified only two weaknesses. First, their value propositions were not as sharply focused or as well substantiated as they needed to be. Second, their proposals just seemed too long. So they worked on improving the value proposition, and they cut down the length by almost half. The result: Over the next six months, they won eleven out of twelve opportunities they went after!

Why would producing a shorter proposal have any impact at all on your win ratio? In a simple experiment we conducted, we asked people who make their living evaluating proposals to review three sample proposals. Actually, we weren't interested in their reviews at all. We just wanted to see which proposal they picked up first. One of them was twenty-five pages long, one was fifty pages, and one was one hundred pages. Which one do you think they reached for first? That's right—the short one.

Why does that matter? Well, let's suppose that you produced the short proposal. And you organized it using the persuasive paradigm, so you have focused on the client's needs, detailed the outcomes, recommended a solution, and substantiated it with convincing evidence that you can do the job on time and on budget. In addition, you've developed a payback calculation that's quantified and based on the client's own data, and you've linked that payback both to your differentiators and to credible evidence suggesting that this client is likely to see the kind of return you're forecasting. If this is the proposal your client reads first, what will he or she think of the bloated, unfocused, unpersuasive proposals that come second and third? They will appear worse by the contrast and will be evaluated even more harshly.

Lots of people pay lip service to short, direct, clear writing, but the reality is you don't see much of it. Within the business, scientific, and academic communities there seems to be a cultural bias against clarity and simplicity. Some of that may stem from insecurity. Writers don't feel confident about their knowledge, experience, or company reputation, so they try to impress the reader with big words, long sentences, and lots of extraneous content. Sometimes bad writing stems from laziness. Sloppy, careless writing takes less time and effort, even when it produces longer documents, than carefully edited writing. And sometimes bad writing is the result of bad training. Many of us remember English classes in which "good" writing seemed to be synonymous with big words, complicated syntax, and convoluted thinking. Even today there are books and audio tapes designed to help you develop a "power vocabulary," which basically seems to mean using lots of big words.

Overcome your anxiety and insecurity. Make the effort to write the kind of prose you want to receive—clear, compelling, and concise. And put behind you the bad training and wrong-headed advice you received from your English teachers. Your proposals are too important to your career and the success of your business. You must write them as clearly and economically as possible.

Here are some tips that will help you keep your proposals short and simple:

1. **GYST.** Don't write anything until you "Get Your Stuff Together." Lots of gas-filled balloons are launched from word processors by people who began to write before they really knew what they were talking about, why they were talking about it, or to whom they were talking. Analyze the client's business problem or need. Take the time to create a cognitive web so you have a basic outline to guide your writing. Give lots of thought to your decision maker's personality and priorities before you commit yourself to paper.

2. **Watch your words.** Churchill once said, "Short words are the best words, and old words, when they are short, are the best words of all." Great advice. Whenever possible, use everyday language in your writing.

   As a rule, use one- or two-syllable words. In fact, use them about 90 percent of the time. Can you still write a powerful message using such everyday words? Well, think about Churchill, rallying the United Kingdom in its darkest hours. Throwing a defiant challenge toward Hitler, he said: "We shall defend our island, whatever the cost may be, we shall fight on the beaches, we shall fight on the landing grounds, we shall fight in the fields and in the streets, we shall fight in the hills; we shall never surrender." You can feel the power that short, everyday words can generate.

3. **Use short, simple sentences.** A sentence is an idea. Sentences work best when they contain only one idea. And they work best of all when they're short and simple.

   Try to keep your average sentence length between fifteen and eighteen words. To determine the average sentence length, use the grammar checking function in your word processor. For example, if you use Microsoft Word, highlight the passage of text you want to check, then click on the spelling and grammar checking function. (Make sure that you have selected "Show readability statistics" in the Tools/Options/Spelling & Grammar menu.) By doing that on this paragraph, I found that the average sentence length is 16.8 words.

   When I recommend that you write simple sentences, I am referring to the syntactical patterns you choose. If your sentences contain a lot of subordinate clauses, particularly clauses placed in the front part of the sentence, as I have done here, you will increase the complexity of the sentence and slow down comprehension. That sentence isn't horrible. You probably understood it all right. But a steady diet of sentences written like that will tire you out.

4. **Write in a natural voice.** Your writing will be easier to understand if you write in a natural, conversational rhythm to the extent possible. And try to say things in a positive way whenever you can.

   Don't think writing short, simple proposals will be easy. You're probably surrounded by bad examples. Writing simply and concisely takes conscious effort. It requires more skill than simply rambling on does. But the effort is worth it. In fact, if your proposals embody the KISS principle, your readers may be so pleased they'll want to give you a kiss in return. Or better yet—a contract!

19 *Word Choice:*

Six Traps to Avoid

The English philosopher John Locke wrote in *An Essay Concerning Human Understanding*:

> *Vague and insignificant forms of speech, and abuse of language have so long passed for mysteries of science; and hard and misapplied words, with little or no meaning, have, by prescription, such a right to be mistaken for deep learning and height of speculation, that it will not be easy to persuade either those who speak or those who hear them, that they are but the covers of ignorance, and hindrance of true knowledge.*

Even though Locke was writing in 1690, it sounds like he was pretty sick of people who use pompous language to impress others instead of to communicate. I guess it's just another sign that some things never change.

In their effort to be impressive and to sound smart, writers often fall into a number of verbal traps. Sometimes they are covering their own ignorance; sometimes they are trying to pretend that they have "deep learning." Sometimes they just can't write worth a darn.

Here are some common traps to avoid.

Trap 1: Using Jargon

We've already said elsewhere in this book that using jargon the customer doesn't understand is a bad idea. The problem is that our sensitivity to in-house jargon, that sharp awareness of it that we have as new employees, quickly fades. And that's when jargon becomes dangerous for you as a proposal writer. When you no longer recognize jargon for what it is—the specialized technical language of a particular company, department, industry, or field of experience—you are most likely to misuse it. Salespeople, proposal writers, even marketing professionals almost always *overestimate* the customer's level of understanding and familiarity with jargon. Seek insight into your customers and their level of understanding, and exercise judgment and common sense in using jargon. If you're looking for a general rule on jargon, here's one: *If in doubt, leave it out.*

Unfortunately, sometimes you need to use it. So how can you introduce jargon into your proposal text without confusing or alienating the reader? You must focus on the functional meaning of the jargon, not merely its lexical definition. By that I mean it's not enough to simply explain what the letters of an acronym stand for, nor is it enough to define a term's meaning by substituting other jargon in its place. Help your customer understand the term's significance at the outset of your proposal. Then you can use it throughout.

Trap 2: Dangling Your Participles and Other Embarrassments

When I was teaching English at UCLA, one of the students in my composition class submitted a paper in which he asserted:

After rotting in the cellar for weeks, my brother brought up some oranges.

I had a hunch I knew what he really meant to say, but then I hadn't seen his brother, and in southern California one never knows. So I wrote in the margin of his paper: "Please do not allow your brother to visit this campus."

What my student had created was, in grammatical terms, a dangling participle; in human terms, it was an embarrassment. *Dangling participial modifiers* are one of the most common and amusing mistakes people make when writing. Other howlers include *squinting modifiers* and *misplaced adverbial modifiers.*

It's easy to create these things. Everybody who writes produces one occasionally. That's why everyone who writes has to edit. Understanding them will help you avoid creating them and, thus, will keep you from embarrassing yourself in your proposals and undercutting your credibility and professionalism.

Dangling Participles

The most egregious of these constructions is the participial phrase that introduces a sentence. Whatever that phrase modifies has to follow immediately after it, because that's how the reader's brain will decode it. For example:

Featuring plug-in circuit boards, this server offers maximum flexibility and growth potential.

That's okay. The participial phrase "Featuring plug-in circuit boards" explains something about "this server," and the noun "server" immediately follows the phrase. So it's clear. It's unambiguous. It works.

But consider this one:

*Featuring plug-in circuit boards, we can strongly endorse this server's flex-
ibility and growth potential.*

What do we have here? A robot proposal writer? We can fix this one by
rewriting it:

*Because the server features plug-in circuit boards, we can strongly recom-
mend it for flexibility and growth potential.*

Once you catch on to the dangling participle, you'll start noticing them
everywhere. They're usually good for a few laughs, as long as they're not in
something you wrote.

Squinting Modifiers

A squinting modifier is a word or phrase that could logically modify two
different parts of a sentence. For example:

*Clients who process data after hours frequently will save money by using
the batch processing option.*

"Frequently" is the problem here. It's squinting between two parts of
the sentence, either of which it could modify. You could be saying that
people who make a habit of processing data after hours will save money by
using the batch option. Or you could be saying that even one instance of
after-hours processing will probably be cheaper if done in batch mode.

The sentence should be rewritten to clear up the ambiguity. That means
moving the squinting modifier:

*Clients who frequently process data after hours will save money by using
the batch processing option.*

Or:

*Clients who process data after hours will frequently save money by using
the batch processing option.*

Misplaced Adverbial Modifiers

This last construction is hard to describe but easy to demonstrate. You see
them in job titles occasionally, which means they might sneak into the
project team or resumes section of your proposal. For example, a company
in my city employs "Vibrating Structures Engineers." The local university
refers to one of the young women in its employ as a "Dishonored Check

Collector." It's hard not to feel sorry for these people, isn't it? Perhaps appropriate medication will help those vibrating engineers, but probably nothing but time will heal the check collector's sense of shame and betrayal.

Be careful when lumping words together to form job titles or project titles. We want our readers to enjoy our proposals, but unintended laughter is probably not a good sign.

Trap 3: Creating Noun Clusters

Living languages change constantly. That's how you know they're alive. Certainly the English language, and particularly that version of it spoken in the United States, has changed in many ways just within our lifetimes. For example, people no longer say "I shall" and "you or he will" for future tense. Now, all of us "will," and we leave "shall" to imply obligation. That's cleaner than the old rule, which never made much sense anyway.

Other changes have affected our vocabulary. I recently read an amusing essay by the British novelist and critic David Lodge, "Where It's At: The Poetry of Psychobabble," which was first published in 1981. In it he analyzed and explained a slew of "deviant constructions" that had apparently emerged from California pop culture. Some examples:

- "I know where you're coming from," which Lodge translates as "I understand what you mean."

- "Heavy" meaning *important* or *serious*

- "Off the wall" meaning *spontaneous* or *eccentric*

- "Up front with" meaning *honest*

- "Run [it] by" meaning *show* or *explain,* but which we would probably also recognize as having the sense of seeking *feedback*—another "deviant construction"

The point is that these expressions, which seemed so odd and almost poetic to Lodge, have become part of our ordinary, informal vocabulary.

However, not all language changes are improvements. One of these changes for the worse is the introduction of what I have called "noun clusters" into written and, occasionally, spoken English.

I had to invent the term "noun cluster" because this construction didn't have an official name when I first started complaining about it. Other writers have called them "jammed modifiers" or have referred to these constructions as "noun stacking" or "nominalization." But I called them noun clusters because that's what they are: a cluster of nouns all wadded together, a bolus of incomprehensibility.

To form a noun cluster, you simply string a bunch of nouns together. That's it. There's no special talent required for this activity. In fact, it probably helps to have no talent, or at least no ear, for language.

You see noun clusters frequently in technical proposals and technical documentation. For example, here's a title that appeared on a proposal I received:

FAX TRANSMISSION NETWORK ACCESS COST
OPTIMIZATION PROPOSAL

Isn't that a jewel? Or how about these beauties:

■ Last year, we published the earth resources satellite field station implementation, maintenance, repair manual.

■ It is a direct drive remote terminal software modification package designed by our internal software applications development management group.

■ Nova offers specialized technology solutions integration services.

■ Personnel development in our company is guided by an employee testing training skill development program.

Bear in mind, it has always been legal in English to use one noun to modify another noun. The first noun functions as an adjective in such a construction and is usually called an "attributive noun." Examples are *telephone company, cellular phone, bus stop, marriage certificate, book store,* and *materials laboratory*. The problem arises when a whole slew of nouns are crammed together. The poor reader's brain has no way to decode this mess until he or she has already gone through it once. Then the reader has to go back through, figure out which nouns are functioning as nouns, which are adjectives, and what goes with what, and try to make sense out of it.

If you catch yourself writing a noun cluster, what should you do? First, identify the key noun in the sequence. Then put it up front. Look for an opportunity to use a verb, and don't hesitate to link your words with a few prepositions.

Take the first example, the proposal title. As you can see, there's no verb at all in the title. What is the writer trying to say? That we can "optimize" the costs of accessing network service for transmitting faxes. Maybe. But do we want to "optimize" costs? That's ambiguous enough that it might mean costs are going up. After all, optimized costs from the vendor's perspective would be higher, right? Anyway, let's assume the writer is trying to suggest that his or her proposal will enable us to save money when we send faxes over the company's network. Instead of using the buzzword "optimize," let's try some ordinary English:

REDUCING THE COSTS OF NETWORK ACCESS
FOR TRANSMITTING FAXES

Or maybe something even simpler:

REDUCING THE COST OF SENDING FAXES:
A PROPOSAL TO ENHANCE YOUR NETWORK SERVICE

Take a look at the second example. How can we straighten out that pretzel? In this sentence, the key noun appears to be "manual." So let's move that up front and then ask ourselves, what kind of manual is it?

Last year, we published the manual for implementing, maintaining, and repairing the field station for the earth resources satellite.

Voila! English!

In the third example, the key idea is probably the fact that our group designed the software. So let's put that up front.

Our development group has designed . . .

Now try to rearrange the remaining nouns in short phrases, using prepositions to show linkage and converting some of the nouns to participles:

Our development group has designed a modification package for software used on direct terminals in remote locations.

That's a little better, I think, a little easier to understand the first time through. The final phrase, "on direct terminals in remote locations," still sounds awkward, but the whole sentence begins to resemble plain English rather than some weird technospeak.

Avoid noun clusters in your proposals. They're difficult to understand, they slow down the reading process, and they sound awful.

Trap 4: Using Knotty Words Incorrectly

I remember reading a cover letter that stated how much the RFP had "peaked" the writers' interest. Hmmm. I don't think so. It probably didn't "peek," either. Maybe what they were trying to say was that the RFP had "piqued" their interest.

Another proposal writer slipped into the common mistake of using a currently popular buzzword in his writing without really knowing what it means or how it's spelled. He wrote: "This application is ideal for use in a nitch market." *Nitch?* Have you ever seen a "nitch market"? Do you think one could buy a nitch on sale there? Of course, the writer meant *niche*. But the damage is done.

Here are some knotty usage problems that can pop up in proposal writing. Maybe a few of them bother you.

Affect/Effect

This pair drives people nuts. *Affect* is usually a verb: "Your choice of a motorized log splitter will inevitably affect the logging camp's productivity." *Effect* is usually a noun. "Your choice will also have an effect on safety." One way to remember which is which: think of *"the effect."* "The" can't precede a verb, so link the "e" at the end of "the" with the "e" that begins "effect." (Sometimes people who speak in psychobabble use "affect" as a noun to refer to a person's emotional state. And sometimes lawyers like to use "effect" or "effectuate" as a verb, meaning "to bring about or execute." Ignore these people. Nobody ever learned to write clearly by imitating lawyers' or psychologists' styles.)

Anxious/Eager

People often write that they are "anxious to work on this project." To which the reader might reasonably ask, "Why? What aren't you telling me?" *Anxious* means nervous or concerned. You will communicate more forcefully, with less ambiguity, if you say that you are *eager* to work on the project, not *anxious*.

Assure/Ensure/Insure

All three of these words mean about the same thing: "to make certain or secure." *Assure* refers to people, though, and suggests putting someone at ease, reducing anxiety or worry. *Ensure* and *insure* both mean "to secure from harm," but *insure* has a stronger implication. If you *insure* something, the reader may take that as your guarantee of a positive outcome, whereas *ensuring* or *assuring* may imply serious effort on your part but no guarantee.

Compliment/Complement

Have you ever seen a menu that promised an appetizer or salad that would "compliment" your meal? But when you ordered it, what happened? Nothing. It didn't say a word. No compliments. No pleasantries at all. A *compliment* involves "flattery" or "praise." A *complement* is something that completes a whole: "The program modules complement each other."

Data is/Data are

Everybody who took Latin in high school, and even a few former altar boys and girls, love to pounce on your throat if you say, "The data is in the computer," or whatever. "Data," they snootily inform you, "is the plural form of datum. Therefore, it must take a plural verb." Yeah, well . . . Maybe that's why Latin is a dead language. Those Romans were too uptight about these things. In fact, *data* as used in English is a "collective singular noun," which is grammar jargon that means it's the same kind of word as *jury, committee, team, staff,* and *humanity.* If the data you're writing about is a homogeneous whole, use a singular verb: "The billing data is backed up daily." But if the data in question is a hodgepodge, use a plural: "They discovered that their sales and customer support data were located in different parts of the system."

Imply/Infer

Inference is a mental process. You *infer* something when you reach a conclusion on the basis of observations. Only people can infer: "The client inferred from our documentation that system training would proceed quickly." Implication is a state of being. Data of any kind, including the attributes of people, can *imply* things: "The disheveled condition of my desk implies that I am a slob. The disgusted looks on your faces imply than you are not."

Interface

Computer systems, hardware, mechanical parts all *interface.* That's fine. The word *interface* has become an accepted bit of IT jargon, although *connect* or *link* might sound less pompous. But people don't interface. It sounds ludicrous to say, "Our technical team will interface with your project management team."

Its/It's [also, Whose/Who's]

One of these is a contraction, one is a possessive pronoun. The contraction is the one that has an apostrophe in it. It's a shortened version of *it is* [or *who is*]. I think the confusion arises from the fact that in English we form possessives with nouns by adding *'s,* as in John's coat, the chair's padding, the company's financial reports. But we don't use the apostrophe when we form a possessive from a pronoun: *ours, yours, hers, theirs, its,* and *whose.* Why? Don't ask. It's a tale of greed, stupidity, and squalor that has been an embarrassment to grammarians for hundreds of years.

Lay/Lie; Raise/Rise; Set/Sit

These are about as knotty as words get. People make mistakes with them all the time, and usually their readers or listeners aren't certain what's correct, either. The second of each pair, the ones with an *i*-sound, are all intransitive verbs. Big help, right? Well, what that means is that they do not take an object. Each of them is something you do to yourself: "You lie on the couch. You rise for dinner. You sit at the table." (Or somebody else does these things to himself or herself: "She lies on the beach. They rise from their pew. He sits on the board of directors.") The first of each pair are transitive verbs, meaning they are actions performed on something else: "I lay the book on the table. They raise orchids. She set the bags of fertilizer on the driveway." Good luck.

Lead/Led/Lead

The preceding heading looks like a typographical error, but it's not. There are two different words spelled *lead*. And that's the source of the problem. The first form of *lead* is a verb, pronounced with a long *e*-sound, meaning "to show the way," "to guide," or "to direct." The past tense of the verb *lead* is *led,* which is pronounced exactly the same way as the second form of *lead.* That *lead* is a noun, is pronounced with a short *e*-sound, and refers to a soft, dense metal. The point is that thousands of proposals every year say something like, "Many of the projects listed below were lead by Dr. Stanhope." No, they weren't. They were *led* by Dr. Stanhope.

Oral/Verbal

Oral means with your mouth. *Verbal* means with words. Spoken language is oral. Hence, people give "oral presentations." But both written and spoken language are verbal (unless you write in hieroglyphics or ideograms). A verbal contract could be either spoken or written. An oral contract is spoken only.

Parameters

This word means a variable or a constant in a mathematical expression. If you have a system characterized by a number of variables and you hold them all constant except one, you will obtain parametric data for that one variable. Fine. So if you're writing about parameters in that sense, go for it. But if you're using the word because it sounds kind of smart in a high-tech sort of way, and if you're using it very loosely to mean "scope" or "limits," then shame on you. You're thinking of *perimeter,* a different word entirely.

Principal/Principle

Most of us recall from grade school that "the principal is my pal." (At least until you were sent to his or her office, that is.) It might be better if we also remembered "the principal is the main thing." Because that form of the word *principal* means the main or primary element. The *principal* is the chief administrator in a school. Your *principal* is the main amount of money on which you're earning or paying interest, and the *principals* in a law or accounting firm are the chief partners. *Principle* means a basic truth, an axiom, a guideline, a firm belief. In the wake of the Andersen affair, we could say, "Some principal partners had no principles."

Serve/Service

Do you *serve* your customers or do you *service* them? I suppose it depends on what kind of business you're in. Here's the point: *serve* is a verb; *service* is a noun. "We will serve the interests of our customers and shareholders alike by delivering the best customer service possible."

Simple/Simplistic

Don't write in your proposal that your solution is "simplistic." Don't say, as I saw in one executive summary, that you have spent extra time developing a "simplistic project plan." Being *simplistic* in this context is not a good thing. *Simplistic* means shallow to the point of stupidity, and simplistic solutions ignore the complexities of reality. I think this mistake arises because people mistake *simplistic* for the superlative form of the word: This is *simple*, that's *simpler*, and that is *simplistic*. Wrong.

Trap 5: Converting Verbs Into Nouns

Here's something odd: For no apparent reason, people like to take perfectly good verbs and turn them into rather puny, ineffective nouns. For example, they convert:

discuss into *have a discussion*
meet with into *hold a meeting*
act into *take action*

There are many more examples of this phenomenon. It's not a good idea, because most business writing is woefully short of strong verbs anyway. Taking the few good ones we have and turning them into nouns drains the vitality right out of prose. Avoid this tendency.

Trap 6: Riding the Cliché Pony

Our firm is uniquely qualified for this project. We offer best-of-breed products and world-class service in a state-of-the-art package that will deliver exceptional results.

Are you impressed? Probably not. We've heard it before. It's the same old marketing fluff. Your built-in B.S. detector is probably going off. The main problem is that it's built on tired, meaningless clichés.

Suppose the sentences were written as follows:

Our firm has successfully installed more than 500 airport security systems in North America, more than any other firm. We offer the latest technology, including digital scanning and face recognition systems, and we back our products up with a one-year, unconditional guarantee and a service department that is available 24 hours a day, 7 days a week. As a result, by implementing our recommendations, you will achieve three important outcomes: First, your facility will be in full compliance with new federal safety regulations. Second, the installation and training process will be handled seamlessly. And third, your total cost of ownership and operation will be the lowest possible.

Now you'd be a bit more impressed, right? It's all in the details.

20 *Sentence Structure:*
Maximizing Your Clarity

M ost lousy proposals have a few characteristics in common. By now, I'm sure you know what they are as well as I do: They're product focused rather than client focused. They're factual rather than persuasive. They're disorganized. They lack a clear value proposition. But there's one characteristic we haven't looked at yet: They use pompous language to impress or intimidate the reader rather than writing clearly to communicate.

Assuming that you subscribe to the linguistic version of the Golden Rule, "Send unto others what you would like to receive yourself," the question arises: How can you write proposals that are clear and easy to understand? And what is clarity, anyway? How do you know if something is clear or not?

Here's my definition of clear writing: the reader understands what you wrote after reading it once. That's it. If the reader has to go back over something in your proposal and reread it to figure it out, you messed up.

In this chapter we'll look at some simple techniques that will help you maximize your clarity.

Avoid Complicated Sentences

Have you ever found yourself reading something complicated, straining to understand, when your brain suddenly goes "blue screen"? You go back to the beginning of the passage and start over again. You reread the material, not because it was so enjoyable going through it the first time, but because you just couldn't fuse it into anything that made sense. Usually when that happens, you have run up against a poorly constructed, overly complicated sentence, and your brain simply couldn't decode it. The sentence was too complex to make sense.

Sentence complexity is a function of two elements: length and syntactic structure. **Length** is simply a matter of how many words your sentences contain. Keep them short. Strive for an average sentence length of fifteen to eighteen words for maximum readability. Here's an example of a sentence that's way too long:

> *For this program, it is proposed that the kick-off meeting be one day in length with the first half of the day consisting of the following activities: [list follows]*

It is proposed that . . . ? By whom? *One day in length?* As opposed to what—one day in width? This bloated sentence is bordering on silliness. Here's a rewrite that cuts it from twenty-seven words to eleven and gets rid of several other problems, too:

> *We propose a one-day kick-off meeting. The first half will cover: [list follows]*

Syntactic structure is a matter of how many embedded elements the sentence contains. The more complexity in your sentences, the more difficult they are to decode. Please understand that I'm not suggesting you write in a Dick-and-Jane style. But unnecessary complexity and sloppy syntax won't help you win any deals, because they are likely to confuse, even alienate, the reader.

Often the quickest way to simplify your writing is to break a long, complicated sentence into a couple of shorter, simpler ones. For example, look at this sentence which appeared in the executive summary of a proposal written by a major consulting firm:

> *The dimensionality of expected project problems coupled with the limited time available for preparation means that choices will have to be made to assure viability of the most critical analytical processes.*

As soon as you saw the word "dimensionality" you probably knew we were in trouble, right? But this sentence drags itself back and forth across the page, turning back on itself a couple of times, until it's so twisted and we're so confused that nothing makes sense.

What is it trying to say? This is only a guess, but I think it means:

> *This project is tackling a number of big problems. Unfortunately, time is short. As a result, you need to decide which problems are the most important to keeping your business running.*

You can see how breaking it into three shorter, simpler sentences and using simpler words made it more readable.

Avoid Passive Voice

In English, you have two options for creating declarative sentences (that is, sentences that make a statement): the active voice or the passive voice. The term *voice* is a piece of grammar jargon that refers to the relationship between the subject in a sentence and the verb. In the active voice, which we use the vast majority of the time, the subject does the action expressed in the verb. For example:

Our sales team visited the client's site.

"Sales team" is the subject. And they're the ones who did the visiting.

To say the same thing in the passive voice, you put the recipient of the action in the subject slot. That inverts the typical relationship between subject and verb. For example, here's our sentence above, rewritten in passive voice:

The client's site was visited by our sales team.

Here "site" is the subject and it received an action, namely, it "was visited." There's nothing ungrammatical about that sentence. It's perfectly legal. So what's wrong with using passive voice? The main problem is that because we don't hear it or read it very often, it's harder to decode. Our brains do a little skip step to sort things out.

Another problem with passive voice is that you don't actually have to say who did anything. Passive voice is the language of nonresponsibility and is frequently used as a way to communicate bad news:

A decision has been made to terminate your employment.

Combine these weaknesses of passive voice with a long sentence, throw in some big words and some jargon, and you have a recipe for incomprehensibility. Here is a prime example, again drawn from the executive summary of a real proposal:

A leveraging of problem similarities and process relationships to allow sharing of resources and solutions, will be needed to contain cost and staff expenditures and assure maximum payoff from effected solutions.

There are lots of problems in that sentence. The wandering comma is odd. It just shows up randomly in the middle. Maybe the author thought it was time to take a breath. Anyway, it's wrong, but it's the least of the problems. It's too long: it runs on for thirty-one words— nearly twice as long as the average length I've recommended. It contains some very odd word choices and usage ("effected solutions," "leveraging of problem similarities"). And it's written in passive voice: "A leveraging . . . will be needed . . ." By whom?

People normally use passive voice about 10 percent of the time. That's a good percentage for your writing, too.

Put the Important Stuff Up Front

You should put your key points in the most prominent position. In business writing and presentations, that's first.

Whatever the audience sees up front in our proposal, whatever they hear first in our presentation, they assume represents our primary focus. It's a good idea to put the most important facts, information, opinions, or observations up front—that is, the things that are most important to the decision maker. This applies to the document as a whole, to sections within a document, to paragraphs, even to sentences.

Proposals and presentations will be most persuasive if they are organized in terms of what matters to the decision maker. That's why the persuasive paradigm works. (You can see why it's deadly to start a proposal with your company's history or an overview of your products.)

Sections of proposals will be easier to read and understand if they start with an overview. The overview should indicate what this part of the proposal is about and how it's organized. Be sure to put a strong selling statement at the outset of each section, too.

Paragraphs make more sense when they start with a clear topic sentence.

Sentences also benefit from following the primacy principle. For example, consider this:

Providing senior leadership during some of the recent projects presented in the table below is Mr. Ralph Brown.

Doesn't that sound odd? (It sounds like Ralph is in the table, doesn't it?) If we put the important point, namely Ralph's leadership, up front, it will read much better:

Mr. Ralph Brown provided senior leadership for some of the projects listed below.

Apply Sant's Law to Every Sentence

What is Sant's Law? Well, in all modesty, it's the most important breakthrough in writing clear, direct prose since the invention of the simple sentence. Okay, maybe I'm not being all that modest. Or all that honest, either. But it is a technique that can help you identify whether your sentences are well constructed. And it's pretty easy to use.

Here it is in a nutshell: *To write a clear, direct sentence, make sure the key idea is embedded in the heart of the sentence.*

What's the heart of the sentence? It's the subject, the verb, and the complement—usually the direct object or indirect object.

That's the first step and, to apply Sant's Law, the only step you have to take. All that matters is this: Does the subject/verb/complement communicate the key idea?

Perhaps you'll run across a sentence like this in one of your proposals:

It would appear that enhanced access to the database on the part of our key executives is desirable.

Can you even find the subject and verb in that thing? Well, the grammatical subject is "It" and the verb is "would appear." Not too exciting, is it? Not very clear either.

Try to rewrite the sentence so that the key ideas are in the key grammatical slots. Something like this would work:

Our key executives need better access to the database.

If you apply Sant's Law, what do you get? The subject is "executives," the verb is "need," and the complement is "access."

Executives need access . . .

Is that the key idea? I think so.

21 *Editing Your Proposal*

So you want to be a good writer? Then force yourself to be a rewriter. That's where good writing happens.

A lot of people apparently believe that good writers don't need to revise, that excellent proposals simply pour out of them in their complete and final forms. Trust me—that's a delusion.

How Much Should You Edit?

How much editing should you do? As much as you can. I know that's a bit vague, but I'm sorry to tell you that there's no magic formula, such as "five minutes per page" or "15 percent of the total time allocated to document development."

Another way of asking "how much" is to ask yourself: "How good is good enough?" When is your proposal good enough to go to the client?

First, you need to recognize that perfection is not a realistic goal. Instead, the goal should be *excellence*. We want to deliver a proposal to our client that is truly excellent, that is in the top 1 or 2 percent of all the proposals he or she receives.

To define excellence, we can consider six levels of "correctness," listing them in order of increasing difficulty of achievement:

1. There are no mechanical, spelling, or punctuation errors and no typos.

2. There are no obvious errors of fact, content, or logic.

3. The proposal follows an effective and appropriate structural pattern and has been adequately divided into functional units so that the reader can understand and use it easily.

4. The proposal writing is clear and concise, free of needless jargon, ambiguities, or possible misinterpretations.

5. The proposal has been slanted correctly in terms of the primary audience's level of expertise, personality, and values.

6. The proposal is intelligent, written in a crisp and interesting style, and delivered in a format that makes it easy to use.

So—how good is good enough? Lots of technical or business profession-als are satisfied if their documents reach level 2. If it gets by on the first reading, it's good enough for them.

From a reader's point of view, however, nothing less than level 4 will do. And for a proposal, where the reader is making a buying decision, you shouldn't tolerate anything less than level 5. So how much should you edit? Enough to get to that level of excellence.

Editing: A Five-Step Process

Perhaps an even more important issue than how much editing you should do is how you should do it. Most people were never taught true editing skills. Instead, what they learned to do was proofread.

Proofreading is part of editing, the final step before you print and deliver the proposal, but it's not the whole job. In fact, there are four other steps that must precede proofreading.

Warning: Don't Edit Immediately After Writing. You must let your writing "cool" before you edit it. If you look at it immediately after finish-ing the first draft, you'll miss a lot of errors and problems. Apparently, this is a variation of the Gestalt principle of completion of form. Because you know what you *meant* to say, you are unable to see what you *did* say. You read what you think should be there, rather than what is actually on the page.

When you have gained sufficient detachment (or found somebody to do the editing for you), cover all five steps of the process, even if you do some of them simultaneously.

Step 1: Go through the first draft quickly and ask three questions:

1. Have I said anything obviously dumb?

    Misplaced modifiers, incomplete thoughts, errors in logic, the wrong cli-ent's name—all of these qualify as dumb.

2. Have I written with a consistently client-centered focus?

    Challenge yourself: Is this information necessary? Does it address the client's needs, problems, interests, values?

3. Can I cut any of this material without interfering with the reader's un-derstanding or my ability to persuade?

    Be ruthless. Many proposals are bogged down with a clutter of details.

You will probably find it helpful to read through the draft out loud. When you have to say the words, you hear them more accurately and the rough spots become more obvious. Read quickly. Don't stop at this point to fix things. Just mark whatever you notice.

Step 2: Read through the proposal more slowly now and focus on orga-nization and structure. You're still not rewriting. You're trying to figure out if the content flows in the clearest and most persuasive way. Ask yourself:

1. Structure:

   ■ *Have I used the persuasive paradigm to structure the proposal as a whole?*

   ■ *Is the overall proposal unified? Is there one central value proposition, idea, or focus to which everything is related?*

2. Organization:

   ■ *Have I used the P-A-R format to organize my case studies?*

   ■ *Did I use the three-part pattern for my important RFP answers?*

   ■ *Does the sequence of content in my resumes put the most important facts up front?*

   ■ *Are the various parts of the proposal arranged in a coherent, logical order? Do they match the order specified by the client, if any?*

3. Is the information easy to find?

   ■ *Did I create logically sequenced sentences, paragraphs, and sections?*

   ■ *Are the key ideas up front whenever possible?*

   ■ *Do the major sections start with an introduction?*

   ■ *Have I used plenty of highlighting?*

Step 3: During the third step, work on clarity, conciseness, precision, directness, and emphasis. In particular, make sure you have adjusted your proposal to suit the audience, then take a close look at your word choice, sentence structure, and overall readability. The goal is to communicate the information so clearly that your customer can read it once and understand it.

1. Audience:

   ■ *Did I slant the material toward the audience's*
      Level of expertise?
      Personality type?
      Role in the decision-making process?

   ■ *Did I prioritize content so that what the audience thinks most important appears first?*

2. Word choice:

   ■ *Work on the words or phrases you marked during your initial review of the proposal.*

   ■ *Challenge jargon and acronyms. Are they necessary? Are they defined clearly?*

   ■ *Review the chapter on word traps in this book. Correct any of these mistakes.*

3. Sentence lengths and patterns

   ■ *Check for passive voice. Revise passive constructions into active voice.*

   ■ *Check the verbs. For sentences where the main verb is a form of "to be," rewrite the sentence so that it contains a strong verb.*

   ■ *Use the grammar checker in your word processing software to determine your proposal's average sentence length. Is it near the fifteen- to seventeen-word range that's most accessible for adult readers?*

   ■ *Have you minimized compound/complex constructions?*

   ■ *Have you avoided long dependent clauses, particularly at the beginning of the sentence?*

4. Readability

   ■ *If your word processor contains a readability tool, use it. Is the readability of your proposal appropriate?*

   ■ *Spot check the most important parts of your proposal —the cover letter, the executive summary, the section intros.*

5. Make information easy to understand

   ■ *Focus on simplicity: in vocabulary, sentence structure, and organization.*

   ■ *Keep the proposal as brief as possible.*

   ■ *Be specific: Use details, not clichés, to make your points; use graphics to illustrate concepts; include examples, comparisons, and analogies to make your ideas clear.*

   ■ *Keep the proposal relevant—no tangents, nothing extraneous or unnecessary.*

Step 4: During the fourth phase of editing, work on *style*. In particular, look for generic, bland descriptions of your products or services that you can make vivid by linking them to the customer's business, specific needs, or desired outcomes. Also, watch for the typical business clichés. Is there a way to make your point more emphatically by using specific details? What about a metaphor or analogy, particularly for a level one reader? You might even look for an opportunity to use humor or a bit of drama.

Step 5: At the fifth level of revision, a writer looks for *mechanical or typographical errors*, the mistakes of carelessness or neglect. Errors in spelling, punctuation, grammar, and other small mistakes can communicate to a reader that you are careless, hasty, ignorant, or disrespectful. Besides—such mechanical and grammatical mistakes are nothing but background noise, which can interfere with your message getting through.

Measuring Readability

Your car may be capable of going 150 miles an hour, but that doesn't mean it will benefit from continuous operation at that speed. Likewise, you may be capable of reading at the level of a college graduate, but that doesn't mean you'll want to all the time. Most people find it easier to read if the text is a couple of grade levels below the level of reading mastery they have achieved. In a proposal, you want to focus your reader's energy on understanding your ideas, not on the task of reading itself, so you should write at a comfortable, easy level.

Readability formulas measure how difficult or easy a given piece of writing is likely to be.

You can measure readability very easily by using tools built into your word processor. For example, if you use Microsoft Word, open the "Tools: Options: Spelling and Grammar" box and select "Show Readability Statistics." The next time you use the "Tools: Spelling and Grammar" option in Microsoft Word, you will see a chart that tells you more than you probably ever wanted to know about your writing. This chart, titled "Readability Statistics," tells you the percentage of passive sentences your writing contains. It also gives you the Flesch Reading Ease index and the Flesch-Kincaid Grade Level index. These numbers measure how easy or hard the writing is to decode. (WordPerfect users have a similar tool that also yields a Flesch-Kincaid Grade Level index.)

When I run a spelling and grammar check on the previous paragraph, I get this summary:

Readability Statistics	[?][X]
Counts	
Words	123
Characters	641
Paragraphs	1
Sentences	7
Averages	
Sentences per Paragraph	7.0
Words per Sentence	17.5
Characters per Word	5.0
Readability	
Passive Sentences	0%
Flesch Reading Ease	50.7
Flesch-Kincaid Grade Level	10.5
	[OK]

There's a lot of useful information here. I can see that my average sentence length is about right, and that I've completely avoided passive voice constructions. But what about the Flesch Reading Ease and Flesch-Kincaid Grade Level numbers? Are they good or bad?

The Reading Ease score is based on a standard of 100. The higher the number, the easier the writing is to understand. In business writing, which includes proposals, of course, a good score would be somewhere between 50 and 70. Based on that score, my paragraph is all right, but it could be simpler.

The Flesch-Kincaid Grade Level measurement indicates the equivalent U.S. grade level of reading competence that someone would need to read a particular passage easily. Note that this is strictly a measurement of the complexity of the writing. It does *not* mean the content is appropriate for someone at that level.

The chart below shows you how various grade levels correlate to mass-market publications. Note that grade level twelve is the danger line. Above that line, reading becomes uncomfortable for the majority of readers. Above fifteen, almost nobody is comfortable reading. Just because your reader has a Ph.D. doesn't mean you should write at a grade level of twenty. In fact, almost nobody enjoys reading for extended periods above an index of ten.

INDEX	READING LEVEL BY GRADE	READING LEVEL BY MAGAZINE
17	College postgraduate	
16	College senior	(No mass-market publication
15	College junior	is this difficult.)
14	College sophomore	
13	College freshman	
12	High school senior	*Scientific American*
11	High school junior	*The New Yorker, Atlantic Monthly*
10	High school sophomore	*Time, Newsweek*
9	High school freshman	*Sports Illustrated*
8	Eighth grade	daily newspapers
7	Seventh grade	*People*

Other Ways to Improve Your Readability

Other factors besides sentence length and word choice will affect the ease with which your readers understand what you have written. Here are some you can control:

Legibility. Is your type easy to read? Don't use a font that's too small, because reading it will become a strain. Don't print type on a colored background that doesn't offer sufficient contrast.

Interest. If your reader is interested in what you're writing about, he or she will read comfortably at a slightly higher level than normal. That's another reason to lead with the content that is of greatest interest to your decision maker, rather than starting with your company history or an overview of your technology.

Format. Incorporating plenty of white space into your page design can make your text seem more readable. Headings, subheadings, the use of color, the use of sidebars, and illustrations can also help.

Simplicity. Presenting too many new ideas, new concepts, or new acronyms in a short space can discourage the reader. Most people have trouble, for example, keeping track of more than three or four new acronyms in a page of text before their mind goes blank and they lose the thread of your message.

Red Teaming Your Proposal

A red team review is an exercise which involves reading and scoring the final draft of the proposal as if the customer were looking at it. It's a dry run that gives you the chance to improve your proposal before you send it into the fray.

Your red team should consist of people who did not write the proposal, so they will look at it without any preconceived notions. Ideally, they should be individuals who can play the role of customer in terms of expertise, personality type, and priorities.

Prepare your reviewers so they understand their role. Make it clear that they are not expected to edit or proofread. Their job is to score the proposal as though they were buyers. Provide them with a copy of the RFP and with the scoring system the customer will use in evaluating submissions. Make sure that the red team reviewers have no contact with the proposal team while they review it.

The job of the red team reviewers is to be as objective, factual, fair, and specific as possible. The responsibilities of your red team reviewers, in order of priority, include:

1. Checking for compliance with the RFP requirements

2. Checking for clear, compelling win themes

3. Reviewing the proof statements and evidence: Are they relevant and convincing?

As they evaluate the overall proposal, they should examine other issues, too:

1. Is the proposal client focused? Does it show that your company understands the customer's problems, goals, and values?

2. Are there any words or phrases that catch your attention or stand out in any way, either good or bad?

3. Are the themes consistent throughout the proposal and well integrated into the total proposal?

4. Does the executive summary use the persuasive paradigm effectively? Does it make a convincing business case?

5. On the basis of the opening, what impression does the proposal create? Are you more "with" or "against" the writer?

6. Does the proposal persuade throughout or are parts of it merely informative?

7. Are there parts of this proposal that are dull or confusing?

8. Does the proposal present clear differentiators and tie them to value statements that will appeal to this customer?

9. After reading the proposal, are you convinced that your company offers the best solution and highest value?

10. What is the key message of this proposal? Can you summarize the recommendation and value proposition in thirty seconds?

11. What else do you wish you knew or had available that's not in the proposal you just read?

As your reviewers make observations, they should try to offer constructive, specific feedback, such as the following:

Transportation planning experience is not highlighted enough in the resumes. Add a separate heading just for that category.

So what? You mention these features, but how will they help? Why should a customer care? Am I paying extra for them?

Simply saying that a section is "weak" doesn't help anybody.

How Your Customer Reads and Evaluates Your Proposal

You and any team members who help you edit your proposals will do a better job if you know how your customers interact with the documents they get. In general, evaluators try to be fair and objective. They also try to look at each proposal on its own merits, but in reality that's impossible. Evaluators are only human, and they quickly become subjective in reviewing proposals.

The basic process for evaluating proposals is as follows:

1. A responsible person—for example, the project manager, contracting officer, RFP manager, or an outside consultant—does an initial read-

through of each submission. His or her job at this point is to identify any submissions that fail to comply with the mandatory terms and conditions of the bid. Proposals that fail to comply may be eliminated at this point. Evaluators are not required to read or score the entire proposal if they have identified a major weakness.

2. If cost is handled as a separate issue, the cost volume will be separated from the rest of the proposal and delivered to the individual or team responsible for financial analysis.

3. Once those proposals that are clearly noncompliant have been eliminated, the survivors are often evaluated against a set of criteria. Even when these criteria are very specific, with numeric values or weights, the process rapidly becomes subjective. Evaluating proposals can be fatiguing work, and after the first few documents, evaluators get tired. When they are tired, they're more likely to be critical and to make snap judgments.

4. Some tips for getting a better score:

Submit the briefest proposal possible. Short proposals are read first and then become the unconscious standard by which all subsequent proposals are judged.

If your proposal is easy to read, your recommendations will seem to make more sense.

Link your deliverables to the benefits your customer seeks and then to your differentiators. This will help separate you from competitors and will make your recommendations read more like a solution, one that the customer can get only from you.

Avoid promising benefits without substantiating how you will deliver on those promises:
- Provide proof statements for each material feature, function, or requirement
- Provide relevant references, testimonials, case studies, and statistics

What Evaluators Like and What They Hate

A few years ago, we conducted a survey of people who make their living evaluating proposals for the federal government. We wanted to know the things they like to see in proposals and the things that they hate. Here are some findings from that survey:

What They Like:

1. They like proposals that follow the directions in the RFP.
2. They like compliance matrices. A compliance matrix saves them time and indicates you've been thorough.

3. They like proposals that clearly identify the vendor's differentiators and indicate why those differentiators matter.

4. They like section summaries.

5. They like well-organized and consistent proposals. They believe a professional-looking document shows good project management and thoroughness.

What They Hate:

1. They hate proposals that are wordy.

2. They hate poor-quality proposals—unreadable graphics, spelling mistakes, typos, poor photocopying, and so forth.

3. They hate proposals that are weak or vague in responding to the RFP requirements.

4. They hate proposals that take a poor or unproven approach to solving the problem.

5. They hate proposals that have inherent deficiencies—missed requirements, inaccurate data.

A Proposal Writer's Checklist

Here's a checklist you can use to determine if your proposal is "good enough." It covers the major points we've talked about in this book. If you can say "yes" to each of the questions in this checklist, you probably have a very good proposal. Print it and send it! And good luck!

The Development Phase

■ Have I analyzed the client's needs and desired end result thoroughly and creatively?

■ Have I turned the statement of need into an overall strategy?

■ Do I know what the customer's decision criteria are?

■ Have I assembled all the necessary information?

■ Have I accurately identified my audience?

   1. Personality style

   2. Level of expertise and familiarity

   3. Role in the decision process

■ Have I developed a cognitive web of the overall proposal?

Style

■ Have I used a natural, friendly tone?

    1. Have I avoided clichés and jargon?

    2. Have I used active voice?

■ Have I expressed myself clearly?

    1. Do I understand my subject thoroughly?

    2. Are my sentences reasonably short and simple?

    3. Have I used specific words?

    4. Have I adapted my vocabulary to suit the reader?

    5. Have I eliminated jargon?

    6. Have I eliminated unnecessary detail?

■ Have I expressed myself with precision?

    1. Are my ideas in logical and effective order?

    2. Have I provided the necessary definitions, details, and examples?

■ Have I written with proper emphasis?

    1. Did I reinforce the win theme throughout the proposal?

    2. Does my executive summary make a strong, concise case?

Structure

■ Have I used the persuasive paradigm to structure this proposal?

    1. Did I restate the customer's needs clearly and accurately?

    2. Does the proposal state the customer's general goals and specific objectives?

    3. Does the proposal contain a clear, targeted value proposition that is meaningful to the customer?

■ Have I organized the content from the reader's point of view?

■ Have I highlighted my key points and made it easy for the reader to skim the proposal?

Mechanics

■ Have I included all the necessary mechanical and prose elements?

■ Are my headings and titles clear, properly worded, and parallel?

■ Have I keyed any tables or figures into the text and discussed them adequately?

■ Have I proofread the manuscript completely?

Index